Praise for *Trivium 21c*

Martin Robinson sets out on a quest to discover the kind of education he wishes for his daughter and we all learn a great deal in the process. I love his writing: wise, well informed, provocative, thinking-out-loud. Robinson engages his reader from first to last. A terrific feat.

Melissa Benn, writer and author of
School Wars: The Battle for Britain's Education

Part reflective autobiography, part educational manifesto, *Trivium 21c* is both a richly erudite and engagingly relevant exploration of the purposes and philosophies underlying the enterprise of education. From ancient Greece through to contemporary controversy, Robinson draws resonantly on his experience as a student and a teacher to demonstrate that the 'trivium', the 'triple way', of grammar, dialectic, and rhetoric, still lies at the heart of a 'good education', albeit in new forms. With refreshing realism, he recognises that teachers in their work in the classroom often transcend many of the political storms about education. Citing almost every contemporary protagonist from our own era, he advances an approach which he describes as 'progressive traditionalism'. *Trivium 21c* is essential reading for all educators and observers of the seemingly endless public debate about education who wish to go beyond simplistic polarities and find a way to integrate and relate, in a historical context ,seemingly contradictory approaches.

Ian Bauckham, Head Teacher and President, Association of
School and College Leaders (ASCL) 2013–2014

In schools today, a focus on contemporary relevance too often trumps educational depth. Martin Robinson makes a compelling case that turning instead to the tradition of the liberal arts can open the minds of a new generation.

Marc Sidwell, co-author of *The School of Freedom*,
Managing Editor, City A.M.

This is a charming book which is fun to read; it is contemplative and self-reflective and at the same time it is well-researched, informative, and genuinely scholarly. What the book does very well is to unpick the tensions between educationalist progressives and traditionalists and it attempts to identify differences but also importantly to seek common ground. Indeed it is a historical tour de force examining the origins and development of the 'liberal arts' from the early Greeks through Shakespearian times to the present day. What makes the book so readable is that it is a journey of self-reflection on what it means to be educated from the point of view of the author as a schoolboy, a teacher, and then a parent seeking an appropriate school for his daughter.

The early part of the book looks at the author's own schooling and the frustrations he experienced. Learning appeared to be chaotic and many pupils were apparently left to 'fail' by not being equipped with the skills necessary to succeed at school. The book then traces his later employment and his experiences as a schoolteacher and how he changed the way he taught to make learning more meaningful and authentic for his pupils. His journey is one of becoming a teacher who adopts innovative approaches to teaching: teaching for meaning, values, and deep learning.

The argument of the book is for a 'trivium' of grammar, dialectic, and rhetoric. The three elements of the trivium would be developed simultaneously, and once mastered it is expected that a student would have acquired the knowledge, the reasoning skills, and the ability to communicate well, which would stand them in good stead for a good life. What Robinson is asking for is the building blocks for thriving at school, the underpinning principles of learning that many teachers assume that pupils already possess but which many do not. I am not convinced that this book will unite traditionalists and progressives in a mutual quest of school improvement, but for the open-minded reader there is much to learn. I agree with Robinson that for students to acquire a sound blend of knowledge, questioning expertise, and communication skills (i.e. the trivium) is the basis of a great education.

Dr Jacek Brant, Head of Curriculum, Pedagogy and
Assessment (CPA), Senior Lecturer in Business Education,
Institute of Education, University of London

Martin Robinson embarks on a highly engaging personal quest to discover what matters in education. By drawing not just on lessons and frustrations from his extensive experience as an educator, but also on the hopes and anxieties that he feels as a new parent, he transcends the often stale trench lines of many arguments about education between traditionalists and progressives, recognising that rival important insights about the foundations of learning and knowledge need not be polar opposites. Robinson's own synthesis offers an ambitious vision of how to pursue an educational ideal as a practical project. Anybody interested in education, citizenship, or how we want our children to learn would find this a thought-provoking read.

Sunder Katwala, Director, British Future

TRIVIUM
21c

preparing young people for the future with lessons from the past

Martin Robinson

foreword by Ian Gilbert

 Independent Thinking Press

First published by

Independent Thinking Press
Crown Buildings, Bancyfelin, Carmarthen, Wales, SA33 5ND, UK
www.independentthinkingpress.com

Independent Thinking Press is an imprint of Crown House Publishing Ltd.

First published 2013. Reprinted 2015.

British Library Cataloguing-in-Publication Data
A catalogue entry for this book is available
from the British Library.

Print ISBN 978-1-78135-054-6
Mobi ISBN 978-1-78135-084-3
ePub ISBN 978-1-78135-085-0

Edited by Peter Young

Printed and bound in the UK by
Bell & Bain Ltd, Thornliebank, Glasgow

For Lotte

In 1842, a young Karl Marx wrote:

> 'It will become evident that it is not a question of drawing a great mental dividing line between past and future, but of realizing the thoughts of the past … it will become evident that mankind is not beginning a new work, but is consciously carrying into effect its old work.'

In a letter to Arnold Ruge

Foreword by Ian Gilbert

It's difficult to read the news these days without seeing some story on education being played out in governments, think tanks, conference rooms, staffrooms, classrooms or even streets somewhere in the world. And rightly so. Education is both a mirror of society as it is now and also, crucially, a reflection of what that society will become. What we do with the minds of our young people today will come back to help us – or haunt us – for decades to come.

Or, in the words of Christa McAuliffe, the teacher on board the ill-fated Challenger space shuttle expedition in 1986: 'I touch the future ... I teach'.

Often, though, when education is being talked about there is no agreement as to what, specifically, is actually being discussed. For example, when teachers talk about education, they are more often than not referring to a process in which they teach and children learn. All being well. When the politicians and strategists talk about it, however, they are often referring to the system within which that teaching and learning process operates. Parents may mean something else altogether, perhaps more related to discipline, employment chances, and life skills. And the young people themselves? Well, often they never get the chance to voice an opinion about just what exactly they are spending the major portion of their first 20 years or so doing.

Yet beyond the world of processes and systems – or maybe underpinning them – there is another debate too, one that goes on often unnoticed and yet has vexed some of the greatest minds for millennia. It is the question of what we want schools and schooling to achieve for our children, of what having 'an education' entails, of what 'being educated' actually means?

It is a debate over which the ancient Greeks battled and that still fills the letters pages of national newspapers and the comments sections on news websites and blogs today. And it is a debate that is very much at the heart of this fascinating and important book.

Through a combination of extensive historical research, face-to-face dialogue with some of the main protagonists currently in the debate and his personal experience both as a teacher and as a parent desperately trying to find the right sort of education for his daughter, Martin weaves a complex and compelling story. It is a journey that stretches back to the ancient Greeks and the 'fork in the road' they encountered that evolved into the trivium of the medieval world and that rages in the 21st century educational diaspora of academies, charter schools, free schools, national and common core curricula, standardized testing and assessment, and practically every aspect of educational policy and discussion worldwide.

If you are involved in education in any fashion – from teacher to parent to governor to educator to inspector to policy maker – and you have an opinion about what 'an educated person' should look like, then you have joined the debate. What's more, that opinion means you will have taken sides, whether you know it or not. This book will help you make the right choices for the right reasons and, who knows, may even help us create the sort of consensus that will bring all sides together. In doing so, we can all help forge an education system and an education process that genuinely does what we want it to do – bring the very best out of, and put the very best into, every child.

Ian Gilbert
Hong Kong

Contents

An Unexamined Life is not Worth Living

It is our moral obligation to give every child the very best education possible.

Archbishop Desmond Tutu

It has often been said that history is written by the winners. The same could be said about education. Articles, books, exams, courses, academic studies, textbooks, books on pedagogy, and even policies, are usually written by those who have a clutch of worthwhile exam results at secondary, university, and post-degree level. This, of course, makes a great deal of sense, but it does mean the system has a flaw. The voices of those who have not benefitted from schooling are not usually heard in the great education debate. If real change is going to happen, then those who have struggled in the system need to be heard; their experiences and ideas should be at the centre of the debate and not ignored at the margins.

I was what you would call a school failure. Yet somehow I ended up as an advanced skills teacher and an assistant head in East London. This introduction is not the story of how I arrived at those dizzying heights, but some background detail that explains why I have written this book.

Failure

My parents moved house when I was 12 and I took the opportunity to reinvent myself. My first year at secondary school in a large comprehensive on the outskirts of Oxford had proved instructive. I had been a good student: I did my classwork and my homework and I played the violin. In 1974 this was not a good combination and I had been marked out as an easy target for those who, shall we say, had a slightly more philistine view of the world. Although they were not outwardly violent, the threat was sufficiently compelling to force me to cut the horsehair of my violin bow and to acquiesce to having my exercise books ripped to pieces and thrown out of the window of the school bus. Even though this wasn't the reason my parents decided to move house, I was glad that we did. I started at my new secondary school, a rural Oxfordshire comprehensive, with one thing on my mind: I did not want to be the target of any vitriol due to a love of learning and playing a musical instrument.

Grammar School for No One

Luckily for me I wasn't challenged in my new school to do much study. It was 1975 and the school had recently become a comprehensive: a girls' grammar had amalgamated with a boys' secondary modern with predictable results. This traditional 'grammar school for all' hadn't bargained on the 'all'. The senior management team were almost entirely drawn from the girls' school and had no idea how to cope with boys, let alone those who'd had their expectations shaped by being confined to a second-rate education. It was glorious, awful chaos. As I was a new boy, untainted by any particular history, I was immediately put in the bottom set for everything, until they realized that perhaps I had 'potential', and I was then immediately moved into the top set for everything. Even though I had missed out a couple of months learning, no one thought to help me catch up. I didn't care anyway; I had already ingratiated myself with some of my fellow bottom-setters; two in particular had already asked me for a fight. One of them

I dispatched with relative ease in the school washroom, and the other, who had challenged me on the staircase, foolishly from a lower position, was easily toppled. This was going to be easy!

The chaos of the school continued in the classrooms. Teachers who could hack it were OK; those who couldn't weren't. And there was never any backup for those in need. When it came time for the headmistress to retire, the school staff made it very clear what they wanted: a traditional, disciplinarian head who could sort out the boys. I was, by this time, coming up to my O levels and hadn't done much apart from cultivate a rebellious nature, so that when the new head arrived we were not destined to hit it off.

I was not the sort of rebel who would burn down the school; I was far subtler than that. I started a school newspaper, I set up a debating society, and I was trying to set up a branch of the National Union of School Students. In lessons I would ask questions and challenge what was being taught. I was most probably a proverbial pain in the posterior. Despite being put in detention on occasion, and even whacked with a slipper, no one seemed to worry unduly about my incomplete classwork and lack of homework. I sat my O levels and got three at grade A–C and one CSE grade one, which was an O level 'equivalent'. I stayed in the sixth form to do A levels and to resit some O levels; I achieved two more in November 1979. However, my attitude wasn't liked, my refusal to wear the newly introduced school uniform for sixth formers wasn't going well, and when I was told off for not wearing the new tie, I turned up the next day wearing the tie but no shirt. I was sent home.

Rock 'n' Roll

This was all very wearisome, both for the school and for myself, but the roots went further back. At no point had I seen the purpose of this poor 'traditional' education I was being offered. Perhaps, had I arrived at the school five years later, the more ordered atmosphere that was being brought in would have inspired me to be the academic student I needed to be, but I shall never know. After a meeting with the headmaster at the end of 1979 I left 'by mutual consent'. I had five O levels and one grade one CSE. This was my winter of discontent. My education was to be found in the pages of the *NME*, the lyrics of the Clash, Ian Dury, Elvis Costello, and the theories I had come across while researching David Bowie, piecing together learning based on a left-field look at the arts, resistance, and pop culture.

Away from the world of sex 'n' drugs and rock 'n' roll, I worked in Oxford Polytechnic Library, then spent a year trying to get A levels at the college of further education, a place where 'progressive methods' held sway in the arts and humanities. Looking back, I see another wasted year. I was incredulous at the behaviour of some of the lecturers who thought nothing of luring their young female students into bed. I even had the wife of one of these lecturers trying to do the same with me, though somewhat unsuccessfully.

My social life at 17 was far more important to me, so when I got a job at a market in the middle of Oxford selling joke items and novelties, this seemed to me to be far more useful. I worked six days a week, had money in my pocket, and was having fun. The stall's turnover doubled, as did the stall. I discovered I had a gift for retail and stayed there for two years, only leaving it for a job as a window salesman! Again, I was a success, and quickly promoted. However, I knew this wasn't the career for me, so I set up my own business promoting bands and, in between times, being a parcel delivery driver for Securicor.

University: An Act of Belonging or Subverting?

Although I was often in Oxford, my only firsthand experience of the university had come from attending a party at a college where an acquaintance was studying. This was quite eye-opening. A student came up to me, 'Where are you from?' I said, 'Oxford.' 'Oh,' he replied, 'which college?' 'Er,' I said, 'not the university, I am *from* Oxford.' If looks could kill – he stared, incredulously, 'Oh …' And at that he walked off without so much as a by-your-leave – the town versus gown atmosphere of Oxford in the 1970s and early 1980s was so marked. My vision of what a highly educated person looked like and sounded like was shaped, indelibly, by seeing them walking around town as if they owned the place – maybe some of them actually did!

It was at this time that I saw an advert in *The Face* for a degree course at a polytechnic in London, a course called cultural studies. It seemed tailor-made for me. The course director took a punt and enrolled me onto the course despite my lack of qualifications. At the age of 23 I was studying again, for the first time since I was 11 years old. I struggled at first: because I had no academic grounding to fall back on, I had no way in. My poly was an old cigarette factory in Stratford, East London. This was education that didn't look like education; this was education as subversion – just the sort I liked. Miraculously, I got a 2:1 BA honours degree, something I never thought would happen. In my spare time I set up an arts group with others, called The Big Picture, and we wrote, produced, directed, and performed in plays, including a punk musical I wrote that went on to be performed on the stage of the Theatre Royal Stratford East. Now, I was waiting for the world to open its arms and invite me into its inner sanctum. As it turned out, I became an advertising salesperson at *Marxism Today*.

Working in the hub of the Communist Party of Great Britain was fascinating, especially as I was the 'capitalist' wing. I loved the dichotomy. I sold more advertising space for the magazine than anyone else had done before. Strangely, *Marxism Today* seemed to be employing the same Oxbridge types I had come across before, only these were lefty ones. I realized that no matter what your politics were, it was your education that held you in good stead. Yes, I could sell advertising space, windows, and novelties, but being a salesman wasn't going to satisfy me sufficiently; I needed to do something more positive. I was headhunted by a national newspaper – the sales manager had heard I was good at selling. I met him in a pub in London's West End, dressed as poorly as I could, looking like the worst sort of lefty nightmare someone in advertising could come across. It worked; I had broken my ties with that world. I resigned from *Marxism Today* and applied to take a PGCE in that most subversive of subjects, drama.

Teaching

I did my teaching practice in what was then called a 'sink' school in Canning Town. I did well as a teacher and, at the end of the course, I got a job and spent the next 20 years of my life as a drama teacher. Early on, I also doubled as an English teacher, not that I knew how to teach English. In drama I was successful, becoming a head of department, head of faculty, advanced skills teacher, and assistant head teacher. Ofsted always judged my work to be outstanding. Yet, as I continued teaching, I became more aghast at what was happening to education. It had become the opposite of the sink-or-swim experience that I had grown accustomed to during my schooling.

Now, the whole system was so controlling of knowledge that pupils had become totally dependent on their teachers. Data followed each child; if any were in danger of getting a D they would be tracked mercilessly. The exams changed and became exercises in writing only what was deemed acceptable by the exam board. It was the awarding body who told teachers what they wanted to see, and who sold them the textbooks they had produced in order to do it. Successful schools seemed to be those that best played the system. Alas, the children who seemed to do well were those who acquiesced the most. I didn't want spoon-fed factory fodder. I wanted a flicker of rebellion alongside the ability to traverse within society as full citizens. I wanted creative sparks who could also contribute.

Parenting

Then I became a father. Having seen what was happening in education, I now was wondering: what kind of education do I want for my daughter? Certainly not the one I'd had, and also not the systematized schooling that we educators are churning out now. Was there another way?

This then is my aim: I want my daughter and other children to have an education that will enable them to live 'a good life' and attain the necessary wisdom that will equip them for the challenges of the 21st century and yes, though it seems a long way off, beyond.

The Quest

The purpose of education is to change people's lives. How it can best do this is the subject of this book. The question is: how do we want to see our young people change? This book examines some of the history of education to find out what is still valuable and explores how we might use the rich tradition of the trivium to help understand the roots of great teaching and learning. I hope that readers of this book – whether you are students, teachers, or parents – will find something of interest between the covers.

In the process of writing this book I found myself reading books I wish I had been directed towards at an earlier point in my education. I have explored philosophy, classics, art, science, literature, European studies, linguistics, logic, politics, and cognitive psychology, as well as revisiting areas from cultural theory, theatre, and pedagogy. I have been extraordinarily lucky on my journey to be able to count on people with real expertise in all these areas, who were most willing to enlighten me with their knowledge and thinking around the issues I was encountering, many for the first time. Without being able to talk things through with them, I would not have been able to attempt the book and my quest would have remained unexamined.

Chapter 1
A Trivial Pursuit?

Ringmaster: (*with a monkey dressed up as a man*) Roll up, ladies and gentlemen. Examine this beast as God created him. Nothing to him, you see? Then observe the effect of art: he walks upright and has a coat and trousers ...

Georg Büchner, *Woyzeck*

Drama Teacher

Those who can, do; those who can't, teach. With that hoary old adage ringing in my ears, at the age of 29, I entered the teaching profession. Good grief. What was I, an educational failure, doing here in the very profession that had managed *not* to educate me all those years ago? But here I was, employed as a teacher of drama and English. I quickly went about ensuring I got my classroom survival sorted out: not smiling before Christmas and negotiating that bizarre relationship between one adult and 30 teenagers, based on 'Somehow, together, we have to get through this' and, well, generally, we did.

One thing became clear to me: my main subject, drama, was not really a subject in the usual sense of the word. Somewhere along the line it had become 'educational drama', a methodology for exploring sociological issues. On my PGCE I had been introduced to schemes of work covering homelessness, drugs, suicide, and all sorts of other explorations of the seamy side of life. This was drama as social commentary. I was introduced to 'freeze-frames' – where social relations between the powerful and powerless could be explored, and 'conscience alleys' – where two lines of children would watch the protagonist walk between them and they would call out what was in the protagonist's head (usually some utterance about misery due to homelessness, drugs, or suicide). It was deadly and strangely uncreative, and I struggled with this approach during the early stages of my teaching.

In the GCSE drama exam children had to work in groups to prepare, through improvisation, a devised piece of original theatre. I went to see what work schools were producing for these final exams. There would be many chairs, with kids sitting on them, talking of misery. Every now and then a character would die, usually at the denouement, and there would be much wailing and gnashing of teeth. Drama education seemed to be firmly stuck in the black-and-white social realism of the 1960s. Paradoxically, it was also extraordinarily unrealistic and it did not move me; its inauthenticity shone through. I decided then and there that this was not what I wanted to be teaching.

Creative Liberation

My first move was to 'ban' chairs – a ridiculous act, but a liberating one. This was the time when physical theatre was all the rage and I wanted to embrace that energy. Instead of issues, I wanted physicality; instead of talking, I wanted activity. Theatre is a physical subject; I summed this up with the phrase 'Movement First'. Our drama lessons were physical because acting is the art of doing. In discipline terms, this became problematic so I introduced stillness too: the act of 'centring' where the actor stands still with their eyes closed for a period of time. This then became the beginning of lessons. I would wait until every participant had centred before the lesson would start. We were all actors, so we all had to 'act'. I got rid of unnecessary homework: writing about misery and colouring in pictures of misery, and replaced it with a notebook in which kids would be expected to collect fragments of writing, experiences, dreams, stories, poetry, lyrics, history, theory. You name it, they got it.

Method in the Madness

This was to be the beginning of the work, 'Fragments of Movement and Fragments of Text(s)'. We would look at what we had to make sense of – the symbols, the text, the verbal and the physical ideas that seemingly had little connection – and we would try to 'sense' what connections there were. Both the students and I would search for links, no matter how abstract. We were alchemists. There might be connections of sound, physicality, coincidence, or juxtaposition, but mostly we would look for an emotional connection, for the sublime, the beautiful, the surprising, or the funny. We would delay knowing what the final piece would look like for as long as possible; we were looking for 'what the play is trying to say', in the same way a sculptor chips away at a piece of marble before determining its final form. This then was summed up with the word 'Emotion'. We would then use the idea of connecting up 'framed moments' and collect as many moments as we could. We would then perform them slowly, quickly, forwards, backwards, in differing orders, at the same time, or separately. We would then interrogate the piece that was beginning to emerge, looking for logical connections or arguments.

Once we got to know our pieces, then characters and a theme (or themes) would emerge. This we summed up with the word 'Intellect' – this was our thinking about the piece. We would research thoroughly, finding out about what we had and then finally we would pull the process together by honing it as a performance for the practical exam. 'What is your play trying to say?' became, 'If in doubt, spell it out!' We would then refine our pieces for performance. This then became the process: Movement, Emotion, Intellect, and Performance.

Each lesson began to take this basic shape, and then this shape was practised over increasingly longer periods of time, over days and weeks. But the mantra was there at its core – Movement, Emotion, Intellect, Performance

– and the material transformed from fragments to connections. This became the clothesline on which the lessons were hung. We used this ritual, we used it repetitively, and the results were extraordinary. Firstly, literally, the results were extraordinary, but beyond that, and far more importantly, the exam pieces were at their best 'great art', as precise and as moving or funny, as Pina Bausch, Théâtre de la Complicité, or Peter Brook.

Tradition

It was at this time that I launched an A level course in theatre studies, which became an altogether more difficult step for me. I had developed a ritual, a way of working, that was successful for devised theatre, but would it work for an A level? Indeed, the A level included a devised theatre piece, but it also included scripted work. Most challenging of all, there were two three-hour written papers on play texts, theatre practitioners, an 'unseen' piece, and a review of a play.

The results weren't great for the first cohort. I had to do something else, so I went about echoing the devising mantra: we would explore, research, and learn about the texts and practitioners; we would learn the language of the discipline; we would 'give Caliban his language' through the 'semiotics of theatre'. I had absorbed linguistics – how we understand theatre – and developed a shared language to ensure we knew what we were talking about. I then fed this language into the GCSE. Gone were freeze-frames and the concepts of the drama GCSE bubble; instead, in came terms from the rich history and traditions of theatre. We would go and see lots of theatre, from a wide range of performers, practitioners, and authors. I refused to take students to see things they would 'normally' see, so we never went to *Blood Brothers*; instead, we went to see Beckett, Berkoff, and Bausch. We saw Greek tragedy and comedy, Brecht, Complicité, and a writer and a play I fell in love with, Büchner's *Woyzeck*. Here was a moment of inspiration; this play had so much to offer it would become central to my teaching.

Woyzeck: Where Three Paths Collide

As part of the A level course we were expected to teach one practitioner. In those days there were no exams in Year 12 so I took the chance, and we began the course by teaching three practitioners under the general heading of 'Truth'. Each practitioner wanted to communicate their truth in very different ways: Stanislavski in a naturalistic way; Brecht wanted to communicate social truth; and Artaud – well, Artaud wanted a metaphysical truth based on the idea of the energy of life, necessity, or what he called 'cruelty', that we are most 'alive' when we realize our own mortality. Stanislavski helped hone the language of drama and acting; Artaud took my work to another level, the discipline of the art, of the physical, which became even more important; and Brecht helped refine the argument, the dialectic, not only in theatre but in our understanding of how to teach, learn, and challenge by seeing the world in a different 'scientific' way.

We looked at the works of Freud, Marx, Socrates, Saussure, Darwin, Gramsci, Breton, Chaplin, and Büchner to supplement our understanding of these approaches to truth. Artaud and Brecht both cited the play *Woyzeck* as being of great importance, and the implicit naturalism in the play also encompassed the ideas of Stanislavski. Therefore, in *Woyzeck*, the three great practitioners, with their conflicting ideas, had a place where they could 'agree' to congregate, to commune, to argue, and it is this that gave even greater significance to this play and to our studies.

Socratic Method

Other influences came in from the texts we were studying: Sophocles, Shakespeare, Chekhov, and Dürrenmatt. These were weighty subjects; this was not dumbing down. The approach I took was: we would find our language, research our texts, look for ways in, and understanding(s). We would then take an unashamedly Socratic approach: questioning, arguing, and prompting. The kids would do the same with each other, which made our sessions lively and challenging. Finally, we would look at how to take our approach into the written exam, and also the viva and notebook which, at the time, were integral parts of the assessment. The exam was a celebration of our exploration; not a 'jumping through hoops' approach to getting grades. We had found a way to bridge the divide between practical and theory. That year I was told the A level results were among the best in the country, as were the GCSE results.

Creativity

This approach became the basis for my involvement with education in a wider sense. Professor Ken Robinson was working on bringing 'creativity' into the curriculum, and I was invited along to the launch of his report. From this I was asked to become part of a delegation to Chicago to see how a form of 'creative partnership' was being used to educate 'downtown' kids in schools. This was a very odd experience: it was great to be in Chicago, but odd to see what comprised 'creative' teaching. Four actors were teaching science to a very unimpressed group of kids. The lesson was about energy transference and this involved actors pushing kids over (not all the way, Health and Safety …) and, I kid you not, that was it. There was no need for this to be done by 'actors', but I'm sure it ticked a box somewhere: yes, we were creative in science because we got actors in. This was a warning: creativity is neither the sole preserve of artists nor are all artists necessarily creative.

I began to take workshops in other schools and countries in what I was now calling 'creative drama teaching'. My work was controversial, especially in those drama departments where many of the teachers continued with their still images and social work themes. In 2004, *The Guardian* described one of my sessions thus:

'This work is in the tradition of the kind of fragmented or cut-up expression associated with the work of William Burroughs,' he [me] explained as he armed delegates with 'statement cards' and invited them to find the person with the words that complemented theirs.

Of course, there were no obvious pairings and we were off on an afternoon of free association and creativity that would have us dancing, moving, chanting.

Robinson explained how his preferred working practice was to encourage students to remain as intuitive as they could for as long as possible. He described how his students have become used to researching and bringing ideas, actions, music and other stimuli to their group's work while at the same time stalling the desire to define the work in hand for as long as possible. 'In the end, there always comes a time when we have to pause and say, what have we got here? And it is then that they can move on to create something formally for presentation and assessment.'

It was clearly a challenging session for some especially since, as Robinson explained, it relies entirely on the co-operation and commitment of his students – who are required to take wholehearted responsibility for their work. 'It is a sure-fire way,' he emphasised, 'of avoiding clichéd drama work. Of course, preparing the ground so that students are receptive and not alienated by such an approach takes time. But it is worth it – you don't get pastiche EastEnders after several weeks of this kind of exploration.' (Monahan, 2004)

Advanced Skills Teacher

I was now an advanced skills teacher and being asked to use my skills to work with not just drama teachers but with teachers in a wide range of disciplines. The stated aim was: how can we get our staff and the lessons to be more creative? I had visitors to my lessons from Japan, the Czech Republic, and a number of organizations looking for hints about how to *be* creative. Looking back, I'm not sure that the creativity in lessons movement in the UK was after quite the same thing as I was producing. I think many in the educational establishment basically wanted their teachers to be more entertaining because they thought that teachers were boring the kids.

However, my view is that creativity is a disciplined process and can be quite contemplative and even boring at times. This difference in position meant that I was sometimes regarded as an outsider even in the creative education movement. No matter, I carried on developing my approach.

Independent Learners

A visitor from the Good Schools Guide sat in on my lesson, a Year 11 class preparing for their GCSE. We chatted and watched as the 28 kids came in, centred, got into their groups, and followed the ritual of Movement, Emotion, Intellect, Performance. I said nothing, I didn't even acknowledge the kids; they were working, I was chatting. I learned a lesson that day: the mantra had allowed the kids to be truly independent, not at first, no, but by the end, when they needed to be, they were. I had never done this before and, though I didn't show it, I was just as amazed as the visitor from the Good Schools Guide who watched that lesson. We stayed there for two hours before I uttered anything, which was a 'well done' to the class. When the Guide came out later that year there was a special mention for the 'excellent' drama lessons. University professors came to watch my classes; they too mentioned how unusual it was that the methodology I had stumbled across had, in the end, enabled me to step away and for the students to work, successfully, in a manner that showed their ability to be truly independent.

Constraints Can Lead to Creative Freedom

At this time, various gurus were all the rage in education land – and they were talking about how to be creative. These included the aforementioned Ken Robinson and the Six Thinking Hats and Lateral Thinking of Edward de Bono, amongst others. Some teachers interpreted creativity as an example of 1960s-influenced progressivism and the idea of free thinking, which was all about allowing freedom and the ethos of allowing a thousand flowers to bloom.

Although I could see where that was coming from, I was working with the great and eccentric theatre improviser and practitioner Ken Campbell, who had pointed me in completely the opposite direction. Creativity is about constraints, he would tell me. This became part of my mantra; limitations were indeed important, whether you were engaged in a piece of improvised theatre, trying to compose a symphony or a tune with the same eight notes, or making a cake with a list of ingredients. Ken was right: constraints are an essential part of creative expression and freedom. Other drama teachers asked me how we came up with such bizarre and varied work, because whenever they asked their pupils to think of an idea they always came up with the same old clichés.

Competencies

A number of education theorists came to the conclusion that the way forward was to develop competency-based curricula, in order to cultivate within pupils a 'language of learning'. This was fascinating to me, as someone who had developed a mantra in his drama teaching that had enabled students to take control of their own learning; there was something in this. When I was at school I had never really thought about what was lacking in my own education. I just thought that I was belligerent or stupid and that academia was a locked room. I was attracted to competency-based curricula because I knew what it was to be incompetent. So perhaps competencies were the key.

However, there were so many different approaches on the market, all peddling different taxonomies, that it became difficult to know which one to choose and why. Schooling was changing rapidly. We were now examining kids in modular formats. We seemed to be examining and testing them all the time. We were being told to have lesson outcomes and objectives, and to assess them against these objectives. The exams began to define in detail what are called 'assessment objectives', which stated almost exactly what students were expected to write. This was a utilitarian approach to learning, allied to league tables, where departments would compete with each other to drain their pupils of the very fibre of their souls in completing course-work, mock exams, exams, tests, practicals, and controlled assessments. After-school activities became exam oriented, levels were all the rage, and C/D borderline kids were targeted to ensure they became C-grade kids. Against this very uncreative backdrop, I was being asked to look for creativity.

QCA

A new curriculum was on the cards and I was invited by the Qualifications and Curriculum Authority (QCA) to help in the assessment of Personal Learning and Thinking Skills – a kind of language of learning that had grown from the competency-based approaches of key skills and other for-mats. This I did, but I was suspicious of what lay behind it and of the language that was being used – the language of the committee and the bureaucrat. Surely there was something more?

Customers

Most poignantly I was beginning to see the results of the changes in educa-tion: kids were more focused on exams, grades, and learning how to pass, and as a result were becoming less independent and less creative. My meth-ods were going against the tide. This new breed of students were customers demanding a service, and the school was delivering this service to them. These customers sat at the table getting fat on the courses they were being fed, some of them force-fed. No longer were the students expected to enter the kitchen; rather they chose from a menu and expected it to be served up ready-cooked. This is the problem with spoon-feeding: the whole process devalues the making and concentrates on the service.

Prospero Parenting

In 2006 my wife and I became parents. As a father, I did not want my daughter to become a 'customer of education'. I did not want to be regularly updated on what level she had reached, how globally aware she had become, or how good at teamwork she was. I wanted her to be able to talk about the things that matter; not to ignore the latest ideas, but to allow those ideas to emerge from an engagement with great works of culture, art, science, and the historical and literary achievements of … for example, Maurice Sendak, Lewis Carroll, A. A. Milne, and Greek mythology.

I began to consider a 'classical education' – having her engage with the works of the great and the good. But at the back of my mind was this nagging doubt: how do I give her a language of learning, a way of taking control of the process? Is this akin to me, as a parental Prospero figure, imposing a language on my Caliban of a child? Yet it is Miranda, not Prospero, who teaches Caliban to speak. This makes a difference because she has innocence, an ethereal quality, and a far more gentle approach to life. Caliban complains that she has, '… taught me language, and my profit on't is, I know how to curse.' Will this always be the relationship between teacher and pupil?

The utilitarian education establishment wants my daughter to develop the language of skills for the workplace. But surely there must be something greater than the language of the committee and the aspiration of middle management. If I look at language as representing culture itself, and if I consider all the great works from the past – those great creative, artistic, and scientific achievements – then there is a way into this which offers a key that I can give to my daughter so that she can unlock the door and continue to discover life's richness and complexity, long after I have fallen off my perch and shuffled off this mortal coil.

Mantra

There was a clue to be found in something I had discovered in drama improvisation and in teaching theory. This was an approach to learning that could help my daughter process knowledge, relate to truth, and have the freedom to express herself. I began to search for constraints – a mantra that would assist her in her learning and allow her to develop her own voice. It was an attitude to learning that is at once based in knowledge, argument, engagement, belonging, and the capacity to make a difference. I needed to go back to the beginnings of learning inherent in my own conventional schooling. This was a tradition that had failed me because it was taken for granted that I had the key. I didn't.

But here I found it – a key that I only wished I had known about long before: the trivium.

Chapter 2
The Trivium

O, had I but followed the arts!

Shakespeare, *Twelfth Night*

So says the character Sir Andrew Aguecheek in bemoaning the quality of his education. The arts he refers to would not have been the subjects that we would think of today as the arts, but the seven 'liberal arts' that were the mainstay of a grammar school education in Shakespeare's time. The seven liberal arts were divided into the quadrivium: arithmetic, geometry, music, and astronomy, which were more about number and *content*; and the trivium: grammar, dialectic (or logic or *logos*), and rhetoric, which were more about language and *ways of doing things*. The three arts of the trivium would be developed simultaneously, and once mastered it was expected that a student would have acquired the knowledge, the reasoning skills and the ability to communicate well that would stand them in good stead for the further study of the quadrivium.

If there were three ways underpinning my education I was blissfully unaware of them. I was not taught any meaningful grammar; I argued the toss but was not taught how to use dialectic, nor did I understand the purpose dialectic had as an integral part of the learning process; and, aside from a couple of performances in school plays, I was never taught how rhetoric – the need to communicate well whether in written or spoken form – would help me in my future. Perhaps I can join in with Aguecheek's anguish. I can only conclude that the trivium had passed by the teachers in my school.

The fact that in most of my 20 years of teaching I knew nothing of the trivium also makes me wonder why it disappeared from the curriculum. I was attracted to the trivium because it was a mantra, and I had found that a mantra can really help students work independently, creatively, and in a focused way. I was also drawn to this mantra because it was not devised by some learned professor with money to make. No, it was rooted in tradition. Some of the finest minds had learned through the trivium; it had been tried and tested. But – and this is a big but – it had also, obviously, been abandoned. This set me wondering: how and why did the trivium come to prominence in the first place? Why did it stop being the basis of our curriculum? Is there anything from the trivium that survives in our schools today? Should I consider it as the basis of education for my daughter?

I began my journey armed with a library card for the British Library, a list of websites and bookshops, and a gregarious and curious nature, determined to ask questions of people who might have some answers or at least be able to point me in the way of more interesting questions. I started with the question: what are the roots of the trivium, before it even came to be known as 'the trivium'?

I was lucky to hear the classics professor, Mary Beard, give a talk on rhetoric. Afterwards, I approached her and enquired nervously where I should begin my quest. She said, 'Books!' and recommended a couple. I opened the first, a rather large tome, with great trepidation; it smacked of the world of temples, porticos, dusty Oxbridge professors, and their all too confident students. For me, this was a journey into the hitherto unknown. I was apprehensive, but I was curious.

Curiouser and Curiouser

It seems that curiosity, the ancient Greek idea that the world was a question to be answered, is the basis of the Western tradition of a liberal arts education. Sometimes referred to as the first scientist, the Greek philosopher, Thales (c.624–c.546 BCE), asked, 'What is the world made of?' And although his answer, 'Water,' was misguided, his question inspired the idea that young people should be taught to ask questions rather than just be given information to memorize. Could this be the beginning of the trivium: grammar, the art of interpreting the world through foundational knowledge and skills, is joined by dialectic, a way of testing the world through questioning, dialogue, or argument? A nice story about Thales is that he was so curious about the stars, and spent so much time studying them, that while he was looking up at the sky he fell down a well! I don't know if this is the first example of a figure in education making an idiot of himself, but it does show that the pursuit of knowledge is not without its risks. My nervousness at engaging with this knowledge was clearly because I was scared of falling into that well. But perhaps Thales teaches us that wrong answers are an integral part of learning: curiosity, wonder, and uncertainty are as much a part of education as answers, facts, and logic.

Pythagoras (*c.*570–*c.*495 BCE) brought logical and mathematical thinking to the solution of practical problems. Ironically, as a leader of a religious cult, he saw no conflict between his beliefs in the metaphysical and the 'scientific' approach he introduced. This may have been because his questioning of the world brought such extraordinary, universal answers that he thought he was experiencing divine revelation. There is a beauty in the natural world that is akin to a religious experience – a sense of wonder that unites the Archbishop of Canterbury, the Dalai Lama, and Richard Dawkins – and as this beauty unfolds it can arouse the curiosity of any child. What did it for me was seeing the moon landings and that image of our Earth, so small and insignificant from afar. Others have found it in wildlife documentaries on TV, standing on a cliff in a storm, the Gothic splendour of a cathedral, a pin-point pass on the football pitch, a first view of the Rosetta stone, listening to Allegri's *Miserere,* jumping up and down in a mosh-pit, falling in love, or even the first time one discovers the golden ratio.

Facts, questions, beauty, curiosity, and uncertainty; these are a lovely way to start my pursuit.

It's All Greek to Me

Becoming a parent brings together a sense of awe and wonder with the need to take responsibility and build for the future. When my child comes across 'important' things for the first time, I need to develop the empathy to know why that something is significant. She needs to ask questions and make sense of that importance from her point of view; and then she needs to be able to develop the ability to communicate about it using suitable methods in an apt or surprising way to express her newly forming feelings and ideas. Zeno (c.490–c.430 BCE) saw rhetoric, the third art of what would come to be known in the Middle Ages as the trivium, as an open hand reaching out to others. It is this image that can, perhaps, best describe how a child can be encouraged to communicate their growing understanding effectively. I hold out my open hand and she holds out hers, and community is the result. This is how we begin to build our shared experiences, our shared culture.

It's not all nice though. Zeno, considered by Aristotle to be the inventor of dialectic, also saw dialectic as a closed fist. This is the dialectic that can be used to punch the pomposity that sometimes accompanies the teaching of Important Knowledge. It is a skill we all need, especially when we see the emperor's new clothes for what they are. Zeno used questioning in a way that seemed to reduce everything to the level of the absurd. There is clearly a tension between someone telling you what 'the truth' is, and then someone undermining that truth through diligent and persistent questioning. There is a balance to be struck in the art of dialectic: a certain amount of questioning can cause most things to collapse under the weight of absurdity – as any parent knows when they try to answer every 'why' thrown at them by a curious child in their indefatigable and destructive search for meaning.

The questioning approach was to find its zenith in Socrates (c.469–399 BCE) and his desire to examine life in the search of a 'good' one. His endless questioning was to be the basis of not only Western philosophy but also, later, through Bacon, the foundation of inductive scientific empiricism. Unfortunately, Socrates' dialogues got him into trouble with the state authorities for his questioning of morality and his 'corruption of youth'. He was eventually put to death through the proffering of the hemlock cup, a punishment I have yet to see used in contemporary schools!

It is with the Greeks that we see the start of the trivium. We have the art of grammar, learning about the way things were or are; which is challenged by dialectic, questioning the way things were or are; and communicated through the art of rhetoric, showing how things could be. I present them here as though it was the most natural thing in the world that they would come together, but these ideas are not natural bedfellows; beneath them are very different ideas about how the world is organized and understood. Over the years, the three arts of the trivium have been in conflict, they have been responsible for their own decline, and, I will argue, they are still today at the root of many of the problems in deciding what sort of education we want for our children.

Dichotomy: The First Sign of a Problem

If I am to be a good parent, I need to encourage the idea in my daughter that curiosity is not best served by prejudice. If I want her to be an independent and free-thinking individual, I must not model the closed mind of someone who thinks there is only one way to wisdom, one True Path that leads to the number 42 and the Meaning of Life (Adams, 1979: 152). I need to investigate ideas from across the ranges of opinion. The three arts of the trivium challenge because they are, fundamentally, different ways of seeing the world. Just as I saw Stanislavski, Artaud, and Brecht as seeing truth in fundamentally different ways, so do the three arts. It would be far easier to be a grammarian, a dialectician, or a rhetorician rather than being an advocate for the trivium, because such an advocacy requires embracing contradictions and living with uncertainty, even paradox.

Although some teachers want politics out of education, we need to note that education is essentially a political act, as is parenting. Do we want our children to be just like us, or do we want them to be different and thus end up challenging us? This uneasy relationship between control and freedom is played out in every nation, every classroom, and every home. This tension is implicit in the relationship between grammar, dialectic, and rhetoric.

So, how did this tension play out in ancient Athens? The Athenian city-state's impulse to be conservative and ordered was in conflict with Socrates' Promethean impulse to be rebellious and innovative. Socrates might have been killed, but his influence on Athenian life was profound. Was it the ability to hold two or more contradictory approaches to learning at the same time that made Athenian culture so great? In *Full Circle: How the Classical World Came Back to Us*, the Conservative thinker Ferdinand Mount writes about how, in education, the progressive theorists and conservative traditionalists seem to re-enact the ancient falling out between Socrates and the needs of the Athenian state to prevent the corruption of the youth. With the progressives arguing for the importance of critical thinking to allow freedom of thought, and the traditionalists retorting that critical thinkers will end up educating people to be so cynical that they believe in nothing:

'True education does not consist in pumping children full of a mass of unexamined knowledge and prejudice, the critical theorists declare. On the contrary, without a deposit of knowledge and settled moral principles a human being is helpless, the traditionalists retort.' (Mount, 2010: 271)

The killing of Socrates is our metaphor for the battle at the heart of the trivium, the conflict between grammar and dialectic; it is the dichotomy, as Mount points out, between traditionalist and progressive educationalists, which is still relevant to this day. Grammarians were thought of as protectors of the language and sustainers of cultural continuity; dialecticians, such as Socrates, seemed to challenge accepted knowledge for destructive reasons. Maybe these are two distinctive approaches to education and, rather than being two sides of the same coin, they are completely at odds with one another. So, if grammarians and dialecticians have an uneasy relationship, what about rhetoricians?

Classical Rhetoric

The Athenian state educated boys for citizenship through the orator's art: rhetoric. It seems that, possibly because of the battle for supremacy between grammarians and dialecticians, rhetoricians subsumed elements of dialectic (*logos, inventio, disputio*; truth, invention, dispute) and 'good' grammar (including *doxa*, probable knowledge, and *episteme*, certain knowledge) into the art of rhetoric. At its best, rhetoric included a belief in ethics, sound argument, and an appreciation of the beauty of language. This was, seemingly, a version of the trivium, brought together in the name of rhetoric. However, even at this time, people could see that without substance rhetoric could become not only empty but, far worse, a dark art for persuading people to follow ethically unsound ideas.

Rhetoric came to the fore in the Roman world through its championing by Cicero (106–43 BCE). When he was young, rhetoric was not considered appropriate for a Roman to study, but Cicero had received his education in Greece, where he had learnt all the skills he would need to become a great orator. It was because of Cicero's oratorical success that Greek rhetoricians became popular in Rome; many made a living by educating young Romans in the art of rhetoric. Cicero's support for rhetoric included adding the vocational study of law to the Greek tradition and it was through his insistence that rhetoric was deemed to serve the 'common good'.

Education needs a purpose. However, what this purpose should be is still under discussion. Should it be to serve the common good, or should it enable someone to live a good life? Are these two objectives mutually exclusive? A nation state can define the common good according to its own needs, and we can define a good life according to the requirements of an individual. Without purpose, education, like rhetoric, can be empty. By clarifying its purpose we can make judgements about what to bring to the curriculum and how it is best measured. The arguments about exam passes, league tables, and 'evidence-based' education policies can only carry weight if we understand what we are trying to achieve. At the moment, the core of the argument seems to have deserted the visionaries and is mainly in the hands of bureaucrats and data-chasers.

Furthermore, in the 21st century, should we be looking forward and not back? Does our communication age need a formal education system at all? Perhaps the key to learning will become so personalized and so distant from the concept of a ritualized mantra that independence and creativity will be found in each individual rather than in any shared experience. Perhaps teachers will sell their wares over the internet, through blogs, YouTube, Twitter, or their more modern equivalents. Children might have a diet of subject-based and customized knowledge served up on plates, turning them into passive recipients who want nothing more than to know enough to get them an exam pass and a good job, in order to get a wage to pay for second and third helpings. Is this what we want? No.

Can Opposites Attract?

If grammar is represented by the Athenian state, dialectic by Socrates, and rhetoric by citizenship and the future of the community, how can the trivium become a mantra that makes sense today? It clearly has the capacity to be very destructive. If I am right that grammarians seem to be the forebears of today's traditionalists and dialecticians of today's progressives, then part of my quest will need to bring both those traditions together. In order to contemplate this, I will need to know the grammar of the trivium: what were the three arts, how have they changed through history, and where are they now? I need to embrace complexity. And I need to read more books.

Chapter 3

Our Dramatis Personae: The Grammarians, the Dialecticians, and the Rhetoricians

From ancient grudge ...

Shakespeare, *Romeo and Juliet*

Where the Wild Things Are

I proffer my hand; she puts her hand in mine. I clasp it gently but firmly, not wanting to hurt her but not wanting to let go. She looks at me and smiles. 'Instead of going to school,' I say, 'today I am going to take you back in time to find out what sort of schooling you would have had if you were born hundreds of years ago.' She giggles and tells me, 'Don't be so silly, Daddy.'

Perhaps I am being silly, but as we walk we pass Victorian terraces, then on through baroque architecture, past trees planted in Tudor times, climb a hill to view a small relic of the Roman era, and gaze out over an ancient river and the temples of corporate modernity, it is clear that everywhere around us there are traces of the past, easily ignored but not too difficult to find. I tell her we are going way back in time to follow the tangled history of the three different types of teacher: the grammarians, the dialecticians, and the rhetoricians. We are going to find out who they were, what happened to them and their ideas, and how they have opposed and accommodated each other over the years. I say, 'I want to find out why and how this has happened and, by looking at their history, I want to answer the following questions ...' She looks quizzically at me and runs off and climbs a tree.

Hmm, another approach is needed, maybe a bedtime story. That night, with her tucked up in bed, I begin, 'Once upon a long time ago there were three arts ...' 'What, like painting, drawing and ...?' 'Er, no. Three ways of teaching, um, three types of teacher ...' 'Three?' 'Yes, three. The first group were the grammarians, who were like parents; the second type were the dialecticians, who were the Wild Things; and the third type were the rhetoricians, who were like priests, politicians, and the people in adverts.' 'What did they look like?' 'Oh, the grammarians were rather stern looking; they dressed very smartly and never had a hair out of place. The dialecticians were scruffy, constantly moving around and looking for a fight. The rhetoricians were well turned out, friendly, smiling types.' 'Who were the baddies, the grammarians or the dialecticians?' 'Ah, yes, well, in each group there were goodies and baddies, but as they didn't get on, each group thought the other two were baddies, and they would steal some of their best ideas.' 'Stealing is bad.' 'Yes, it is, and they would also do down one another, saying things like, "Grammarians are boring", "Dialecticians don't care about anything", and "Rhetoricians are big fat liars". But one day a man called Boethius brought them together and said, "Hey guys, you should get rid of your bad friends and work together and set up your own school. Grammarians can make the rules, dialecticians can make the kids think, and rhetoricians can help the kids communicate well." So they did that and it was very good.' 'Can I go to that school?' 'Well, no.' 'Why?' 'Well, maybe, one day.' 'Why not tomorrow?' 'Well, because the school closed.' 'Why?' 'Ah, well ...' 'Perhaps there were more baddies than goodies?' 'I don't really know. Let's look at it in a bit more detail.' I turn the metaphorical page ...

The Grammarians

Telling it How it is

Typically, when I begin to talk about grammar, her eyes glaze over and very soon she is asleep. Perhaps she is dreaming of a white rabbit grammarian looking at his pocket watch and muttering about being late – I think of grammarians as sticklers for time. But no matter, let us leave her to her dreams.

A few months ago, I decided to teach my daughter Latin. *Nunc est bibendum* it says on my teacup; it was this bit of writing that started us off on our pursuit, 'What does that mean, Daddy?' I showed her the translation on the other side, "Time for a drink". 'It's in Latin,' I tell her. 'Would you like to learn Latin?' 'Yes,' she says. 'OK, I'll get some books.' As I sit down with my daughter to teach her and, of course, myself, Latin, all sorts of grammatical constructs become clear. As she learns to write and construct sentences in Latin, and translates them into English, we are both learning some fundamental rules, and both for the first time.

And, now, here I am learning about grammar and, thanks to my schooling, for the first time too.

Grammar, it transpires, in Western education, originally meant the study of Greek and only later Latin and Hebrew. It consisted of theory: the study of language; and the practical: the study of poetry. The intention behind the teaching of grammar in the ancient world was to enable people to gain a deep knowledge of literature. Dionysius Thrax (170–90 BCE) wrote the first surviving book on grammar. In it, he defines grammar by incorporating the work of the dialecticians and the rhetoricians. He believed that grammar had six parts:

1   Versification (trained reading)

2   Rhetoric

3   Dialectic

4   Etymology

5   Analogy

6   Drama and performed poetry criticism

If we include etymology and the learning of verse in grammar, analogy in dialectic and drama and performed poetry with rhetoric, we have the trivium. To Thrax, therefore, grammar is more than just 'telling it like it is'. He has included the contradictory and complementary traditions of rhetoric and dialectic *within* the study of grammar. This is clearly not the image of the stern grammarian I had been led to believe in. However, in *On the Marriage of Philology and Mercury* by Martianus Capella (fl. 5th century), grammar is offered by Mercury to his fiancée Philology. Minerva, listening to the equivalent of the PowerPoint presentation at a school's INSET day, quickly interrupts Mercury's presentation saying, 'Stop! Because the Gods are bored!' Something clearly happened to grammar. Why is it often, perhaps unfairly, seen to be dull? Perhaps the answer lies in when grammar became synonymous with the writing down of language.

Written Beginnings

It might come as rather a shock to those of us who love to read to discover that the root of written languages is not the work of the great writers. Writing arose as a utilitarian activity. Phoenician traders traded with the Greeks and introduced them to their alphabet; it was trade, not the desire for poetry, which drove the spread of writing. Poets, whose business was storytelling, might even have seen it as a threat. Plato quoted Socrates, for one, as asserting that writing would destroy memorization. Imagine writing considered as a sign of dumbing down! Religions and leaders, however, soon saw the potential of writing and used it to help establish their own mythology and rules. It was clear that the written word had power; due to its permanence it had become a symbol of authority. This meant that rules could become fixed; something is more difficult to challenge when it is written down. The accountants, bureaucrats, pedantic rule makers, authoritarians, and religious zealots were all early adopters of written language; the poets, dramatists, philosophers, novelists, and journalists were laggards. This monstrous conclusion perhaps could explain the problems that many have with the study of grammar. It is not that it isn't needed and doesn't exist in our utterances, but that the way it is taught – its rules and perceived lack of flexibility – is authoritarian. Some of us react with annoyance. As dialecticians, we hate being told what to do – we want to break rules!

Boring Grammar

Boring rote learning, chanting repetition, ritual humiliation, and a swipe across the knuckles – grammar as learned through a dark, dismal dictatorship. In the western facade of Chartres Cathedral the Liberal Arts are presented in relief, probably dating back to 1145; Grammar is shown holding a book and an instrument of punishment, and two children are cowering at her knees. No wonder kids have traditionally entertained themselves in the dialectical pursuit of undermining their teachers' authority: doodling in their books or scratching graffiti on their desks that mocks their teachers' idiosyncrasies. The cheeky response to the power of the teacher seems to go back a very long way. There is an example of Mesopotamian writing from *c.*1700 BCE: on one side of a stone (the exercise book of its time) a schoolboy has carved whatever the focus of his lesson was and, on the other side, a rude caricature of his teacher. For some reason, the gatekeeper of knowledge, the teacher, always seems to be held in a degree of critical contempt by the person who is meant to receive this knowledge. 'Why should we learn this? It's boring!' could be the cry of a generation who want to make their own impact on the world. To the young, the times they are always a-changin'! Grammar provokes due to its relationship with authority.

Grammar as Cultural Glue

Later in antiquity, grammar became perceived as the first step, the foundational knowledge, not only of language but also of culture. This took grammar away from being purely concerned with the workings of language into the area of our lived experience. In these terms, grammar becomes more contentious because it represents the underlying common fund of knowledge and, consequently, the cultural glue of society for the authoritarian ruling class. The power to decide what is worth knowing, and who should know it, has been contested ever since.

If my daughter is not taught what constitutes the common fund of knowledge, then what should she be taught? Should she be allowed to follow her own path and discover the things that she wants to know about? I am not allowing her to develop completely in her own way, of course. Should she want to run across a road, I restrain her. Should she want to stay up late, I put her to bed. Should she want to eat chocolate, I give her broccoli. I am feeding her cultural practices that I consider important; I am imposing a way of living that is the result of my (however limited) wisdom and experience. Sometimes this experience says, 'No, you can't,' and in others, such as learning ballet, playing piano, or writing poetry, it is, 'Yes, you can.' If we want our children to take part in society, they will need to be able to access certain knowledge and behaviours that will enable them to participate in this culture more easily. However, this relationship doesn't have to be one way and nor is it fixed. It could be argued that Bob Dylan is now part of the establishment that he did so much to undermine. Have the times changed so much that Dylan is now part of 'the old road that is rapidly ageing'?

There are children, schools, and families who respect order and discipline. The youngsters present themselves with their ties properly knotted, every hair in place, and ready to fit into the system. Other young people, on the other hand, who might feel like rebelling, already see the purpose of learning and flourish despite their environment; they are able to ignore some of the obvious contradictions and pedantry. At school, I was rebellious and questioned the whole chaotic system that had tried to impose a facade of order. Now, as a parent, I have to consider: do I want my daughter to be happy and accepting, passively absorbing knowledge as its torrents flow over her, or do I want her to have a rebelliousness that rejects the old with the 'shock of the new'?

The Dialecticians

Dialectic and the Art of Annoying People

Most nights, the bedtime regime goes like this, 'Time to switch the light out ...' She is reading. I love the fact that she is reading, but now it's time to sleep. 'Time to go to sleep ...' Usually she complies, sometimes she does so with a hint of belligerence, and sometimes, occasionally, defiance. This, as ever, is part of parenting. I represent authority, rules, and standards, and I want her to respect that. I have told her I do these things for her own good. How do I cope with rebellion? Don't I want her to have a bit of a creative, divergent, and belligerent spark? If she defies me, isn't that a sign of character? Hmm, maybe, but not tonight. Tonight is not the moment to explore her burgeoning character development, 'No debate,' I say. 'Good night, love you!' 'I love you too,' she says, and my heart melts.

Ignorance

I bet as a young kid Socrates was a nightmare at bedtime. Perhaps it was a childlike quality that made him approach the art of dialectic from the standpoint of one who knew nothing, and to question people who professed to 'know everything', thereby exposing the contradictions and gaps in their knowledge. He insisted he was assisting in 'the birth of new ideas', rather than annoying some rather self-important people. He thought he was the wisest man in Athens, not because he knew everything but because of his self-confessed ignorance, which, paradoxically, was a very wise thing to realize.

The Dichotomy: Grammar and Dialectic

The dichotomy between grammar and dialectic is at the root of a funda-mental and fascinating relationship in education. On the one hand, we have the grammarian idea that education means to pass on knowledge from one generation to the next and, on the other, the dialectician's notion that education can help in the birth of new ideas. Grammar is tradition; dialectic is modernity. Perhaps we can take this further into two views of what an educated person is: the first is the educated person who knows everything and passes all their exams; and the second is the person who professes to know nothing but asks awkward questions and gives birth to new ideas. Confusing? The dichotomy is an old one. Is education about 'putting things in' or 'drawing things out'? Hang on, though: drawing things out implies there must be something in there in the first place in order to be able to draw it out. Did Thales' well have water in it?

I asked Natalie Haynes, the comedian, writer, critic, and classicist, what she thought of Socrates and how he fitted into the education of his time:

Socrates refused to call himself a teacher. He proudly boasts that he's never taken a fee for teaching because he's not a teacher. This makes him differ from the Sophists of the time, some of whom, grammarians, were teaching the right name for things, and rhetoricians, who were teaching rhetoric – both of which they would charge huge sums of money for. If you read Aristophanes' play, The Clouds, Socrates is presented as the über-Sophist who runs the Thinkery, which, in the play, teaches you to be completely immoral. In the play, like the word, educere, to lead out, Socrates would be leading people out of their delusion, but he didn't know where he'd be leading them. The end goal for Socrates was to prove that we all know nothing. He was quite nihilistic, although occasionally that was not true. Mainly he was very negative, very critical.

This is fascinating; our characters are coming alive. The three different types of educator are becoming clearer: the grand style of the rhetorician, whom I can imagine with a resonant and fruity voice; the fact-finding pedantic grammarian; and the most dangerous underminer of all, the person who refused to see himself as a teacher, Socrates, who perhaps saw himself as an enabler. We can also see the debate enfolding about the role of the teacher: we have the grammarian passing on knowledge, the rhetorician passing on skills of oratory, and the dialectician questioning you to the point of ignorance. Socrates used a question-and-answer approach, *stichomythia* (a term from Greek drama in which characters converse by single lines only, a kind of uttered tweet), which was later turned by Lucian (*c.*125–after 180) into satire. I like to think dialectic has been much loved by radicals, revolutionaries, and cheeky school kids ever since.

Dialectic is the Word

Dialectic, though, is not as simple as I have so far made it out to be. Over its long history, it has been variously referred to as *dialectic, logic,* or *logos.* If these words all meant the same thing there would be no problem. However, they are not interchangeable because their meaning has altered over the years. So, which word should I choose? Is that dictionary of etymology going to help me?

Logos is often translated into English from the ancient Greek as 'word'. That seems simple enough. The word *logikos,* or logic, came from the word *logos.* Logikos was about the breadth and depth of all thought and reasoning. It was associated with any spoken thought that grew into narrative, even if this covered the meaning of works of art or myths, and anywhere an idea or opinion is given full rein. The word dialectic comes from the Greek *dialektos,* which meant discourse or even conversation, which seems almost mundane. *Logos,* on the other hand, lends itself towards a religious or metaphysical interpretation of 'truth'. In the first century, the Jewish philosopher Philo of Alexandria (*c.*20 BCE–50 CE) said it was *Logos* ('the Word') that organized the creation of the world under instruction from God. As it says in the Bible:

In the beginning was the Word, and the Word was with God, and the Word was God.

Christians used *logos* to mean 'universal truth'. It was the root of creation and was also Christ: the prologue to John's Gospel states that the Word (*Logos*) is 'made Flesh'. The apostle equates Jesus with truth, with *logos*. This stems from the Platonic idea of *logos* = truth = good.

At root, the three words – dialectic, logic, and *logos* – are quite different and carry very discrete power. *Logos* is the ultimate creator, the 'truth'; logikos is lesser and still represents all thought but seems more human; and dialektos is that most human of activities, a chat. Apparently, it was St Paul's (*c*.5–*c*.67) suggestion that truths in the Christian faith might be superior to truths in rational argument that really opened up a Platonic and Aristotelian schism in *logos*. Now, what on earth does that mean? I think I'm going to have to look at how the two great philosophers, Plato and Aristotle, differ. I warn you, this gets messy, because the words dialectic and logic become interchangeable but, by the end, I hope to have a definition of dialectic, *logos*, and logic that works for me.

Plato vs Aristotle

Plato (*c*.427–*c*.347 BCE) believed that when dialectic is used as an approach to critical self-awareness it could attain insight into one's higher reality or self. As Natalie Haynes put it, 'Plato came along with "the forms", realizing there was a big gap in the core of Socratic thinking, that there isn't an answer, there are just more questions. Plato used the idea of the forms as an answer to that: that we, as "pre-born" people, learn about truths.'

This is one of Plato's key ideas. Maybe the reason that we know how to pick up language, how to feed, breathe, recognize our mothers, and all sorts of other things that seem innate, is because our souls existed before they were planted into our bodies at birth. The rest of our learning is about rediscovering or drawing out what our souls already know. Plato used the word 'dialectic' to describe the ultimate part of the process that leads us to 'the truth' – rediscovering the true, universal essence (for example, the perfect redness of red, the perfect horseness of horse).

Natalie continued, 'In some ways I am quite Platonic. I do, slightly, believe in some things, that there is the perfect answer somewhere. I am not a cultural relativist. I think, for example, advertising is based on a belief that subconsciously, somewhere in our souls, is the Platonic ideal.' Dialectic in this sense is far from destructive. Plato thought dialectic was a way to uncover the greatest truths of all. *Logos* points to higher truths; it is what Heraclitus referred to as the universal, everlasting idea – the cosmos that exists within and without and where *even opposites come together*. Part of this art is how we get from dialogue to *logos* – the holding together of differing views.

Aristotle (384–322 BCE) wrote extensively about logic and turned dialectic into a formal art. Aristotle believed dialectic was a useful approach in everyday discussion about important subjects where certainty was not always possible. He wanted words to describe reality as experienced. Does this mean Plato is rooted in the idea of certainty and ultimate truths, and Aristotle engaged in the cut and thrust of debate on a human level and was happier with uncertainty and doubt?

In order to help me answer this question I needed to understand how Plato's and Aristotle's ideas have affected philosophy down the years. Some philosophy books divide philosophers into two types: those who are mainly Platonic and those who are mainly Aristotelian. As we have seen, Plato believed that there is universal 'true' knowledge or intelligence (*noesis*) that comes from before (*a priori*). Therefore, philosophers who believe in universal truths or solutions that are timeless and beyond what happens in day-to-day life have tended towards a Platonic view. In contrast, Aristotelian philosophers would not philosophize in universal, a priori ways; they would start in the 'real' world as experienced and take an approach more akin to an *a posteriori* (what comes after) view. This is messier and engages with uncertainty, and thus is more likely to go with the flow.

Both Plato and Aristotle are open to the other's way of thinking. Plato wrote about Socrates and his engagements with 'not knowing'; Aristotle wrote extensively about logic and trying to get near to 'truth'. But, generally, the dialectic between Plato and Aristotle is one of *certainty* versus *uncertainty*, the *universal* versus the *particular*. This, I suppose, is typical of dialecticians – they are prone to argue amongst themselves. In order to have a simple way of differentiating these three parts of the dialectical art, I will categorize the Socratic approach as dialectic; the Aristotelian as logic – an analytical or scientific process; and the Platonic process as *logos* (for example, as witnessed in the famous dialogues where Plato uses Socrates as an interlocutor who enters into chats (dialectic) to find truth (*logos*)).

Can our schools be establishments that embrace complexity and uncertainty? On the whole, they tend to be places where certainty rules, 'Write this down, in this way and you get an A. Get an A in this and that and the other, then go to this university and get a good job,' and so on. Do I want my daughter to believe in the certainty that Father Christmas exists, or should she entertain the possibility that he might not? The grammarian will tell it like it is, either by agreed practice or imposed rules; the Socratic dialectician will ask about it until it is no longer; the Platonic dialectician will discuss it until 'ultimate truth' is revealed; and the Aristotelian dialectician will use an approach that should uncover possible truths with differing degrees of probability.

The Rhetoricians

Now You're Talking: The Art of the Orator

The formal teaching of rhetoric seems to be missing from my daughter's schooling; it lives on in the idea of performance. I have seen my daughter perform in nativity plays, music recitals, and dance shows. At home, she has put on her own plays and performs the parts of the three witches in *Macbeth* with frightening authenticity. Performance is an important part of our relationship: it gives her a point of focus and it gives me an opportunity to pause and listen to her expressing herself formally at a given moment. In this instant, she expresses something of herself within a given discipline – she has learnt the 'grammar' of rehearsal and now performs her part.

Cicero (106–43 BCE) highlighted the importance of rhetoric in *On the Orator* (*De Oratore*). In this work he emphasized that by placing the art of oratory in the 'right' hands, rhetoric becomes the highest form of the expression of humanity. Cicero believed that proponents of the specialized arts of philosophy, logic, mathematics, cultural studies, literature, and music were numerous and could reach any target they wished to set themselves, yet would rarely achieve mastery. For Cicero, it was the rarity of great orators that set the art apart. He implied it was the character of cultured and ethical men that enabled them to speak great truths. For him, to be a great orator you needed a formidable quantity of knowledge, the ability to arrange and choose words well, to understand every emotion, have a good sense of humour, be 'appropriately' cultured, quick yet sensitive, and have a great memory. Rhetoric reflects the good and virtuous person who has truly mastered knowledge – the cultured individual, the 'great man'. Do I want my daughter to be a 'great man'? Hmm, there is a lot to unpick here.

Is rhetoric an art to which only a few can aspire? Cicero expands this idea in *On Obligation* (*De Officiis*), in which he sees the search for, and scrutiny of, truth as obligated to wisdom and prudence. For him, community cohesion is essentially part of decency and decorum; justice and beneficence come to be virtues, as do kindness and generosity. Proper behaviour is obligated through the desire for knowledge, and ignorance should be something to be ashamed of. This would make a possibly controversial school motto, 'It is shameful to be ignorant.' For Cicero, dialectic and research are essential but we are obligated to public service, where thinking will be taken up by projects for a good life or through advancing learning and knowledge. Education is tied to virtue and ethics, particularly the idea that the pursuit of knowledge is proper behaviour and that to even contemplate ignorance is reprehensible. Oh, that we keep this wisdom in sight: to be wilfully ignorant is an evil unto yourself; for a school, or any institution, to hide knowledge or make it difficult to obtain is similarly wicked.

Cicero absorbed dialectic into rhetoric through the idea of a debate which presented both sides of an argument. He generally liked to leave these dialogues unresolved, allowing readers and listeners to make up their own minds – something that could be seen as a precursor to a more open-ended dialogic approach. In contrast, the Socratic approach had as its aim the defeat of the interlocutor. Again, this is the idea of dialectic as dialogue, with its etymological roots in *logos*.

Can You Teach Virtue?

Ancient Greek, Roman, and Chinese societies all saw the need to educate young people in the ways of morality and to prepare them for a role in civic society. The first question that Meno asks Socrates is whether virtue is acquired by teaching or by practice. Sophocles seems to be open as to whether it is taught, practised, or even a gift from God. Later, in a dialogue with Protagoras, Socrates seems to say that virtue is based on knowledge and is in fact made up of four virtues: courage, justice, temperance, and wisdom. When, at his trial, Socrates is accused of 'corrupting the young', he retorts that all of society teaches virtue, so it wasn't his fault because, by implication, if the young are corrupted, then we have all had a hand in it.

This defence did him no good, but it is an important consideration. If we are surrounded by crime or anti-social behaviour, do we all have a responsibility for it or can we just wash our hands and blame our schools? Can you have a good school in a bad society? Can you have a good class in a bad school? Can you have a good student in a bad class? Can a good action come from a bad student? Schools can't solve all the ills of society, but they can contribute to them. As a parent, I want to know what are the virtues upholding the school my child attends, what is the ethos, and how are they expressed? This is because, if I know what a school's values are, I can work with them as part of the greater community.

Why Bring the Three Arts Together?

We have the authoritarian grammarians with their 'valued' knowledge and rules. We have the communitarian rhetoricians with their great oratory, who bestow citizenship and are interested in the development of virtuous character. The former tell you what to do; the latter encourage you to get involved. Added to these we have the awkward dialecticians, those who want to enter into debate, dialogue, or even just have a chat. We have the scientifically thinking logicians, all reason and slightly removed. We also have the Platonic dialecticians (*logos*), the believers in higher truths – perhaps they are quasi-religious types or have artistic 'vision'. I might even suspect that they are prone to megalomania. Whatever they do or believe, they operate on a different plane. In the interest of education for wisdom and a good life, all of these come together under the umbrella of the trivium.

However, I can also see how by bringing all these contradictory ideas together we might possibly have the root of the destruction of the trivium. Is it inevitable that the trivium can't work because people are unable to see their way to accommodating different ways of thinking about and seeing their world (especially when you are a school student with no idea about how to articulate some of these differing world views, let alone all of them)? In my own case, as a schoolboy, I was unprepared for any of this thinking.

Chapter 4

The Liberal Arts:
A New Curriculum is Born

And Prospero the prime duke, being so reputed
In dignity, and for the liberal arts
Without a parallel; those being all my study

Shakespeare, The Tempest

The Spread of Christianity and its Grammar

Throughout the early Middle Ages, the so-called Dark Ages, Christianity proliferated rapidly throughout Europe. At this time, Christian texts were written and memorized in Latin. There was an urgent need to educate people in religious ideas, so it was necessary for them to learn Latin in order to read these sacred writings. Consequently, the learning of Latin and Christian doctrine used up most of the time on the curriculum, and instruction came from didactic grammarians who taught in repetitive and boring ways. The Church frowned upon the idea of two-way dialogue, preferring the one-way catechism (literally 'to sound into ears') by which the master instructed his pupil. Even the word 'dialogue' was understood as a one-way tool for transmitting 'truth'. In order to teach Christian dogma, grammar became the main art of learning. Significantly, the study of grammar was not only used for the literal and allegorical interpretation of the Bible but also a few other classical texts. And thus began the canon of the great Western tradition.

Although much maligned by modern-day progressives, a canon brings together the concepts of rules, the sacred, and the authentic with ideas of quality. How a text enters the canon is controversial. It can be accepted because it is genuine or because of its accuracy or value. Once a text has entered the canon, it is treated as authoritative. A respected canon is certainly useful because it makes the teaching of children much easier. All a teacher needs to say is, 'Here is a work of quality. Now sit there and realize why. And if you don't, then you are at fault for not having the necessary taste and sensitivity to accept or understand quality.' Can this one-way process truly be called an art? And can teaching be a one-way street? Perhaps, in the Middle Ages, it was possible because what was being taught was new, exciting, and 'the truth', and mainly was taught to boys as a vocation. My daughter, however, is not being brought up within a vocation, or in a world where one book dominates, or where the 'truth' goes unquestioned. She is faced not with simplicity but complexity.

Augustine's Argument on Dialectic

When instructing children, you soon realize how complicated even the simplest things can appear. The pulpit approach to teaching works to a degree, but the neo-Platonist, Augustine of Hippo (354–430), thought that complex spiritual ideas needed to be taught in different ways. A fraught relationship with faith led him to pray, 'Lord make me chaste, but not yet!' Augustine believed it was possible to know things; he was not a sceptic. He thought about the use of language and whether it was simple or complex. He defined a simple word as meaning 'one thing' and a complex word as meaning 'more than one thing'.

By implication, the grammarian approach works reasonably well when language is describing simple things, but is found wanting as the level of complexity increases. Complexity, for the Milanese professor of rhetoric, meant there was a need for dialectic, which he described as the art of arguing well. Augustine's approach was to adopt Plato's idea of education as 'leading the truth out from within' rather than 'pushing it in from without'. In order to awaken what was already within the pupil's mind, he began with the familiar and moved on to the unfamiliar. He decided that students should be actively engaged in the learning process and he used the trivium in a flexible way, rather than just starting with grammar and shovelling it all in. This challenges the idea of the trivium as being used in a particular order. The ritual of the trivium, once understood, is infinitely adaptable.

In Augustine's time, the Ciceronian idea of the discrepancy between a writer's intention and his words became reinterpreted as the difference between literal and spiritual explanations. It is through this distinction that Augustine was able to connect classical Platonic thinking with Christianity. He thus brought together simple grammar and dialectic for more complex ideas, with the idea that rational thought served faith, but did not surpass it as God was always and ever will be 'truth'.

So, perhaps, the teacher can begin with didacticism: there are certain simple things that can be taught, but because the world is, and always has been, complex, there are ideas beyond the simple and these are dealt with through dialectic. We start with the simple that can be known, move on to the complex that can be discussed and investigated, until we reach another, more metaphysical understanding. This I take to be *logos* – faith or universal essence – which is known or felt.

The Seven Liberal Arts

Grammarians, dialecticians, and rhetoricians – along with astronomers, architects, and others – relied on Greco-Roman institutions to ply their trade, and this brought these different types of teacher together. The classical liberal arts education was on the rise. In classical antiquity, a variety of subjects comprised the liberal arts, but it is generally down to two men that the seven liberal arts came to the fore. These founding fathers were the neo-Platonist Roman philosopher Boethius (*c.*480–*c.*525), who had translated

Aristotle's work on logic (the only work of Aristotle to be translated at the time), and Martianus Capella (*c.*430–*c.*500), who was responsible for *On the Marriage of Philology and Mercury*. But even as some young people were beginning to be taught these seven arts, Boethius was imprisoned by a group of conspirators and wrongly accused of treason. While in prison he wrote *The Consolation of Philosophy*, a book that, apparently, did nothing for his cause; he ended up being executed. Not much consolation there.

Other influences on the liberal arts were Augustine's *On Dialectic* and Varro's (*c.*116–27 BCE) *On the Latin Language*. Significantly, Varro also wrote nine books (now lost) on what he referred to as the 'disciplines'. The first three books were about grammar (which he also called 'literacy'), dialectic, and rhetoric; the others were arithmetic, geometry, astronomy, music, medicine, and architecture. The use of the word 'discipline' rather than 'art' is significant. Isidore of Seville (*c.*560–636), who is known as the last scholar of the ancient world, drew on these works and others for his *Etymologies*, in which he dropped the more vocational disciplines of medicine and architecture.

The first part of Isidore's *Etymologies*, Grammar, starts by looking at distinctions between art and discipline. He explores the idea that 'discipline' (drawn from the Latin for learning, *discere*) is where 'the whole thing is learned', and 'art' (drawn from the Latin *artus* (strict)) is defined by strict precepts and rules. Isidore also points out that the Greek word for virtue is ἀρετή (*arete*), which is the word the ancient Greeks used for 'knowledge' and is another possible source of the word art. Art, for Isidore, who was influenced by Plato and Aristotle, was drawn from opinion, resembled truth, and meant that things can end up with a variety of different outcomes, virtues, or meanings. In contrast, the word discipline was based on 'true' arguments, meaning you could reach only one outcome or meaning. This distinction is vital. It allows for the possibility of the student either having to find their own way through the 'arts' or developing in a more rigid way by means of the 'disciplines'. The trivium, being the basis of the liberal *arts*, is therefore a process in which a student begins a subject or topic by learning about its language – the rules and precepts. They then develop their own ideas and begin to express themselves in a variety of ways. The liberal arts are open-ended. A *discipline* on the other hand would be illiberal by having pre-ordained outcomes. This brings out the reasoning behind the trivium: grammar, dialectic, and rhetoric are arts through which we are taught a way of thinking that is liberating. An art offers an open-ended approach, as opposed to a discipline where we are trained to follow one path, which is closed.

How do we want our children to be when they leave school: open to possibilities or closed to follow one path? Our Western cultural tradition chose to situate education in the liberal arts rather than the disciplines. The mantra that the trivium delivers is one that enables free thinking – its essence is creative. So, should schooling ever be about fixed outcomes, such as answering exam questions in 'correct' ways by responding to a limiting list of assessment criteria? Or should we be looking to our schools to encourage variable outcomes and to develop virtuous characters with mindsets that are creative, open to challenge, and able to change?

The Trivium: Where the Three Roads Meet

Boethius and Martianus Capella defined the liberal arts as the four *calculating* arts (arithmetic, music, geometry, and astronomy) and the three *philological* arts (grammar, rhetoric, and dialectic). The word 'philology' meant a mix between literary study, history, philosophy, and linguistics. However, it was not until medieval times that the term 'trivium' itself would come to prominence and the seven liberal arts would be established as the basic curriculum. Perhaps it was the trivium that helped unleash the huge step forward in art, ideas, and literature in what is known as the Carolingian Renaissance (*c.*800–900).

It was trade with the Orient (where ancient Greek heritage and manuscripts had been preserved) that brought further changes and challenges to Western European culture and, consequently, to education. In Islamic culture, Aristotle was known as the first teacher and his teachings had quite an impact. The excitement around such pagan texts was understandable, considering the importance of education in a modern, dynamic 12th-century Western society. When more of Aristotle's works were translated into Latin they caused great consternation in the Christian world: his ideas on experience and reason challenged Christianity's view of the fundamental truths.

The grammarian Hugo of St Victor (*c.*1096–1141) proposed that secular learning was a necessary foundation for religious understanding. This meant that as well as the study of religious texts, grammar and the canon were being opened up to a number of secular or pagan texts. Hugo said that the purpose of the liberal arts was 'to restore God's image in us'. This is significant as he is suggesting that a worthwhile aim is to aspire for something beyond the particular, something more than ourselves. We need to see study as a restorative, a way of finding God within us – or, as we might put it in our rather more secular age, fulfilling our potential or allowing ourselves to be more than who we think we are. It is necessary, therefore, to consider what our aims and purposes should be.

The Purpose of Education

The trivium was now becoming the foundation of all learning, so it is important to clarify the benefits of educating pupils in this way. John of Salisbury (*c.*1120–1180) talked about the power of the trivium to create independent learners, 'Those to whom the trivium has disclosed the significance of all words … do not need the help of a teacher in order to understand the meaning of books and to find the solutions of questions.' He went on to suggest that grammar, dialectic, and rhetoric are arts because they 'delimit' the self: they nourish, they enable us to grow, they strengthen the mind towards wisdom from rules or virtue, all of which result in our 'liberation'. A laudable aim; this is the arts as cultivation, as the roots of culture. And, as we increase our understanding of the vast complexities of culture, so we will define what education is for.

Autodidacticism, the art of teaching yourself, is something we all need to be able to achieve. I do not expect my daughter to leave school knowing everything there is to know, but I would like her to acquire the habit of learning on her own, of having knowledge, processes, and criteria by which to judge what she is yet to learn. The trivium is a *way* of learning rather than just the *what* of learning.

In ancient Greece, the arts equated knowledge with virtue and gave a purpose to study for the good of all, not just the self. Plato's aim for education had been that it 'should be for its own sake' and result in freedom. But freedom for whom? Those to whom full citizenship was bestowed were men, not women, and were free, not enslaved. Socrates desired that these free men use their leisure time productively in thought. Aristotle made a further distinction between the superior pure forms of art and the more practical, inferior arts of designing and making. Thus the liberal arts became associated with a privileged education for the independent elite – another schism that abides to this day.

For my daughter, independence – an ability to understand and find solutions – would seem to be a good thing, and I would like her to love learning for its own sake. We are lucky to live in a culture that recognizes the rights of women to be educated as free citizens. I would like her to be educated to spend her spare time in worthwhile activities, including a pursuit of the pure forms of higher culture. However, I would also like her to have experience and skills in the so-called inferior arts, such as an engagement with a craft in which the authentic experience of doing is as important as thinking.

This is a notion that I need to make clear: the breadth of study I am arguing for is not purely academic. Nor do I support the idea that the well-to-do should solely study the academic superior arts and the poor the inferior arts. If we are to retain private schools, they need to produce as many good bricklayers as bog-standard state schools produce Nobel prize-winning authors and scientists. Schooling is reflective of our civilization and our values. Schools are not places which absolve us of our responsibility for the education, care, and behaviour of all our citizens. Schools can help shape the future, but not without the help and examples set by all.

The Conflicts Continue

With the trivium firmly in place it was perhaps to be hoped that the three roads would settle down in harmony with each other. The story of what followed shows that at times this was possible, but at other times contradictory tensions would rise to the surface.

Abelard and the Importance of Dialectic: Castration and Scholasticism

In the early Middle Ages, boys alone were taught in cathedral schools, unlike monasteries where both sexes were taught. It was at Notre-Dame Cathedral that the Aristotelian Abelard (1079–1142) was a teacher. Twice condemned for heresy, Abelard's preference was for dialectic over all other parts of philosophy, and this emphasis put him in direct conflict with older and more traditional grammarian teachers. Although his work resulted in a very masculine world of verbal sparring, later institutionalized in the universities, Abelard's best student was a woman. Her name was Heloise. It is thought that somehow she attended some of Abelard's lectures and they fell in love. Abelard, 20 years her senior, was appointed as Heloise's tutor by her uncle. They married in secret and had a son together, Astralabe. Abelard's role in the battle between dialecticians and grammarians was such that, it is reported, he shouted, 'Heloise, dialectics has made me hateful to the whole world!' One cannot be sure that it was Abelard's insistence on using dialectic that caused Heloise's uncle to attack and castrate him one night, or the anger her uncle felt about the seduction of his niece. Either way, Abelard's interest in Heloise's claims that passion led to devotion waned somewhat after the incident. This may have given rise to his coining of a new word, 'theology', by which he meant the use of rational argument to sort out acts of faith. This dialectical form of knowledge was now to be exclusively the preserve of men and definitely devoid of passion. Abelard's famous work, *Yes and No*, listed the contradictions of the Church, using this as the basis for exploration rather than as a threat. Consequently, medieval thinkers began to embrace the plurality of truth and the importance of reason. Crucially, some universities were now able to operate as semi-autonomous centres of learning in pursuit of truth and rationalism, rather than just institutions of religious dogma. Into this atmosphere the new translations of Aristotle were welcomed with open minds.

Some universities in the 12th century excluded grammar from their teaching, relegating it to the new grammar schools, where it was taught to students in order that they would have the knowledge necessary to enable them to face the more challenging dialectical approach of the universities. However, these schools were few and far between. The idea that schools should teach the more simple grammar to prepare students for the more complex dialectic of the universities is something that, it could be argued, remains to this day. So, if my daughter doesn't attend university, does this mean she will have only a limited experience of the trivium? After all, attending a grammar school and learning 'stuff' turns you into a vessel, and by learning grammar alone this vessel is not balanced enough to navigate the complexities of the world.

What balance do we require? The idea that (grammar) school prepares you for university presupposes some kind of progression, a learning journey through which one moves from simplicity to complexity, from facts to wisdom. There is the danger that, if these stages can only be reached through formal education, if we leave education early on we will lack the tools to reach the next stage. I would advocate that *every* stage of schooling should prepare students for becoming wise, knowledgeable, and virtuous.

Aquinas and the Rise of Aristotle

Most universities were not so progressive. The study of Aristotle was banned in many, although some radical teachers ignored this ruling. Albertus Magnus (*c.*1206–1280), a religious man who, like Hugo of St Victor before him, insisted on the importance of secular learning. Crucially, he was the teacher of Thomas Aquinas (1225–1274). It was because of his teacher's influence that Aquinas was able to create a Christian Aristotelian philosophy to defend the Church's doctrine and faith. This was to be of momentous importance in philosophy and education, and by doing so he helped set in motion a scientific revolution.

Aquinas thought reason was the highest state of being. This contradicted Augustine's more Platonic view that reason was subservient to faith. Aquinas felt that philosophy and religion are separate, but that it is through reason that man would find God, thereby uniting certain Platonic approaches with Aristotle's views. Aquinas thought that the highest ends were reached by humanity striving towards them.

Aquinas, who coined the term *tabula rasa* (usually attributed to Locke) was in conflict with more conservative theologians who had reacted to the difficulty of uniting Aristotle's thinking to Christian grammarian orthodoxy and the dangerous outbreak of thinking that had occurred in some of the universities. He asserted that all of our knowledge of the world came from reflecting on our experience. Aquinas's thinking is highly empiricist. Despite the knowledge gained through our senses we cannot prove that God exists, and although we might see that things can and do change, those things were made by other things and not by God. However, if we were to keep going back we would find the first thing that occurred, the beginning, and that would be because of God. So to Aquinas, if we reason correctly, we cannot come to any other conclusion than that there is a God. Aquinas's nuanced thinking brought together philosophical thought and Christian belief.

In December 1273 Aquinas had a breakdown, and in 1274 he was summoned by the Pope to explain his ideas, but he collapsed and died on the way. Was this a sign of God's anger? Four months previously, during mass, Aquinas had experienced such a cathartic episode that he said it made all his work seem like straw. What that experience was we shall never know. His death saw the Church revoke much of his teachings and widened the schism between the dialectical scientific thinkers and the more grammarian traditionalists. His work was condemned in the universities of Oxford and Paris, despite Aquinas having studied and been a master there.

The great contribution that Aquinas made was to set the mind free, allowing people to explore their humanity, whilst at the same time still holding onto their faith. The Church took time to accommodate Aquinas's way of thinking, as did some universities. Paris revoked its condemnation 50 years later, although Oxford has yet to take this step. The Church was now able to take on Aristotelian ideas, bringing together grammar and dialectic, faith and reason, but there was an inherent paradox. With the benefit of hindsight, it was this freeing of thought that ultimately enabled people to later challenge both the teachings of the Church and Aristotelian philosophy, and helped lead to the decline of the trivium.

Common Good

To Aquinas, the common good of the community was superior to the common good of the individual, meaning that virtue was both outward looking as well as an intrinsic good. He took on Aristotle's idea of the virtues (although he changed the virtue of intuition to understanding) and went on to describe the superior cardinal virtues: courage, justice, prudence, and temperance, and the secondary virtues: art, science, understanding, and wisdom. He thought you could become a good artist or thinker through the secondary virtues but you could only become a good person through the cardinal virtues. Above these qualities come the theological virtues of faith, hope, and charity.

This idea of the virtues reaching outward is inherent in the idea of rhetoric, for it is in community that we are most human, and it is in the conversation with humankind that we reflect most on ourselves. By taking on the idea of the liberal arts as arts we encompass an idea of virtue, although the arts liberate the idea rather than dictate the terms. If virtue is dictated to us as a set of behaviours which we cannot adapt or change then in itself it is not virtuous.

Ockham's Razor and the Victory of Aristotle

The medieval age finally came to an end when the English philosopher William of Ockham (*c.*1288–*c.*1348) applied his razor; that is, where there are competing theories the simplest answer is often right, thereby fully integrating Aristotelian philosophy and Christian theology in the 14th century. Universal ideas, said William of Ockham, were products of man not God. Nothing relies on anything else in order to exist: we can discover and know things from the application of grammar and logic. For William there were but two realities – empirical scientific truth and religious truth – and the two were separate, with no way from one to the other. In one swift cut, science and philosophy were free from theology and could become part of mainstream thought. The liberal arts tradition began to thrive.

This flourishing of learning led not only to Latin grammar being studied but also national languages. For example, the first grammar schools in France began teaching French grammar in the 1300s, and this practice soon caught on in other countries. National grammar schools began to spring up in most large towns, and they had a need for accessible teaching and learning materials. In the 12th century some grammar books had been written in verse (was this an early example of dumbing down?). By the end of the 14th century, thanks to these schools, students arrived at university far better prepared than before. This meant there was more time for students to study at a higher level. This scholasticism saw the liberal arts enshrined in the curriculum at the universities of Oxford and Prague, and both flourished as places where intellectual freedom was cherished.

Renaissance, Petrarch, and the Return of Plato

Petrarch (1304–1374) saw the medieval emphasis on Aristotle as a period of decline in thinking, literature, and morality, and declared the previous thousand years to be a 'dark age'. He wanted to move beyond Aristotle, demanding that a wide range of classical works, including the work of Plato, should be studied on their own terms, without having to be 'Christianized'. Petrarch added to the great Western canon the works of Cicero, Virgil, Homer, and Plato, amongst others. Petrarch had begun a new education, reuniting grammar, *logos* (as opposed to just dialectic or logic), and rhetoric. Added to the trivium was the *studia humanitatis* (philosophy, history, and poetry), which, I argue, is also an extension of the trivium, with history pertaining to grammar, philosophy to dialectic, and poetry to rhetoric.

Petrarch also restored the ancient Greek creative tension between Aristotle and Plato: the particular and the universal, reason and imagination, exterior and interior. That this creative dialectic brought forth the Renaissance was also mirrored in the figure of Petrarch himself – his spiritual, psychological, humanist, and aesthetic approach to the world made him, arguably, the first Renaissance man. Petrarch also admired Socrates and was a major force in seeing his age as a rebirth of classical times. The Renaissance was to unite the intellect, the imagination, and the spiritual in a neo-Platonic combination of contradictory creative forces. Pythagoras was again in vogue, influencing Copernicus (1473–1543) to use mathematics to measure the world. This was history as cyclical rather than linear. Promethean man had returned, but now, significantly, it was divine genius that could drive a man to create wonderful things. No longer was divine creativity the sole preserve of God (or gods); truths were to be found in art and literature. The Renaissance shifted mankind towards exercising the critical faculties for uncovering greatness and universal truths, but these were now the truths of humanity rather than of the gods. Platonism saw beauty as an essential part of the search for truth. For example, the Renaissance humanists had a desire for rhetoric to be persuasive but also to be convincing through its aesthetic, its elegance, and its eloquence. This attitude led to a revitalizing of poetry – and grammar – in the reading of the great texts.

The Renaissance began in the 14th century in times of turmoil and economic depression. There was tension between East and West, corruption in the Church and State, violence and disease, the decline and rise of new nation states. Against this backdrop there were many new inventions, including that most transformative agent of change, the printing press. The liberal arts flourished. Cicero's work on the importance of good character, virtue, leadership, and versatility in times of change was rediscovered, and this led to the adaptable liberal arts coming to the fore in education.

In 1479, Rodolphus Agricola (1443–1485) set out a method for reading a text dialectically. In Florence, the trivium held sway and soon enabled a fertile breeding ground for contradiction and argument. In the 15th century, a fully fledged Platonic centre of learning was founded under the patronage of de'Medici family. The de'Medicis were famously a family close to the papacy, especially the Borgias; this comradeship brought the Church fully on board. The trivium had reached another high point, as evidenced by Thomas More's letter to his daughter in 1517 in which he wrote, 'I see … you have not left aside any of your usual pursuits, either in exercises of logic, in the composition of declamations, or in the writing of verses.' Now, if I were to write a letter to my daughter, what would I comment on? The usual pursuits in contemporary schooling do not lean towards logic and declamation.

Tensions, of course, remained. Erasmus (1466–1536), the Schoolmaster of Europe, wrote many books for use in grammar schools. An old grammarian, he was intent on re-establishing grammar in a world where dialectics and rhetoric held educational sway. The writer Rabelais (c.1494–1553) attacked the humanist neo-Platonic curriculum as established by Petrarch and his followers, protesting that there was so much content in the course of study that pupils would have no time to think. For him, education meant liberation. Montaigne (1533–1592) agreed with Rabelais and wanted to educate the whole person, with the emphasis on understanding rather than simply knowledge. The trivium retains this debate at its core: the balance between what and how much to learn, how much time for thinking and criticizing, and how much for developing your own ways of communicating – how to be a free-thinking citizen. In other words, we have the eternal compromise between free individuals and the demands and mores of the community.

Milton: Of Education

By the mid-17th century, Milton (1608–1674) had written, in *Of Education*, that a virtuous and noble curriculum should include the study of Plato, Plutarch, Aristotle, Demetrius, Longinus, Hermogenes, and Cicero, and that the purpose of education was for the good of the state. He believed novices should start their educative journey to mastery with the laborious study of 'some good grammar'. They would then reach the more fertile slopes of the hillside, by reading some Socratic discourses, tempered by lectures and explanations that would 'draw them into willing obedience'. As they become 'enflam'd with the study of learning', by which they may 'delight in manly and liberall exercises', they would come to use eloquence and persuasion. They would then learn ethics and morality and the 'knowledge of personal duty'. Milton was a great believer in the importance of exercise, diet, music, and other activities, such as travel, in forming character, or 'breeding'. However, he did not think every teacher would have the wherewithal to teach this form of education, which was heavy on knowledge and included 'the queen of the arts', logic. Logic, he believed, was especially ill-served by poor teaching. Crucially, in *Of Education*, Milton showed his idea of the journey of education – learning that progresses from sense experience through the abstract to citizenship.

The Good Life

The three ways of the trivium – knowing, questioning, and communicating – had come together as the basis of a great education. *This* is what I want for my daughter. I want her to know about things and how to do things. I want her to be able to question, both to find out more and also to realize that some things aren't known, can't be known, or aren't fully understood.

I want her to communicate about things she has discovered, surmised, or created in the way of an open hand to the world. Finally, I want all this to have a purpose, which can be summed up by the phrase 'a good life' (because I certainly don't want her to have a bad one). When I look at the three arts of the trivium and the pursuit of a good life, I wonder why it was beyond the wit of my school to give me this grounding, and why it shouldn't be the grounding for a great education now. Surely, there is nothing that could stop the trivium from being the foundation of schooling for my daughter in the 21st century?

Chapter 5

The Rise of the Rational: The Fall of the Trivial?

So throughout the world children are spoon-fed all the opinions under the sun before they are able to acquire the capacity to make judgements.

Voltaire

The trivium, as a child of philosophy, was enhanced both by the thinking that brought Aristotelian philosophy and the Christian religion together in theology, and by the burgeoning educational institutions. It was the other children of philosophy – science and rationalism – that would threaten the trivium, and then destroy it as the avowed basis of the curriculum. The modern era rejected many of the ways of thinking and communicating based on traditional classical or religious knowledge and reasoning. Added to this, the economic need for society to educate more of its citizens to ever higher levels would mean that what and how to teach would take on a more utilitarian purpose; that is, how to educate children to become productive, malleable workers and managers rather than independent thinkers.

Nowadays, education is almost wholly a ticket into the world of work. No longer is the emphasis on the idea that we are to be educated in order to attain wisdom or to live a good life. The focus has shifted from educating for your leisure to educating for your wallet. The liberal arts have become disciplines. Education is dominated by discussions around the right systems, subjects, and skills in order to achieve the closed outcomes of high test scores in a global marketplace. This has raised the question of whether there has been a decline in standards. Grammar, ethics, aesthetics, virtue, citizenship, creativity, character, contemplation, critical thinking, imagination, innovation, independent learning, and communication skills have all been neglected, at various times. The 'education debate' has become a topic of discussion, where politicians and educationalists let off steam to ease their frustration. Want a scapegoat for all of society's problems? The easy target is to blame schools or teachers for today's ills, from too many teenage pregnancies to the financial crash …

Behind all this is an important question: what is education for? Do we want our sons and daughters to leave education fully up-to-date with the 21st-century skills necessary for the workplace that we envisage and able to specialize in just one or two areas? Or do we want them to be polymaths, with wide and adaptable expertise, particularly ranging across the sciences and the arts, with an ability to think for themselves, and to be fully engaged citizens who live flourishing, virtuous lives on the way to achieving wisdom? Do we want our children to study hard traditional subjects or soft modern subjects? Do we want them to be trained in soft skills – such as empathy and working in teams – or to know their times tables and be able to use the possessive apostrophe? Do we want our young people to know key dates and events from history or to be able to use the internet to find out anything they want to know? Often referred to as false dichotomies, these choices are very much part of modern educational discourse and have become ever more urgent due to the perception that widening access to knowledge has completely changed what and how we should teach our young people.

There is no doubt that technology has inexorably altered our lives. Perhaps by being interconnected on the internet our children have access to the democratic wisdom of crowds, which gives more importance to knowledge emanating from a popular authority than that acquired through expertise. In our social media age, information comes from sound-bites, aphorisms, and rhetorical flourishes rather than by recourse to any particular authoritative body of knowledge. The ignorant become just as respected as the wise, and in many cases far more influential. For example, in January

2013, James Argent, from the popular television series *The Only Way Is Essex*, had more than a million followers on Twitter, whereas the controversial scientist Richard Dawkins had to make do with less than half that number, and the popular philosopher, Alain de Botton, about a quarter. If each tweet is a portion of the knowledge of our age, democratically accessed from computer or mobile phone, which knowledge has the most effect? Without hierarchy do we have a democratic levelling of knowledge where every brick can be perceived as great art?

This means that the trivium is relevant because we live in a more democratic, scientific, technological, and culturally relative age. Does the trivium need the cultural authority that comes from a limited Christian and classical canon and access to 'truth', but which has also rendered it useless in the march to modernity? What were the main challenges to the trivium that eventually led to its downfall? It was the modern age that was to see the decline of the trivium. An increasingly secular age, believing in the power of science to discover truth and measuring value through the market, would not be satisfied with the old ways of learning.

The Republic of Letters, the Challenge to Aristotle, and the Triumph of Science

Harking back to Cicero's ideal of a *respublica literaria* (the equivalent of a Facebook group of interested and engaged people), an international community of learning uses written rhetoric to knit its community together. The Republic of Letters (dating between the late 17th and 18th centuries) included many Renaissance polymaths and others who had been enriched by a liberal arts education and the trivium. In their number were philosophers and early scientists: Copernicus, Galileo (1564–1642), Bacon (1561–1626), Descartes (1596–1650), Locke (1632–1704), and Newton (1642–1727). Throughout the modern era, science would challenge the authoritative knowledge of the Church. Galileo, inspired by Pythagoras and Plato, and in opposition to Aristotle, was imprisoned by the Church for his heresy in questioning one of the basic tenets of faith –

that the Earth was the centre of the universe. This argument between belief and knowledge threatened the basis of a classical liberal arts education. Copernicus's publisher saw the danger and tried to save the liberal arts by claiming that the sun-centred universe was but a set of 'novel hypotheses'.

Paradoxically, this scientific thinking was also threatening the very philosophy of those who had been at the forefront of the epistemic approach: Socrates, Plato, and Aristotle. As reason and rationality became the new buzzwords, it was the trivium's link to Christian theology and education that was trivializing it. But why did this happen? Is the trivium really only of use in a time where knowledge is fixed and authoritative, where there is but one God, one Book, and one set of transcendent values? If dialectic is used to prove one 'truth', to reach one 'true' conclusion then, indeed, the trivium does become problematic in a world of uncertainty.

The Trivium in Decline: The Trivial, Grandmothers, and Sympathy for the Devil

Evidence that the trivium was in decline during the 16th century can be seen in the literature and vocabulary of the period. For example, in *Doctor Faustus*, Marlowe (1564–1593) ensures that Faustus dismisses logic on his way to making a pact with the devil.

Settle thy studies, Faustus, and begin
To sound the depth of that thou wilt profess;
Having commenced, be a divine in show,
Yet level at the end of every art,
And live and die in Aristotle's works
Sweet analytics, 'tis thou hast ravished me!
(Reads) Bene disserere est finis logices.
Is, to dispute well, logic's chiefest end?

Affords this art no greater miracle?
Then read no more; thou hast attained that end.

Marlowe was educated at Cambridge in rhetoric and dialectics, and there is much in the play that reflects Marlowe's education. Could Faustus's pact with the devil be an allegory of the demise of the trivium? Probably not, but it is clear that belief in the trivium and its component arts was on the wane. In the 16th century, rhetoric first began to be regarded as artificial or ostentatious, and the whole of the trivium itself became associated with the modern interpretation of the word 'trivial'. In 1589, the first use of 'trivial', meaning ordinary or common, is recorded and, soon after, Shakespeare reflected a further decline in the status of the trivium: in *Henry VI, Part II*, the first recorded use of trivium meaning 'insignificant' occurs. In Act 3, Scene 1, Suffolk says, 'And yet we have but trivial argument'. For the trivium to be seen as trivial, in its modern sense, is devastating. Both the idea that it is common and that its study leads to nothing of any particular importance, ensures that it is open to further adjustments and attacks.

The Advancement of Learning: Knowledge is Power

Was the trivium dead or was it adapted for new times? Science would slowly outgrow philosophy and, eventually, to all intents and purposes, make a land grab for all of philosophy's concerns. In his work *The Advancement of Learning*, the grammarian Francis Bacon, considered by many to be the originator of scientific method, refashioned the trivium for the modern scientific age. He was concerned with rational knowledge and how to transfer it to others. This was an inductive, logical way of thinking, drawn from the pre-Socratics, which linked philosophy and mathematics. This undid much of the medievalists' work linking theology with the trivium. He called this rational knowledge 'tradition' (in effect, the trivium renamed). The three component arts were Organ, Method, and Illustration. Organ was speech, including gesture and words, and is more akin to our contemporary understanding of grammar. Method was no longer dialectic or *logos* but 'empirical logic'; that is, teaching a form of argument in order to secure reason (not to be confused with abstract principles), or moving from deductive methods to inductive ones. (Deduction is reasoning from the general to the particular; induction from the particular to the general.) Illustration was to fill the imagination with reason and to communicate in such a way as to adapt to your audience – in other words, rhetoric.

Bacon was so distrustful of the dialectical model that he said it should only be used to remove pre-judgements, and not to administer doubt and dispute. He believed there was a moral imperative to secure emotions to reason, implying that reason was far more important than emotion. He felt that emotion should not distract man from the pursuit of wisdom. Bacon thought that the followers of Aristotle knew how to collect data, but they didn't know how to read it. He asked that people take the same empirical approach, no matter what the subject matter. He disliked the way that different types of proof were sought in different subjects, saying that, 'the rigour and curiosity in requiring the more severe proofs in some things and … contenting ourselves with the more remiss proofs in others, hath been amongst the greatest causes of detriment and hindrance to knowledge' (Bacon, 2002: 229).

Bacon wanted to focus on facts and wished to avoid theorizing, 'analyse experience, take it to pieces and by a due process of exclusion and rejection, lead to an inevitable conclusion' (ibid.). He is suggesting that an inductive, empirical approach that avoids abstraction will lead to rational conclusions. He thought that by beginning in doubt, one ends in certainties. This reflects a belief that the world can be categorized and understood, and that empirical science can bring us to certain truths. So, although the movement from deduction to induction is significant, Bacon inhabits a world where we might begin a quest with uncertainty but end it with certainty. Even results that showed a hypothesis was wrong were of interest to Bacon: if something was proved to be false it could be dismissed. It was this idea, perhaps, that would be of greatest interest to a man who would be influenced by Bacon's ideas and who will come into our story later, Karl Popper.

By 1672, traditional grammar had become the object of Molière's (1622–1673) satire. In *The Learned Ladies* (*Les Femmes Savants*), he continued the long line of those who enjoyed satirizing the grammarians. *Grammaire* had now become *grand-mère*, a grandmother whose offspring would grow up and live in a very different world than the one she recognized. This issue is still very current in the 21st century, where modernity seems to remake the world with alarming rapidity; one becomes a grandmother all too easily. As technology and culture change, it doesn't take long for us to become out of touch or to hanker for a past that has already passed us by.

For the trivium, there is a problem with a world that seems to be changing ever more quickly. For example, how can grammar – which needs a certain amount of stability and authority – retain relevance in a world where capitalism, technology, globalization, and mass communication threaten its claims to correctness, rule making, and belief in tradition? In an ever-shifting world, the young are more likely to look to each other as travelling companions, rather than listen to the sage-like advice of grandmothers sitting at home telling them how things were better in her day.

I Think, Therefore I Don't Know

It is from the Enlightenment that the challenges to the ideas that underpin the trivium – authoritative knowledge and dialectic leading to certainty, and rhetoric communicating that truth – would now come thick and fast from philosophy, science, and commerce. Using the scientific method, Descartes wanted to learn whether there was anything we could actually be certain about. He argued that anything based on our senses and beliefs are open to doubt except one, and that is, 'I think, therefore I am'. Reason was the only way to acquire knowledge, which he called rationalism. Descartes thought that dialectic could contribute nothing to the discovery of truth and declared that it should be a branch of rhetoric. Dialectic was only to be used to explore truths that were already known; everything was to be in doubt until one found certainty through deductive reasoning.

Conversely, Locke thought that we are born with our mind a blank slate or *tabula rasa*, and although we have innate capacities, we do not have innate ideas. He judged that everything we know is gained from experience: a pure empiricism. Newton, who believed that we stand 'on the shoulders of giants', thought that the real reason we could see further was because of the enlightened, rational approach – and this would bring about the triumph of science. His scientific method was to harness both the induction beloved by Bacon and deduction revered by Aristotle.

David Hume (1711–1776), however, echoing Locke and reaching back to the ideas of Sextus Empiricus (*c*.160–*c*.210), believed that we should be sceptical and opened up 'the problem of induction'. Hume viewed human perception of nature as intrinsic to our understanding. He understood it as our first perception, the strongest perception. This awareness comes before, and connects ideas through, memory, imagination, or reflections. Influenced by Bishop Berkeley (1685–1753) – who thought that if empiricism was fully taken on board then this would mean that all things exist in the mind rather than outside of it – Hume stated that impressions come first and ideas second, and are experienced as a faint copy of the impression.

Hume's greatest contribution to philosophy is his theory of causality. What causes these impressions? His answer was chaos. He thought chaotic whirlwinds of sensations leave impressions, and from these impressions ideas are formed, which occur as they are ordered in the mind. The fundamental importance of this view is that our ordered ideas come from our imagination, rather than a relationship to any truth beyond those impressions. Hume's fork separates reason and enquiry into two prongs: *relations of ideas* and *matters of fact*, something *demonstrable* and something *probable*. In mathematics, we can demonstrate 2 + 2 = 4, which is an example of a priori, deductive logic. To Hume, these relations of ideas are worked out in thought and need not tell us anything about our existence. We can only demonstrate whether matters of fact are probable if we provide empirical evidence for them. Now, this is taken a step further when Hume looks at the way we infer things from evidence in the past. Just because something has always occurred when an event is observed, does not mean it always will, and this becomes the problem of induction. For example, if every swan you see is white, it does not mean logically that the next one you see will also be white and not black.

Hume's theory of causality means induction, and therefore science itself becomes difficult to justify. In order to deal with this, Hume argues for a 'mitigated scepticism' where common sense tempers the excessive scepticism, or Pyrrhonism, which holds we cannot ever know truth. These opinions are ordered in our minds into narratives that become our world view. We rationalize that view, and by seeing the world from our viewpoint, we convince ourselves that our thinking is based on reason. This reason becomes our custom, our way of doing things – which, of course, can be wrong. Custom and tradition are important as they shape our world view and also, thanks to this conservative philosopher, we can also see that we need to question our traditions, our grand narratives, and be sceptical about how we view the world.

Rousseau (1712–1778), who famously wrote, 'Man was born free, yet everywhere he is in chains', thought that education corrupted man's nature and perpetuated the evils of modern society. He believed that education should be guided by the senses rather than thought: heart not head. Some see Rousseau as the harbinger of the progressive education movement and all that is wrong with modern education methods.

The Challenge from the Specialization of Labour

Education during the Enlightenment was to be based on pure reason. Adam Smith (1723–1790) wrote about rhetoric, describing it, at its best, as a form of communication that expresses the thoughts of its author precisely. And the model for rhetoric was to be found in trade. For Smith, rhetoric was a necessity because of the need to communicate about new inventions and through more complex trade relations, just as had been the case in earlier times. He thought that beauty should still be central to rhetoric, but that this could be found more in the simple than in the ornate; that is, less is more. This is a very clear break with the rhetorical flourishes beloved of the classical and Renaissance eras.

Another challenge to the ideals of a classical education was Smith's philosophy on the specialization and division of labour. These were the opposite of the ideal of the Renaissance man or polymath. Smith recognized that early specialization in education would not produce fully rounded human beings. Although he dismissed the study of Latin and ancient Greek languages as 'primitive', he understood the need for a Greco-Roman style liberal arts tradition, which would be provided by a truly national education system, available to all, through small local schools.

Kant Criticizes Pure Reason

After the salvoes from Bacon and Descartes, dialectic was to suffer a further setback from Kant (1724–1804). In his *Critique of Pure Reason*, Kant posits a problem with dialectic as, possibly, 'The logic of illusion'. How many times have we heard or been involved in a dialectic or argument that seems to love the sound of its own voice more than it has anything to do with 'fact'? Again, Kant: '[dialectic, for the ancients was …] a sophistical art of giving to one's ignorance … the outward appearance of truth.' (Kant, 2007 [1781]: 92). Troubled by Hume, and drawing on Plato's work, particularly on that which was related to metaphysics, dialectical criticism was, for Kant, essentially exposing the contradictory character of knowledge, especially when shown in the light of a single principle. Metaphysics was, therefore, beyond reason. For example, we will never be able to prove or disprove the existence of God.

Kant's synthesis of rationalism (the idea of reason leading to knowledge) and empiricism (knowledge comes from experience) led to his concept of transcendental idealism (both reason and experience are vital for knowledge). For Kant, what we are conscious of is always evolving. This would, in turn, lead to a rebirth of dialectic through Hegel (1770–1831). One of the main results of Kant's work is that 'pure reason' would come to be viewed as more subjective and relative. Relativism would go on to become the great enemy of the authoritative, classical Western tradition.

By the 19th century, rhetoric had lost its place in the curriculum – it was viewed suspiciously as an (unscientific) art of persuasion. With its demise went the last vestiges of dialectic. However, a significant change in the dynamics of the educational world appeared at this stage – the intervention of the state into mass education. This was driven by the needs of the industrial age and the desire for a suitably educated workforce, and would bring a new tension to the education debate: how to educate the masses rather than just a privileged elite? The utilitarian desire for the greatest good was split between the Benthamite ideas of relativism and Mill's belief that there was a hierarchy of knowledge and skills.

Utilitarian arguments still echo in educational discussions today. Jeremy Bentham (1748–1832) believed in 'the greatest happiness for the greatest number', regardless of the quality of the pleasure. Learning about authoritative, high culture – the canon of the Western tradition, for example – could be as important as eating a Big Mac; all knowledge and skills were as important as each other. Education is now seen as a journey towards employment rather than wisdom, and is clearly distinguished from the idea of a liberal arts education for its own sake. Grammar, in its widest sense, loses its authority based on quality and tradition. It becomes, at its core, a more democratic ideal: culturally relative and reflects the practices and interests of the young. A curriculum without any sense of value or authority is no curriculum at all. Some people bemoan this lack of hierarchy, as well as the utilization of knowledge for the means of succeeding in a capitalist world – rather than in the more thought-provoking, but less economically viable, pursuit of, for example, reading and appreciating the great 19th-century novelists. Another utilitarian, John Stuart Mill (1806–1873), argued that 'education for all' would improve general happiness, but he differed crucially from Bentham in that he believed in a hierarchy of pleasure, with the higher intellectual pleasures more important than lesser ones. Mill advocated the idea that pleasure can either be immediate or worked towards, and that, of the two, delayed gratification offered the greater and higher form of enjoyment. This idea of difficulty as a way of accessing greater pleasures might give succour to high-minded intellectuals whose work is often perceived by the general population as inaccessible. But it might not be welcomed by those who make more populist art, with its more immediate and emotional connection, which could be regarded as easier to access and therefore somewhat lacking. The 'T. S. Eliot is better than the Beatles' argument is worth having in education, because what to teach is always, at root, about our attitudes to culture and values, and how they relate to who we are.

We need to be able to enter into that debate, but are we able to have a similar discussion in areas where knowledge is more fixed? Where is the room for doubt with a priori knowledge, where the truth is predestined and imbued with authority? Or in extreme fundamentalist religions, where it appears there can be no doubt? The same might be said for mathematics. Mill even argued that experience was at the root of the 'necessary' truths of maths and logic, which meant, rather controversially, that arithmetic, for example, is a posteriori rather than a priori. This is extreme empiricism, indeed, but it opens up certain areas in logic for doubt to be encompassed. Although challenging the trivium and its adherence to vestiges of truth, it does provide the space for challenge and change even in the most disciplined of forms.

The Disappearance of Grammar

The 1944 Education Act (in England and Wales) guaranteed access through the 11-plus – to all students who could pass it – to a kind of liberal arts education in grammar schools; meanwhile, more vocational, manual 'illiberal' studies would occur in secondary moderns. The use of the word 'grammar' emphasizes that these schools tended to put great store by one aspect of the trivium and taught it through the learning of Latin and its grammar, as well as through traditional English grammar. Later, as comprehensive education came to the fore, Latin began to disappear from the state sector, as did the teaching of traditional English grammar. Comprehensive schools, first devised in the 1920s, came to prominence in the 1960s. Fuelled by the modernity movement and the 'white heat' of technology, the promise of a more meritocratic age enabled the 'comprehensivization' of schools to continue apace.

Between 1965 and 1975, virtually all state secondary schools in the UK went comprehensive. Offered a chance to knock down the old class barriers, most people saw that the stuffy grammar schools (which seemed to represent an outmoded tradition and had failed to keep up with the times) and the 'dumping ground' of secondary moderns (which had failed to fulfil the ambitions of many parents for their children) were both ripe for renewal. But there was more to the revolution than simply types of schooling. Comprehensive schools became places where progressive educational ideas would take root. If grammar schools were the preserve of the grammarians and authoritarian traditions, then comprehensives, instead of being 'grammar schools for all', would soon be seen as the preserve of the progressives, and would offer an alternative view of what an education should or could be. This shift echoed ideas from Rousseau. The progressives wanted to challenge society and the stifling chains it wrapped around the young. The chances are that if you were educated in an English comprehensive between the 1960s and 1990s you were not taught traditional grammar at all, and other parts of the canon were under a relativist attack: why study stuffy old classics when there was rock 'n' roll?

Political Divide: Stability vs Change

Do the traditionalists of today have their forebears in the Athenian state and grammarians of yore? Are our contemporary progressives the sons and daughters of Socrates and the dialecticians? Over the years, each has borrowed from the other, and although both sides find adherents across the political spectrum, it can be broadly held that traditionalists are from the right and progressives from the left. The grammarian traditionalists value a world of rules, stability, and examinations that measure worth in terms of our ability to absorb the knowledge and narratives of the past. On the other hand, the dialecticians seem to delight in the language of change and see the need for a new paradigm in education to cope with the new challenges of the 21st century. The grammarians trust the methods of the past and are sceptical of academic intellectuals, whom they accuse of dominating the educational establishment. The progressives, however, look at the traditionalists as representing the knowledge of a bygone age that has no relevance to the needs of today.

With the changes that happened to dialectic from Francis Bacon, Adam Smith, and Jeremy Bentham onwards, we also have the progressives (along with libertarian conservatives) finding an accommodation with science and vocational and soft skills, and seeing these as a worthwhile way of enhancing the market and our country's ability to compete internationally. With the traditionalists looking on doubtfully, the progressives' language is all about skills, creativity, vocational and technical qualifications, and the need to educate young people for the world of work in a high-tech future. They also have faith that advancing technology will disrupt the need for a hierarchy of knowledge and, in some instances, the need for knowledge at all. They assume that information will be picked up as and when it is needed. Old-school traditionalists regard this with horror, wondering why what was deemed good in the past, all of a sudden, has no purchase in the present. The data set they cling to is the highly academic exam with its emphasis on reproducing knowledge. And, as far as they are concerned, standards are falling. The progressives, with academic data technologists on their side, point instead to evidence-based approaches that 'prove' that the new ways are best. So, although both sides borrow each other's ideas from time to time, the two cultures in education are as far apart as they have been through most of history.

As we have seen, the trivium tends to divide opinion. The three arts are incompatible with each other, and there is no simple way of bringing them together. The grammarians hark back to an age of authority, the dialecticians see only the never-ending modernity implicit in scientific thinking and the rhetoricians find themselves split down the middle. On the liberal side they lean towards ideas of citizenship and the importance of communication technology; the traditionalist rhetoricians tend towards promoting the learning and recitation of approved poetry and the idea of character-building activities.

There are some individuals in the 20th and early 21st centuries on whom we can draw. Some were rooted in one of the trivial arts, others saw beyond the conflict and in reinterpreting the trivium they showed how the arts and the trivium could be relevant to our age. However, their ideas have not become part of mainstream educational practice. The reason is probably political. There is a large and almost unbridgeable divide at the heart of education: both sides wish to treat schooling as a simple ideological battle; they are unwilling to embrace the resulting complexity that emerges when the competing sides are brought together.

I need to find out if it is possible to refashion the trivium in the modern age in a way that unites right and left, traditionalist and progressive. For without accord, education will continue to be knocked around in the maelstrom of politics. To avoid or minimize such a buffeting, education needs to absorb the political world into its workings. This means our schools need to embrace a culture that is at once traditionalist *and* progressive.

Chapter 6
Trivium: A Clash of Cultures

And we are here as on a darkling plain
Swept with confused alarms of struggle and flight,
Where ignorant armies clash by night.

Matthew Arnold, *Dover Beach*

By the end of the 17th century, the trivium was struggling to compete with the new enlightened and progressive science, and its ability to unearth and deal with 'true' knowledge rather than superstition. The call was, 'We need 17th-century skills!' The trivium had been formed in an age when religious beliefs had a stronger hold on the transmission of knowledge and the concept of truth. That was now beginning to change.

A similar argument is occurring now. Some argue that the 21st century is so different from previous periods, in terms of its technology and fast-moving culture, that it requires a completely new way of educating young people. This challenge arises because, in these days of globalization and mass communication, information is no longer protected by gatekeepers of knowledge. In their place the internet – with its new gatekeepers, Google, Wikipedia, and so on – has democratized knowledge. The skill of finding out has become easier; a more 'trivial' way of learning has replaced the traditional methods that required making an effort to access a particular body of knowledge, whether through books, libraries, lectures, or courses. Instead, lots of 'stuff' is now available on a device you can carry around in your pocket or bag.

This dialectical challenge to institutions, authority, even to knowledge itself, is seen by some as a threat to our very culture. Instead of facts stored behind closed doors, we access knowledge on our smartphone or tablet computer. The modern-day progressives say that all we need to know are the skills of accessing knowledge; we don't need to 'know' anything else. This attitude has been responsible for numerous moral panics, and the traditionalists have fought back to protect our culture from the liberal attack. So, out go skills and in comes Our Island Story; out goes enquiry learning and in comes a body of knowledge including good Victorian stalwarts like Florence Nightingale and kings and queens. At least, that is how the spin in the tabloids goes.

As we have seen, this argument between traditionalists and progressives has a long pedigree. However, if we perceive culture as a battleground between two world views, where one side must win, do we really want to accept the destruction to the 'losing' side that this would entail? Can we really envisage all schools being progressive schools where only skills are taught, or all schools being traditional schools where only knowledge of the distant past has dominion? What would be the relationship between our schools and our society if one side were to 'win' the education game? This debate is not just about our schools; it is about our very culture – and our culture thrives on the tension between the two.

Grammar, Dialectic, Evolution, or Revolution?

Throughout its history, dialectic was often problematic for those in authority in that it enabled inherited ideas to be questioned and turned in new directions. Dialectic can challenge the traditional with the force of the modern. The German philosopher Hegel rejected some of the ideas of the Enlightenment thinkers, such as Descartes and Kant. In particular, Hegel believed that the way we experience the world changes; not only in terms of what we experience, but that our consciousness itself evolves, and it develops in a dialectical way. Dialectic for Hegel (and also for Marx, Engels, and Darwin) is similar to the Greek concept, but it differs from Latin, medieval, and Renaissance ideas.

Hegel revelled in dialectic's 'ability to cause change'. His dialectic, as expounded by Friedrich Schiller (1759–1805), works like this: firstly, an idea is given the appendage of truth (Hegel called this *thesis*). The thesis is then tested with an equally logical *antithesis*. Although these opposite views are seemingly incompatible, Hegel thought that we should look for a *synthesis*, and it is through this process that we are on our way to gaining knowledge. Each synthesis becomes a new thesis, and thus the dialectic keeps going until 'ultimate knowledge' (*Geist*) is reached. Hegel believed that the search for *Geist* was what drove history, and although we couldn't control it, we are always driven by the 'spirit of our age', the *Zeitgeist*.

Hegel influenced two other greats: Karl Marx (1818–1883) and Charles Darwin (1809–1882). Marx, along with Friedrich Engels (1820–1895), revered dialectic because it not only allows change, thanks to its Socratic ability to expose contradiction, but because it can cause conflict and therefore function as the 'motor of revolution'. Darwin saw dialectic as development that keeps on going – the 'motor of evolution'. For Marx, however, the *Geist* should be fought for and would result in victory for the revolutionary class and 'an end of history' in the form of a communist state. That went well.

The Hegelian dialectic gives an insight into how the arts of the trivium might relate to each other – with grammar as thesis, dialectic as antithesis, and rhetoric as synthesis. So, it seems there is yet another process at work in the relationship of the three arts; for Hegel, this is how history moves. In the trivium, therefore, grammar represents the past, dialectic the challenge of the present, and rhetoric is synthesis, bringing the other two together to make the future. This is the trivium as conflict and resolution.

Dissenting Voices:
The Challenge to Utilitarianism

In the 19th century, as the state began to educate more children, the ever-present dissenting voices became louder. This dissent was anti the status quo and it was rooted in cultural and political values. The questions – How should we live? What values should we have? What should we know? What skills should we have? – all became vitally important. Increasing state involvement in education led to a greater need for accountability and assessment. If government invests money, it wants to know immediately how its investment is doing. This, in turn, led to objections about how education was no longer serving the greater good, but had started to serve the needs of commerce. The Industrial Revolution seemed to be mirrored in industrial schools. Cardinal Newman (1801–1890) talked with despair about the birth of the 'exam factory', and John Ruskin (1819–1900) wrote that the creature can be made into a tool or a man, but cannot be made into both. These more 'romantic' voices included Thomas Carlyle (1795–1881), who came up with the term 'industrialism'. Carlyle, championed a grammarian pragmatism, suggesting that the alphabet was 'the indispensable beginning of everything'. To this he added, hinting at the ancient trivium, 'The beginning of merest logic ... to impart the gift of thinking to those who cannot think' (quoted in Williams, 1958: 82), and he wanted all this to be provided through popular education.

Crucial in this movement against industrialism and materialism was Matthew Arnold (1822–1888). He was the chief inspector of schools and the son of the famous headmaster of Rugby School, Tom Arnold. Arnold wanted to spread 'sweetness and light' instead of what he saw as the inadequate education of the barbarians (the upper class) and the philistines (the middle class). He wanted to strengthen the liberal arts tradition, perceiving culture as a civilizing agency that, through its pursuit of perfection, would enable people to leave the world a better place. Arnold thought that education should be about the study of 'the best which has been thought or said'.

This idea that learning should be qualitative and improve people's lives is a persuasive one. After all, no one wants learning that is damaging. Although

Arnold understood that rational, scientific knowledge should be a part of education, he thought it should be included alongside literature and should never be the main focus. This was education as cultural capital for all, cultivating character as well as intellect in order to help eradicate human misery, rather than unleash anarchy in society. Arnold's thinking was to find support from both traditionalists and progressives, and his critique of industrialism is an almost quintessential British sensibility. Our national character distrusts the 'dark satanic mills' of technological change but has a romantic view of the rural idyll, 'the green and pleasant land' of our collective cultural memory.

That this view of our rural past seems to ignore poverty is not the point here. Our 'myths' can be highly significant, rooted in a collective and contested idea of the essence of the past. They might not be real in a factual sense, but they are genuine in how they feel. The myth of St George and the dragon is as much a part of our history as the Battle of Agincourt. The Edwardian children's history book, *Our Island Story* (Marshall, 1905), starts with mythology: the story of how Neptune made his fourth son, Albion, king of this island. How much of our collective past is in fact 'fact'? Perhaps the greatest myths of all are the stories of King Arthur and Robin Hood. We even communicate an idea of 'Britishness' to the rest of the world through fictional characters such as James Bond and TV series such as *Downton Abbey*. Education is a fundamental part of how we perceive our shared culture and values; how we view culture, and write and rewrite our myths and narratives, makes education intrinsically political.

Education in England continued to evolve, shaped by Matthew Arnold's romantic and anti-utilitarian desire to ensure individuals are touched by the best that has been thought or said. Albert Mansbridge (1876–1952) established the Workers' Educational Association (WEA) with this very much in mind. He wanted the working class to 'imagine the rivers of learning and purity in the world and bathe yourself in their living waters'. As one of his tutors, R. H. Tawney (1880–1962) put it in his essay, 'An Experiment in Democratic Education' (Tawney, 1914), the WEA provides a university education in difficult circumstances. Tawney wrote disparagingly about the '[b]ad utilitarianism, which thinks that the object of education is not education, but … professional success or industrial leadership' (quoted in

O'Hear and Sidwell, 2009: 186). Tawney looked on admiringly at the workers 'who pursue knowledge with the passion born of difficulties' (ibid.: 187). For him, this knowledge should always be for its own sake. What this information should be was not really questioned; it was generally accepted that people knew what the best that has been thought or said was, and by teaching the workers about high culture their lives would be improved.

The romantic view of culture and education also seemed to downgrade the sciences. Grammar schools were for everyone who passed the 11-plus. In practice, that meant mainly the middle classes, so grammars would teach sweetness and light to the sons and daughters of the well-to-do. Secondary modern schools would teach lower-level technical and vocational skills and subjects to the horny-handed sons and daughters of the hoi polloi. Science and engineering struggled to find a foothold: the third part of the tripartite system was intended to be secondary technical schools – where scientists, engineers, and highly skilled technicians would be educated – but few of these actually saw the light of day. The root of this issue goes back centuries; the 'grammarian' schools mistrusted the progressive 'modern' skills training. The grammar schools, although they embraced mathematics, taught science in a way that seemed to mistrust the logician's approach of enquiry and concentrated instead on rote learning the principles. When practical demonstrations occurred, these were to be precisely noted down and learned by heart. Inevitably, a purely grammarian approach to science ignored the scientific method. This cultural attitude towards science triggered a very significant spat that still has echoes to this day.

The Two Cultures

In 1959, Charles Percy Snow (1905–1980) gave the Rede Lecture at Cambridge University. C. P. Snow was a chemist and novelist; from this viewpoint he straddled the two worlds of science and the arts. In his famous lecture he proposed the thesis that, intellectually and practically, Western society had been split into two opposing factions. On one side were the literary intellectuals, and on the other were those from science.

Both sides, he posited, had a mutual dislike and incomprehension of the other.

Snow noted that scientists had very little interest in the arts, apart from music, and, conversely, that traditionalists – the literary intellectuals – had the attitude that their culture was *the* culture and therefore tended towards developing a superiority complex. Snow argued that the two cultures needed to clash along together rather than view each other with suspicion from afar. He contended that creativity is produced through the clash of the two cultures.

Snow went on to say that, in terms of the history of education, we see a chronicle of increasing specialization. He argued that our education system was trying to produce a tiny elite who had been educated in a narrow range of academic skills, whether that was mathematics, classics, or natural science. He claimed that, at 18, the young English elite knew more than their contemporaries about science, for example, but knew very little else. In the United States, he asserted, the opposite was true. They had a looser and more general education system that lacked a certain thoroughness, especially in the sciences. But, at a higher level, say PhD, the US suddenly kicked in with far more rigour. He saw literary intellectuals in the UK, and to a much lesser extent in the US, as natural Luddites, and suggested that if we were to bridge the gap between rich and poor, we would need to bring both cultures together more closely, especially in education. Our most basic needs, he argued, were served by scientific revolution. Snow also maintained that scientific logic needed to be as widely understood as the 'logic of language'. Snow was arguing for a change in education and society, with science as a more progressive and meritocratic force being brought in alongside the more conservative and traditional force of the literary elite.

Frank Raymond Leavis (1895–1978) was livid with Snow's assessment of the problems of the two cultures. Leavis saw Snow as a utilitarian of the Benthamite sort, interested in 'the quantifiable, the measurable, the manageable' (quoted in Collini, 1998: xxxiii). Stefan Collini, in his introduction to the 1998 edition of Snow's *The Two Cultures*, says that not only is the animosity between Leavis and Snow about the romantic versus the utilitarian clash very familiar in British cultural history, but Leavis couched his comments in literary terms (he was a literary critic, after all) and bemoaned the quality of Snow's work rather than addressing its arguments. *What to learn* is central to any argument about education, and so is *how to learn* and *for what purpose*.

Pedagogy of the Oppressed

In *Pedagogy of the Oppressed*, Paolo Freire (1921–1997), a Brazilian neo-Platonist and Marxist, differentiates between the qualities of knowledge learned through cultural ideas and norms, *doxa*, and that learned through *logos*. He describes the ownership of knowledge, where the knowledge of the teacher and the society they represent is learned by rote in order to preserve the dominant culture. But, he says, this is not true culture. That should be explored through dialogue and 'critical co-investigation'. 'The role of the problem-posing educator is to create, together with the students, the conditions under which knowledge at the level of the *doxa* is superseded by true knowledge at the level of the *logos*' (Freire, 1970: 62). Indeed, this is a return to Plato, giving *logos* an authentic level of 'truth' beyond that of the lesser truths, which are, basically, a way of preserving the status quo. Like Plato, he saw dialectic as a way to go beyond the truth of accepted cultural practices into the higher and authentic truth of *logos*.

Now, progressive dialecticians were able to resist the *doxa* of the white, male, middle- and upper-class monoculture. Far from seeing the Arnoldian idea of education as liberating, some progressives no longer accepted that the knowledge of the dominant class was necessarily 'the best which has been thought or said'. Culture became the battleground, and why not? If science can feel that it is an outsider, how did other groups feel when their very identity was marginalized? High culture (in other words, traditional grammar in its widest sense) was under attack from a dialectical antithesis. This confrontation did not involve simply arguing with culture on its own terms, but questioning whether it was right to learn this 'great tradition' at all. The knowledge and values associated with dead white males was ripe for challenge.

In this divide there were more than just two cultures. Ideology began to be questioned on the grounds of gender, race, sexuality, and class; the best that has been thought or said itself was being questioned. *His*tory became *herstory.* The dialecticians were on the rise, challenging the traditional grammarian views, their very ways of thinking. This was a time of upheaval and blessed were the change makers. There was a huge shift on the progressive side of politics. Instead of the WEA's stated desire of bathing in the running waters of purity and knowledge, their aim was the liberation of the individual through the celebration of their very experience – providing you were an outsider. Originally thought of as 'grammar schools for all', it soon became clear that for some teachers, parents, and pupils, comprehensive education had to resist traditional education values. The progressive movement began to gain ground. The question is: did this approach result in knowledge at the level of *logos*?

Perhaps the trivium was informing, however subconsciously, some of these thinkers and practitioners. The Arnoldian romantics were grammarians who had the goal of challenging the utilitarian status quo in order to improve society. Snow saw that this version of culture rejected science and technology and wanted to bring the two sides together to improve society. Freire rejected knowledge at this mundane 'bourgeois' level and wanted the ultimate knowledge, *logos,* to be available to the oppressed. Some thinkers, however, looked directly to the trivium and used it to make their own observations about where education was going wrong.

The Trivium Revisited: Mysteries, Messages, Pragmatism, and Prayers

Charles Sanders Peirce (1839–1914) came from a scientific and mathematical background, yet he came to think that science, on its own, was unhelpful as a way to reach understanding. Peirce was drawn to the trivium and made it a basis of his pragmatic philosophy which he called *semeiotics.* At the core of this theory was his reworking of the trivium into speculative grammar, logical critic, and speculative rhetoric. A lover of triadic constructions, Peirce further divided logical critic into what he called scientific thinking: abduction, induction and deduction – an idea we will return to later. Peirce was enamoured by the creative forces unleashed by the relationship between tradition and modernity, which are exemplified by the core relationship of the trivium between grammar and critic. Peirce believed the master art was speculative rhetoric, and believed our understanding of the world, the real, to be a series of explanations rather than certainties. These explanations are undeniably human in origin and go beyond the purely scientific. For Peirce, mankind is not a detached spectator observing the facts of the world. Rather, we are an engaged participant creating the world around us and then understanding it. This community that creates the world is drawn from the idea of the trivium – as the place where the roads meet. This meeting occurs at a 'common' place, and therefore could be mistaken for being trivial. But for Peirce, this common place is far from marginal. It is a space of understanding; it is our collective knowledge, our community.

Pert Poetic Parrots

In 1947, Dorothy L. Sayers made a speech at Oxford University entitled 'The Lost Tools of Learning'. Sayers lamented the current quality of education and harked back to the need for a revitalized classical trivium. She thought that the trivium constituted the 'tools of learning'. In other words, the trivium was primarily an approach in which pupils would learn how to learn. She interpreted the trivium as: grammar (any language, what it was, how it was put together, and how it worked), dialectic (logic and disputation), and rhetoric (expression). She described how some schools encouraged disputation and rhetoric through debating societies but, crucially, she bemoaned how they were detached from the main curriculum.

Sayers wanted the trivium to be included in all subjects, throughout the curriculum, as an approach to teaching and learning. She saw the three parts of the trivium as stages – which she referred to as Poll Parrot, Pert, and Poetic – through which a pupil must pass. These correspond approximately to the following ages and stages: grammar (Poll Parrot) is Key Stage

2; dialectic (Pert) is Key Stage 3; and rhetoric (Poetic) is Key Stage 4. She explained how each phase would work: grammar would involve learning Latin, English verse, and prose by heart, and the teaching of factual aspects of all subjects, particularly history, geography, science, mathematics, and theology. Dialectic would be the stage of debate: dramatic performance (especially pieces where argument is central), syllogisms, algebra, geometry, ethics, the use of imagination, and so on. Rhetoric would be realized throughout by attempting to show that all subjects and knowledge are 'as one' – interrelated.

Her speech was a passionate call for independent, lifelong learning, and echoes John of Salisbury's belief from 700 years earlier. It finishes with the following flourish:

[The decline in educational standards] is not the fault of the teachers – they work only too hard already. The combined folly of a civilization that has forgotten its own roots is forcing them to shore up the tottering weight of an educational structure that is built upon sand. They are doing for their pupils the work which the pupils themselves ought to do. For the sole true end of education is simply this: to teach men [sic] how to learn for themselves; and whatever instruction fails to do this is effort spent in vain. (Sayers, 1947)

The Trivium is the Massage

Marshall McLuhan proposed that education was shaped like a 19th-century factory where 'information is scarce but ordered and structured by fragmented, classified patterns, subjects, and schedules' (McLuhan and Fiore, 1996 [1967]: 18). In *The Medium is the Massage*, McLuhan suggests that all media are an extension of human faculties; for example, the wheel is the foot, the book is the eye, clothing is the skin, and electronic circuitry is an extension of our nervous system. He argues that when our media –

our tools – change, we change. For example, he understood the spoken word as, 'The first technology by which man was able to let go of his environment in order to grasp it in a new way' (quoted in Gordon, 2010: 58), and that the alphabet was constructed of fragments that need to be connected. This connectivity was the work of grammar, which, due to the dominion of the written and printed word, made sense of our world in a linear way, and led to specialization, as extolled by Adam Smith. The rhetoric, logic, or rationality that followed on from our linear tools depended on the presentation of sequentially connected facts or concepts, which led to the architecture of Western civilization.

However, McLuhan saw that the electronic world was challenging this way of thinking and being by creating a multidimensional space – the 'global village' – in which our experience and environment constantly interplay. In order to understand and make sense of this 'mosaic' we need to create a 'teaching machine' to make 'everyday learning a process of discovery' (McLuhan and Fiore, 1996 [1968]: 68). He thought that our classrooms should move from mere instruction to discovery and the recognition of the language of forms. McLuhan took a neo-Platonist approach to communication and classification: 'the ideas', where facts, principles, nature, and conduct are investigated. This is the role of grammar.

McLuhan described grammar as the 'art of interpreting all phenomena'. The interpretations are then open to disputation and argument, to dialectic: 'Dialectics is, variously, a way of testing evidence or the study of kinds of proofs for an argument, a method of dialogue, or simply logic' (McLuhan, 2005 [1943]): xi). This then allows us to 'live mythically' by 'putting on an audience', a vesture, a whole time, a *Zeit*, which he saw as the role of rhetoric. McLuhan understood that grammarians look for connections and distrust abstraction, whilst dialecticians look for divisions and distrust concrete modes of language. He interpreted the history of the trivium as a struggle for supremacy between grammarians, dialecticians, and rhetoricians. McLuhan, an avowed Catholic grammarian, argued that, on its own, grammar fails to provide a rounded education, unless it is supported by dialectic and rhetoric.

McLuhan perceived that, in our electronic age, young people were disembodied and 'looking for a formula' in order to relate to the universe. What was that formula? McLuhan wanted a radical restructuring of education based on the old idea of the trivium. The trivium was to be the 'new spectacles' that the young need to wear in order to interpret and understand their world. McLuhan saw that world as 'fragments of text', a mosaic through which we give meaning through 'pattern recognition' and through our active participation. We make sense of our experiences and communicate our sense-making through a rhetorical device, 'the probe', which, rather like an aphorism, is sent out into the world to connect with other texts and contexts in our global village.

Voices from the States: Christian Fundamentalism and Classical Home Schooling

In her book *The Trivium*, Sister Miriam Joseph writes that, 'the essential activity of the student is to relate the facts learned into a unified, organic whole, to assimilate them as the body assimilates food or as the rose assimilates nutrients from the soil and increases in size, vitality and beauty. A learner must use mental hooks and eyes to join the facts together to form a significant whole' (Joseph, 2002 [1937]: 7). She goes on to say that this approach (the trivium) would make learning easier, more interesting, and more valuable.

The trivium's links with medieval Christian education has brought it a new lease of life in the United States through Christian schools and the home schooling movement. Many people are now being drawn towards a 'classical' education movement, which extols the virtues of a liberal arts education rooted in Christianity. The educational history of the United States is very different from the English experience. In a nation that was formed through a break from tradition – having dissolved 'the political bands which have connected them with another', according to the Declaration of Independence – progressive ideas seem to have the upper hand. It might certainly help to explain why the concept of a grammarian 'common core' has gained ground.

E. D. Hirsch, Jr. has been a big influence on this movement. He talks of a 'knowledge deficit' in American schooling, and blames romanticism. He is distinctly anti-Rousseau and asserts that the romantic approach leads to complacency in an educator who waits for a child's development to unfold. Taking on the 'history is bunk' ethos, which he believes pervades American schooling, he claims that progressives link 'the acquisition of broad knowledge to "rote learning" of "mere facts"' (Hirsch, 2006: 10). Hirsch sees progressives arguing for the development of critical faculties, but derides their attempts to achieve it without a base in foundational knowledge. He sees shared knowledge and grammar as vital if individuals are to belong to the society in which they have been brought up – because in any society, whether you like it or not, taken-for-granted background knowledge is assumed, whether in vocabulary, history, mathematics, or the arts. Hirsch has created his own inventory of What Every American Child Should Know (although he also acknowledges that his list will change with time).

Susan Wise Bauer and Jessie Wise take Dorothy L. Sayers at her word and build an entire home and self-schooling curriculum based on her approach to the trivium. They consider that the way to approach learning is to obtain facts, analyse and evaluate them, and then form your own opinions. They suggest that schools often jump to the third stage before the first two stages have been covered in enough depth or detail. As such, they believe that the pattern of the trivium 'trains the mind in the art of learning' (Bauer and Wise, 2004: 20).

In the next chapter I will explore how this training could work in our schools today.

Chapter 7

A Crack in Everything:
The Imperfect Arts

Forget your perfect offering
There is a crack in everything
That's how the light gets in

Leonard Cohen, 'Anthem'

Shakespeare's Trivium, 'The whining schoolboy ... creeping like snail unwillingly to school'

If the trivium is 'training' for the mind, then it is worth looking at how someone who was taught through the trivium has used their training in their work. It is not too hard to see Shakespeare in the schoolboy creeping snail-like to school – but thank goodness he didn't play truant. The education he received at Stratford Grammar School is reflected in his plays. The aim of the school would have been to teach Latin and provide a solid grounding in classic Roman, Greek, and biblical texts, as well as teaching ethics and religion. Classes would begin at six o'clock in the morning, with breakfast at nine. This would be followed by more study from quarter past nine to eleven. There would then be school dinner and a break from study until one o'clock, after which there would be further study until five. Finally, this extended school would serve supper, and six or seven pupils would formally present what they had learnt that day – or, on Fridays and Saturdays, review the week's learning. One week every school year would be devoted to the pupils reciting their learning for the year.

The method of learning was through the trivium. Grammar would generally be studied first, in order to learn precepts. As Shakespeare got older, he would have moved on to logic as a tool of analysis and rhetoric as a method of composition. Texts would be studied to look for evidence of how they used the three arts of the trivium (grammar, argument, and style), and then little William would have practised using the arts through copying, writing, and speech making. It is likely that his schoolmasters also taught contemporary literature and debate rather than just logic.

Such exercises in exploring rather than solving arguments are just the sort of thing that might have inspired a young dramatist in his playwriting. Clearly, Shakespeare uses this exploratory art in his most famous speech, 'To be or not to be', in which Hamlet goes through self-reasoning, or *anthypophora*, a rhetorical device he may well have learnt at school. In her superb book, *Shakespeare's Use of the Arts of Language* (2005 [1947]), Sister Miriam Joseph explores how Shakespeare's education – and, in particular, the trivium – is reflected in his plays. This consideration raises the following questions: How much are we a result of our schooling? Would it be possible to educate children in the same way as Shakespeare today? Would my daughter flourish under this form of study? When people hark back to 'traditional methods', do they want to take on those methods lock, stock, and barrel, or do they want to retain the right to pick and choose? It is obvious that the methods used to teach Shakespeare would not work in schools today, but could the underlying method, the trivium, offer a blueprint or a mantra upon which to build?

In *The Well-Educated Mind: A Guide to the Classical Education You Never Had*, Jessie Wise Bauer sums up the trivium as a process that passes through three stages: grammar, where children learn foundational knowledge; logic, where they analyse and criticize information and rhetoric, where they learn how, 'to express their own opinions about the facts they have accumulated and evaluated …'

Classically educated students know this pattern (learn facts; analyze them; express your opinions about them) applies to all later learning. (Bauer, 2003: 18–19)

The Well-Educated Mind has a companion volume, written by Susan Wise Bauer with her mother, Jessie Wise, called *The Well-Trained Mind* (Bauer and Wise, 2009), which is designed around this approach to the trivium. It has been written for those who are home schooling or supporting their children's education. 'Is this trivium the equivalent of McLuhan "spectacles for our age"?' I put Susan Wise Bauer's idea of the trivium to the philosopher Alain de Botton, who also helps run the School of Life, which is dedicated to 'a new vision of education'. He replied:

[This idea of] the trivium presents a very appealing model of how learning should take place, but I wonder whether it is really suited to our times. A number of objections come to mind: there is a lot more to know nowadays. The idea that one might know everything in the first stage of education, then concentrate on analysing it, then speaking properly, seems unsuited to the demands of the modern world. Even if there wasn't so much to know, one wonders why the analysis of facts is given such prestige. Why not, for example, the pursuit of wisdom? Why couldn't that be the next stage, after the facts have been taken on board? There could be a time when the facts are interpreted in a search for a good life (Aristotle's idea). The emphasis on rhetoric is also bizarre: this was fine in ancient Rome, but do we need rhetoric nowadays? Hardly. PowerPoint use perhaps, which takes an afternoon to teach. Also, it is evident that modern society does not want everyone to be questioning everything. It is just too awkward. Therefore, a Marxist would quickly spot that any scheme to raise a self-conscious citizenry is going to run into trouble from the powers that be.

If de Botton is right, and Wise Bauer's take on the trivium is not right for our age, then what is? Perhaps it is a waste of time to pursue the trivium itself and my quest should end here, or maybe I need to think about how to refashion it for our age, as others have done for their ages, whether they are Boethius, Bacon, Sayers, McLuhan, or Peirce. Hmm, I'm clearly not in the same league as any on that esteemed list, but, anyway, I'll give it a go. I have nothing to lose but my … er … Well, clearly, I've *nothing* to lose.

God Help Me

In an extraordinary tour de force, the essay entitled, 'An Apology for Raymond Sebond', Montaigne derides the idea of reason existing on its own in the world and states that craftsmen and ploughmen can be wiser than professors. In the essay, Montaigne addresses how the trivium works, how the logician refers to the grammarian, and the rhetorician to the logician. Then he raises a crucial question: on what is all this philosophy based? To Montaigne, the answer is a Catholic God. But, as a non-believer, I take God out of the equation, so all I am left with is individuals referring to each other. Therefore, is my trivium just an abstraction or is it connected with life as experienced? That would simply be education to fill in time between the cradle and the grave.

So, should education be more than just abstract academic study? I want my daughter to enjoy, be curious, get excited by learning, and have experiences that stay with her for a lifetime. It must offer something authentic, which speaks of the depths and heights of human experience, which can fire enthusiasm or spark the anger of debate, but without the need of an authority figure, a God, giving credibility to the whole enterprise. In a nutshell, is a secular approach to the trivium possible?

Trivializing Google

To be authentic, a contemporary trivium needs to reflect the complexity of our times as well as the complexity of the past. Eric Schmidt, the former executive chairman of Google, has observed, 'We create as much information in 48 hours, five billion gigabytes, as was created from the birth of the world till 2003.' There *is* a lot more information to know about nowadays; the challenge comes from linking ideas and making sense of it. In practical terms, we need to be more selective, more demanding of supporting evidence, and more adept at picking, connecting, and understanding what knowledge is important and relevant to our lives. Just because there is more to know, that does not mean we can switch off because it is difficult to differentiate – and end up knowing nothing. It is extraordinarily difficult to find out useful information if you don't know anything in the first place. What we need is the ability to filter out what is trivial, in the modern sense, and concentrate on acquiring our own wisdom.

Starting with the trivium, is there a way to adapt it so that we can educate our children to be able to continue to educate themselves in successful ways once they leave formal education? Is it possible to find in the trivium an approach to schooling that would be relevant to our times, one that would leave an imprint on the lives of our children in much the same way as the trivium left its mark on Shakespeare? Can the trivium cross the two cultures of science and art? Do we need a new 'educational paradigm' to achieve this?

Any alteration to the landscape of education is extremely disruptive and can create all kinds of unforeseen problems for those involved. It is apt to employ the gardening analogy that Stephen Toulmin uses in his book *Return to Reason* (2003). Up until the romantic period, garden design in Britain was about imposing formal designs onto the landscape. But then along came Lancelot 'Capability' Brown (1716–1783), who revolutionized British garden design, not by means of rational planning and imposition, but by looking at what was there and seeing what offered the 'capability' to be improved.

This is a philosophy that takes what is already there and makes changes that are organic and born of the landscape. This is also important in the field of education. A key part of the trivium is the passing on of the culture and traditions of the past; it would not be in the spirit of the trivium to argue for itself as a new paradigm. The trivium that I am arguing for is one that is drawn from the past but is adapted for the present. Therefore, I have given it the name Trivium 21c. We do not need a new model; our system already has the capability to improve our existing educational landscape. This is truly radical: it is from the root and also progressive.

One Man's Paine Is Another Man's Burke

Edmund Burke (1729–1797) and Thomas Paine (1737–1809) were both fine rhetoricians and, at one time, great friends. Burke is reported as joking, 'we hunt in pairs'. The conservative Burke was more like a cultural ecologist; he believed that society should hand on tradition with its own inherent wisdom to the generations that follow. The radical Paine saw that just because something has tradition on its side, and appears to be common sense, does not mean it is right. In education, this relationship is at the heart of what we do. We pass on our culture to our young people in a way that is respectful, but also so that it can be opened up for criticism. If we are receptive to others reinventing the world, we will welcome our young people criticizing and making new sense of what we bequeath to them – just as we did in our own youth.

Each generation has to adapt, reject, or re-model their view of the world in order to take full stewardship of it in the future. With a sense of duty, we transmit our culture to our progeny, warts and all. As they embrace this culture, we need to ensure that instead of closing down their stewardship (and repeating the same mistakes), they have a collective idea of what is important and valuable, what needs changing, what could be changed, and how they establish their ownership through change. This is not easy. It takes place on our common ground, where we all come together. Within this cultural landscape the young must develop the capability to improve and make an organic difference. We need to ensure as a community, and as educationalists within that community, we help them develop that capability.

Tzvetan Todorov writes, 'Living in a culture is the natural state for human beings and the fact is that culture and, to begin with, language are transmitted by those who came before us ... Tradition is constitutive of human beings; it is simply that it does not suffice to make a principle legitimate or a proposition true' (Todorov, 2009: 42–43). Ensuring that the three ways – grammar, dialectic, and rhetoric – meet in such a manner as to open up education for us all, there is a need for a certain degree of scepticism. As Leonard Cohen sings in 'Anthem', 'There is a crack in everything/That's how the light gets in.' If we can shine a new light on each of the three arts of the trivium, then through their imperfections we should start to see a way of bringing them together.

With this in mind, let us explore the three arts of the trivium in terms of their relevance to the 21st-century classroom – its teachers and its students. And, as the educators of Shakespeare would have done, let's start with grammar.

Chapter 8

Grammar: From Rules of Language to Cultural Capital

Turning and turning in the widening gyre
The falcon cannot hear the falconer;
Things fall apart; the centre cannot hold;
Mere anarchy is loosed upon the world,
The blood-dimmed tide is loosed, and everywhere
The ceremony of innocence is drowned;
The best lack all conviction, while the worst
Are full of passionate intensity.

William Butler Yeats, 'The Second Coming'

The relationship between a parent and child, inevitably, has various tensions which are negotiated over time. The authority of the parent is gradually relinquished whilst the child finds ways to increase their power and to make their own life. In a similar way, a culture has a relationship with its youth; the older, traditional part reconciles itself with the younger, progressive part's desire for exploration and change.

In the process, some degree of anarchy is loosed upon the world. In this way, each of us collectively imprints our culture with a way of being, through which we hope to form the next generation. The new is in perpetual battle with the old, change versus the status quo. It is in realizing a synthesis that the next generation can rediscover the old, and find within it a relevance (or irrelevance) to their lives. Philip Larkin took the whole thing further by writing that:

Man hands on misery to man,

Philip Larkin, 'This Be the Verse'

The poem's famous first line makes the point far more starkly; a nihilistic viewpoint for those who don't see the point in giving anything beautiful or worthwhile to the next generation. The purpose of parenting, and teaching, is to negotiate the relationship between an age that is dying and one that is beginning to reinvent the world. You give of yourself, enthusiastically and wearily, hopefully and painfully, happily and warily, in order that a child might benefit, grow stronger, and be able to fulfil themselves and others by living a good life. This relationship is played out in millions of homes, schools, and institutions, continually renewing and refreshing, losing and forgetting – a movement in personal, regional, national, and global history. In Disney's *The Lion King*, this is called 'the circle of life', and it is the stuff of many coming-of-age stories in the literary canon.

Grammar, *la grand-mère*, is the parent passing on her not-always-explicit rules to a child, for good or ill. We hope that our current culture is somehow right; it seems reasonable to us. Yet, we know that there are cracks in it, because knowledge expands, perhaps methodology and technology improve, and values change. What was the best that has been thought or said justifies itself anew as fresh ideas come along to challenge the old.

The question we should ask is, 'What is worth knowing? Should we teach everything or, at least, the foundational knowledge of everything?' In *Why Don't Students Like School?*, the cognitive scientist, Daniel T. Willingham, writes, 'Cognitive science leads to the rather obvious conclusion that students must learn the concepts that come up again and again – the unifying ideas of each discipline' (Willingham, 2009: 37). This leaves open the question of which disciplines to teach and which ones should make up our common fund of knowledge. Once we have decided what subjects to teach, then all we need to do is select the unifying ideas. But is it as simple as that?

Traditional grammar is associated with the structure of languages and, through this, the learning of languages. But that is not the whole story. Today, we think of this as only part of what is meant by the study of grammar. If we look for definitions of grammar, we find that no two authorities or reference books agree. McLuhan's definition was the 'art of interpreting … all phenomena' (2005[1943]: xi). Grammar can also be perceived as foundational knowledge, not only of language but also of culture.

This notion of foundational knowledge is key: schooling for most people comes near the beginning of their lives and, therefore, along with their parenting, it provides the basis for learning. Grammar, in every subject, discipline, and art, is the beginning of our understanding of all phenomena – it is a way of reading and making sense of culture. From the Middle Ages onwards, grammar came to mean reading the world, as well as reading the word. Children need to learn the basic units of meaning that will enable them to become part of their culture, share its values, and maybe work to transform it for the better.

Achieving Balance

If the grammar of a subject (the foundational knowledge) is 'the unifying ideas of each discipline', what are these ideas? Are they a collection of facts? Are all facts the same? What our culture holds as true, establishes as a fact, or gives importance to, has a lot to do with our explicitly and implicitly agreed ideas as to what matters.

Some of the things I learnt as 'facts' at school have since changed. For example, the capital of China is no longer Peking but Beijing. Other facts had not yet come into existence, such as the internet or the Higgs boson particle. A difficulty arises if we start out with an idea and present it as a priori knowledge or an 'absolute' truth, when it is based on fallible human understanding. At some point this truth will be exposed as 'false', and that can lead to an entire belief system collapsing.

Grammar is not just about literacy, but also cultural literacy. The world of education is but a subset of the world as a whole; it has the same need to resolve the eternal conflict between stability and change, certainty and uncertainty. This affects everything we do and teach. In a practical sense, this means we need to make the contradictions explicit. We must answer questions like: what should a teacher teach and how should they teach it? This must include a sense of the incompleteness, the cracks in our knowledge. Teachers must move away from a position of omniscience.

Much of what passes for the jungle of English grammar is a list of heuristics or 'rules of thumb'. The English language is not sufficiently tightly rule-bound to be without exceptions. For example, when I and my classroom comrades were taught that, in spelling, 'i before e except after c', we were shocked to discover words such as 'ancient' or 'society'. How weird, we thought! And yet this was taught as if it were a priori knowledge. Then we were told that there were exceptions, and the more we looked the more exceptions there were. But because this had been presented as fact, and we had now found out that it wasn't, we became suspicious of *all* the knowledge we were being taught. Hence, our inclination was to argue. The rhetorical question in our heads was, 'Why are you telling us these lies?' It is only now that I am able to codify that experience as belonging to the 'dialectic' stage rather than the 'grammar' stage. So, if we choose 'traditional English grammar' as a unifying principle we can begin to see how confusion might occur and how disputes can arise.

We need to understand that teachers should have the authority to teach, but also to recognize that what they teach is probable, uncertain, open to amendment, change, revision – that no knowledge is ultimate or perfect. Some might argue that, therefore, we should ditch the authority of the teacher (the sage on the stage) and let our children find their own way (with a guide on the side). This is all very well, until the entire class marches off a cliff, at which point the teacher ceases to guide and washes their hands of the entire venture pleading, 'Well, I told them not to, but would they listen?'

When I contemplate teaching my daughter about the world, I baulk at letting her choose to learn about anything she wants. She might just indulge in computer games when I want her to read Shelley's *The Mask of Anarchy*; she might prefer to play with a Barbie doll when I want her to rehearse *The Taming of the Shrew*; or she might stuff her face with chocolate when I want her to cram her mind with chaos theory. Clearly, I would like her to learn about some things more than others. This is why the authoritative figure of the teacher is important.

Dr Johnson and the Dictionary

The invention of printing meant that there was a need for the printed word to become standardized. In writing his dictionary, Dr Johnson was clear in wanting to impose strict rules on the language. In English, inevitably, this would have class and regional connotations. Professor Colin MacCabe writes, 'Dr Johnson makes the point clearly enough in the preface to his dictionary when he ridicules the notion that the middle or working class actually speak English.' He continues, 'Nor are words which are not found in the vocabulary to be lamented as omissions. Of the laborious and mercantile part of the people, the diction is in a great measure casual and mutable; many of their terms are formed for some temporary and local convenience, and though current at certain times and places are in others utterly unknown' (MacCabe, 1982: 11). English grammars were written, 'to divide the nation into those who could speak their own language and those who could not' (ibid. 12).

However, after much work on his dictionary, Dr Johnson realized that his ambition to impose rules, facts, and stable definitions on what he termed 'fugitive cant' was going to be difficult. Instead of giving up, Johnson turned this problem into something positive. In the foreword to a later edition of his dictionary, he wrote, 'If an academy should be established for the cultivation of our style, which I, who can never wish to see dependence multiplied, hope the spirit of English liberty will hinder or destroy, let them, instead of compiling grammars and dictionaries, endeavour, with all their influence, to stop the licence of translators, whose idleness and ignorance, if it be suffered to proceed, will reduce us to babble a dialect of France' (Johnson, 1755: para. 90). For Dr Johnson, 'liberty' in the English language was a mirror of our national 'cultural' identity.

In *The Language Wars: A History of Proper English*, Henry Hitchings links the British constitution to the English language, claiming that just as Britain has no formal constitution, it has no formal grammar. He asserts that the attempts to solidify British national identity through grammar, between 1586 and 1800, produced more than 270 grammatical books, covering 56 different systems, and even those systems that were closely linked to Latin managed to produce 20 different grammatical approaches. Our constitution (and language) has 'evolved for practical purposes. It is amorphous and in many places indistinct, and as a result it is much contested' (Hitchings, 2011: 80–81). It is this fluidity, of not only the language but also of the past, that might have prompted David Starkey to say, 'The history of England is the history of modernism' (Starkey, 2012).

Peter Ackroyd writes in *Albion: The Origins of the English Imagination*, 'There are very few rules in English syntax and grammar which cannot be broken … It is an absorbent medium established upon the imperatives of usage and practice. It carries a pragmatic force, therefore, and may bear certain responsibility for English empiricism itself' (Ackroyd, 2002: 394). The conservative writer Simon Heffer acknowledges the fluidity of traditional grammar. He knows that English is not fixed but at the same time he celebrates the prescribed rules of usage. Despite ongoing change, he says, he knows that at any one time the English language is codified and, therefore, there is no ambiguity. This is neither true nor reasonable; it would be an impossible task to pinpoint the current 'rules' of grammar. As Heraclitus is reported as saying, 'No man ever steps in the same river twice, for it's not the same river and he's not the same man.' And where would the double entendre be were it not for ambiguity? So, how do we address this conundrum?

If the teacher presents knowledge in a way that makes it seem like conjecture, then they provide the space for debate and the challenging of dialectic. This also encourages students to appreciate that they can challenge ideas, if they can muster a sufficient amount of evidence. Such an approach opens up a degree of uncertainty, but it also implants the idea that deeper thinking is needed. Teaching about unicorns is as real as teaching about lions to one who has seen neither. Therefore, the teacher should use language in such a way that ensures uncertainty has its place, explaining the kind of 'truth' under discussion, and casting doubt where scepticism is appropriate. This opens up a world that is no longer 'fixed', where it is possible to examine the framework of knowledge in which something is held as true – the evidence it is based on and the reasoning behind the proposition. But how much doubt and uncertainty should we embrace?

Culture, Conservatism, Class, and Cricket

The common fund of knowledge and the unifying ideas of each discipline are at once our collective cultural history and our sense of who we are. Grammar provides the building blocks for a conversation between past, present, and future. As a parent, I am teaching my daughter both 'how to speak proper' and how to be culturally literate, so that we have a communality of culture. We want to be able to share our ideas and experiences, and we need to have a space where we come together to further the development of our relationship.

To what extent should grammar be prescriptive? In *The Selfish Gene* (1989), Richard Dawkins coined the word 'meme'. A meme is an element of culture or way of living that is passed from individual to individual by non-genetic means. We pass on our memes in order to help us solidify a sense of our cultural and subject heritage, rules, traditions, and qualities. If we pass on our memes in an unthinking way – by just seeing all knowledge as reflecting our contemporary and current concerns – then we will never prescribe codes of behaviour or select knowledge that we think is important. Our memes are passed on, in the main, because we attach importance to particular knowledge and ways of living, either unconsciously or consciously.

In *England: An Elegy*, the philosopher Roger Scruton writes about how his education helped form his view of Englishness and how it shaped his character. He portrays the teachers he encountered at grammar school and university, and describes the importance of culture and his 'ideal' England, which in his view is being discarded. He also discusses the importance of myths that tell us truths about ourselves, 'The global economy, the democratization of taste, the sexual revolution, pop culture and television have worked to erase the sense of spiritual identity in every place where piety shored up the old forms of knowledge and local custom fortified the moral sense' (Scruton, 2000: 246). To this conservative thinker, the 'grammar' of national character needs a reverential foundation on which to justify and build itself.

The memes that Scruton wishes to pass on are threatened by the memes of the market. If 'all history is bunk', then it is the progress offered by unfettered capitalism and a Benthamite utilitarianism that drives us into abolishing a shared past and sense of belonging. Grammar cannot exist in a never-ending present; it needs a relationship with the past to shape the present, and through this it helps prime our future. Grammar works by transmitting its memes. It cannot just be reflective; it has to prescribe its rules and commonality of practice, or else it is completely given over to the whims of fashion.

During the time of the British Empire, certain disciplines, codes of behaviour, unifying principles, and foundational knowledge were taught and imposed at home and throughout the colonies. It is a history of occupation, cultural imperialism, and other awkward truths. In Ireland, Éamon de Valera would, after independence, see to it that most of the trappings of Englishness, both in terms of governance and culture, would be rejected or downgraded and replaced with Irish cultural practices.

De Valera included sport in his pursuit of Irish identity, lauding Irish sports over British ones. In other countries that had been colonized, however, the 'civilizing' sports of the occupier became, literally, the fields of resistance. Take the quintessentially English game of cricket: in his book *Beyond a*

Boundary, the Trinidadian C. L. R. James talks about cricket, aesthetics, class, race, politics, and colonialism. In a telling passage, he writes:

> between the ideal and the real fascinated me and tore at my insides ... thus the cricket field was a stage on which selected individuals played representative roles which were charged with social significance. (James, 2005: 87)

The unifying principles of cricket became the field of play for 'ownership' of knowledge, of the sport. Later on, the West Indies would teach England a thing or two about how to play the game the English had invented.

Sunder Katwala is the director of British Future, a think tank looking at issues around British identity, integration, migration, and opportunity. Prior to this, Sunder was general secretary of the Fabian Society and a writer at *The Observer*. In my interview with him for this book, he said that he would be 'quite attracted to the idea that there is a tradition, and that it is an evolving tradition, where the synthesis comes out of the traditional and the modern. If you are going to rip up the rules of literature, you need to know the rules of literature. Experimentation tends to be rooted in the traditions it is rebelling against.'

This is my point exactly. It shows the intrinsic nature of the relationship between the modern and the traditional, between the dialectic appetite for destruction and newness and grammar's insistence on what came before. Katwala continued, 'I think the tradition versus modernity argument in British society sometimes involves an assertion of tradition.' It is this assertion of tradition, and that it is good for you, which is problematic, especially if you are an 'outsider' to that tradition. Katwala added:

> *The liberal instinct is that tradition looks like it is not including people; what about the people it doesn't include? The progressive project seemed to say 'for inclusion to work, tradition has to go'. So you end up with a grievance of the large constituency for the traditional, who see that the price of*

inclusion is to not be 'you' anymore and instead you have to be part of this totally cosmopolitan thing. It was not a necessary move, yet Labour modernists seemed to feel it quite strongly and they went for a year-zero version where you end up saying, "Let's celebrate what's great about this country – come and look round the Millennium Dome," and some people said, "But you haven't put anything in it!"

I put it to Katwala that, in education, we seem to be very much in that mode – the traditional versus the progressive. Some progressives are arguing for a new paradigm, and this worries me; movements that call for a year-zero option can end up tearing down some good things that are already there, like replacing old housing stock, some of which is now highly sought after, with tower blocks. Katwala replied: 'The tower blocks are a very good example of that "Fabian progressivism", a sort of done to, not done by. I'm basically sympathetic to the small "c" conservative idea that you need to know the traditions you are operating within if you want to make some radical move.'

It is possible to be radical, and still take people with you, through organic change. I asked Katwala how he saw the English curriculum, and especially the history syllabus, which tends to be one of the more sensitive areas in which this debate plays out:

I think there was definitely a view in the kind of inner-city Birmingham classroom of the 1980s that it was a very good idea not to talk about the history of Empire and colonialism, because people thought it was going to be divisive for the children in that classroom. The counter-argument to that would be to say, "In which case, society is never going to know how the children in that classroom came to be in that classroom." I think there was a latching onto Nazi Germany and the American civil rights movement as a way of telling a human rights story. But there aren't many people on the 'Nazi' side of the question; it's a goodies and baddies view of history. It's taught as a morality tale where everyone is always on the same side. I think it's a fantastic mistake not to teach colonialism, because the reason you're not *doing it is actually the reason you* should *be doing it. I think it's brilliantly captured in literature like [Andrea Levy's] Small Island, where you arrive at the mother country from the Caribbean and you're expecting that because you know all about it, you're expecting it to know all about you, which sets up a set of assumptions about the task that needs to be done. The encounter is incredibly 'othered' and we embark on this 'difference' anxiety.*

I asked the Conservative Member of Parliament, Elizabeth Truss (who since this interview has become parliamentary under-secretary of state at the Department for Education), what she felt the balance between tradition and modernity should be:

The process of education itself is the advancement of human knowledge. You should teach things based on their inherent merit. How good it is. Maybe how important it is to the fabric of society. Shakespeare is clearly integral to that, and I don't think that just because somebody comes from a different background that they may take something in a different way and that some 'particular' type of poetry may not be appropriate to them. You shouldn't make too many assumptions about what children are capable of taking on.

I then invited her to suggest what should be in our current curriculum:

We can over-focus on literature and history at the expense of mathematics and science. I think education is a good thing in itself, but you do have to keep an eye on exactly what the application of it is and understand that, if the country is failing to produce people … and you are having to import a vast number of people with a particular type of skill, you have to ask yourself the question: Why are we not teaching that in our schools?

So, if there is a balance to be achieved between what the state needs and wants, as well as what the individual wants, what happens when it comes to shaping culture and character? Truss said:

Some things about culture and identity come from education but a lot of it comes from outside the education system. It is from our broader culture as a country. Education is about character, yes, but being a parent is also about character. Therefore, where there is poor parenting – or no parenting – education takes on an even more important role.

Here we can see the tensions between the traditional and the modern revealed. Sunder Katwala is conscious of how sensitivities towards Britain's past led to a year-zero approach in schools where anything could be studied, as long as it didn't cover 'British' culture in too much detail. Instead of examining our own history, some schools looked at themes and issues from other cultures to avoid the difficult questions that are at the heart of being British. Elizabeth Truss sees the importance of teaching subjects of individual merit for the advancement of knowledge, but she also sees a tension between the teaching of humanities and the arts and the utilitarian necessity of teaching mathematics and science. Hers is an interesting view on what the state wants from our kids. The state takes on an authoritative or parental role in deciding what is best for its own needs, and then tries to convince children that what is best for the state is also best for them. This is the relationship between the falconer and the falcon again. Grammar is not really *une grand-mère*; it is everyone's parent, full of the difficulties and tensions that the role entails. And love?

Civilization: Are We in Chains or Can We Become Our Ideal Selves?

As parents, teachers, and citizens we face a fundamental question, 'What should my child (and every other child, for that matter) know? What manners, what words, what books, what formulae, what history, what behaviours, and what facts should we hold up as exemplary? What are the memes we wish to pass on?' Our answers are charged with social (and cultural) significance.

The Marxist thinker, and one-time leader of the Italian Communist Party, Antonio Gramsci (1891–1937) wrote a series of essays while imprisoned by Mussolini, which become known as *The Prison Notebooks*. In one of these essays, *On Education*, he wrote, 'In the school, the nexus between instruction and education can only be realized by the living work of the teacher. For this he must be aware of the contrast between the type of culture and society which he represents and the type of culture and society represented by his pupils, and conscious of his obligation to accelerate and regulate the child's formation in conformity with the former and in conflict with the latter' (Gramsci, 1971: 35–36). This question needs to be addressed in every classroom: who and what does the teacher represent?

When we teach our children manners, and tell them off for bad behaviour, are we making cultural judgements? We value certain types of behaviour, knowledge, and ideals, which make us who we are and who we want our children to be. We do this to ensure that our children conform to moral codes and cultural practices that we assume will stand them in good stead for their future. We want to civilize our children to share in the culture and society of which we are a part. And we civilize them with our memes, which are, by definition, historical.

Yet, it is through understanding our civilization that we decide which disciplines we value and, therefore, teach. We select the relevant foundational knowledge and unifying ideas that we feel are important. Although I have sympathy with Rousseau's romanticism and his ideas on the importance of self-expression and freedom, I find it difficult to believe that civilization is always something through which man becomes chained. Gandhi's observation that Western civilization 'would be a good idea' strikes at the heart of the difficulty inherent in the idealized concept of tradition. It is fundamental in all cultures and civilizations to present an ideal through which we can aspire to be the best that we can be and learn the best that there is to learn. Education (and parenting) might be forms of cultural imperialism, but they are stronger and more important because this authority gives structure to the young, through which they can find themselves. Remember the idea of the liberal arts – how from these rules and precepts freedom can grow.

In his *In Search of Civilization: Remaking a Tarnished Ideal* (2010), John Armstrong writes about the importance of the pursuit of higher things. There is a fundamental importance for humans in feeling uplifted by achievement, beauty, wisdom, love, and in the significance that these experiences have for us. I will address this in more detail when I look at *logos* (see Chapter 9), but here let us get some idea of what schools should be teaching. Schools should be involved in the pragmatic nitty-gritty of the mundane, but they should also aspire to these higher ideals. One of the ways to do this is to ensure that the grammar taught in schools relates to the best that has been thought or said. As Armstrong puts it, 'We are taken up: subsumed into and absorbed by something that seems greater than ourselves, but in which we can participate – which is why we are enlarged … In thrilling to grandeur, we become grand' (Armstrong, 2010: 178).

To Niall Ferguson, who echoes Elizabeth Truss's concerns, civilization is, 'as much about scientists' laboratories as it is about artists' garrets … as much about sewage pipes as flying buttresses … [as much about] some understanding of the economic, social and political institutions which devised … paid for … executed … and preserved … the eye-catching achievements' (Ferguson, 2011: 2–3). All this, and more, will be relevant as we move into an uncertain future. The individuals with the most to offer will probably be those who have the ability to adapt themselves across disciplines, including those not yet thought of; those who can adapt the knowledge of the past to shape the knowledge of the future; and those who will aspire to be the best they can be. This is why the polymath who spans two (or more) cultures will be particularly advantaged.

Cultural Capital

Young people can easily acquire knowledge from many sources. The de-schooling and un-schooling movements trumpet the idea that children should be left to learn at their own pace, asserting that their natural curiosity will enable them to grow up in the way they want to. By taking them out of factory schools, they believe, children will develop their own learning webs based on their own curricula (and nowadays they have many opportunities to do this). But, what if they were to respond to this freedom by spending all day playing computer games or calling up for pizzas? Should we allow them to carry on?

Pierre Bourdieu (1930–2002), a leading French sociologist, argued that neo-liberalism was killing culture in the name of making a fast buck. A man of the left, Bourdieu thought that the teacher's role was essentially traditionalist. He came up with the idea of 'cultural capital' – that the accumulation of cultural wealth is a major way in which the middle and upper classes (the bourgeoisie) maintain their position in society. For those who are denied cultural capital, in some or all areas, formal education should provide the key to unlocking the closed doors to the high culture that is so often unavailable to those who believe it isn't for them. As Roger Scruton puts it in *Modern Culture*, 'A high culture is a tradition, in which objects made for aesthetic contemplation renew through their allusive power the experience of membership' (Scruton, 1998: 39). Bourdieu describes how the bourgeois home environment, which values books, reading, art, theatre, science, mathematics, and foreign travel, will ensure that the bourgeoisie continue to dominate.

Make no mistake about how this works. If a school or a child's parents were to ignore cultural capital, this would not free their child from the chains of civilization. By providing cultural capital for your children, you bequeath to them the ability to take part in experiencing, learning, and conversing about culture confidently. Possessing a wide vocabulary and knowing how to communicate about a variety of subjects, forms, ideas and artefacts from both 'high' and 'popular' culture helps enable a child to develop as a culturally literate person, and able to feel at home in a variety of different environments. Caliban learns many 'languages' and the children who inherit this wealth of knowledge and tradition will continue to pass on these cultural memes to their children. Therefore, if we live in a society where we want individuals to be able to traverse class distinctions, we need to ensure that the allusive power of membership is made available to all. Formal education can help to widen the constituency for cultural capital.

Tradition

So, grammar is tradition; it is our cultural literacy and history in all fields, subjects, and domains. It crosses and links them as well as defining their differences. In a stable society, mastering that culture's knowledge and rules was all that was needed. Now, in a less stable world where – as Marx put it in *The Communist Manifesto*, 'All that is solid melts into air' – young people can take part in a great conversation by developing knowledge and rules from a wide experience of culture, and with the idea of the possibility of change and likelihood of ambiguity. Although much of what they learn will be pragmatic and address their day-to-day existence, we should also aim to teach them a qualitative sense of the best they can be, whether that is based on higher truths or on the dominant, hegemonic values of our society.

On a visit to the Yad Vashem Holocaust Museum in Jerusalem, I was struck by the tendency of the Nazis to log everything. For some reason the bureaucracy shocked me. It was as though I needed evil to be disordered rather than be revealed through the mundanity of measurement and counting. This reinforced for me why I prefer the messy to the messianic, the difficult and contradictory over the easy and certain. Let it never be forgotten that the British devised the concentration camp and were deeply involved in colonialism and the slave trade. Reading Goethe or Shakespeare, or listening to Beethoven or Purcell, does not automatically mean you will be a good person. Civilization is a constant source of debate.

Tradition is also a dialogue. It was exemplified in the opening ceremony for the 2012 London Olympic Games: it was a discourse between past, present, and future, as well as our interpretation of all three. Watching that ceremony, I was moved but I was also aware that this was part of the job of education – to enable that dialogue to take place, to present that information, to share that collective knowledge and more, in a way that is just as awe inspiring, emotional, and enabling. British children should be able to engage with all the references that were made in the ceremony because it should be part of them. If it isn't, then it should be.

Vertical Transmission

The 2004 tsunami delivered a 9-metre high wave to the Andaman Islands in the Indian Ocean. Indian Government officials feared that the isolated tribes on the islands would suffer heavy casualties, but this wasn't the case: the tribes' oral traditions told them to escape to the high ground if the sea retreated. While recent settlers suffered terribly, the tribespeople found safety in the hills.

Jonnie Hughes, *On the Origin of Tepees* (2012: 269)

Can we detect in this passage a problem with our knowledge age? Yes, and it relates to how we make meaning of the vast amount of knowledge that is being shared in ever more ingenious ways. This sharing allows the memes to breed in ever-faster ways, connecting horizontally from person to person. We are all quickly communicating our opinions via Twitter, YouTube, Facebook, blogs, texts, email, and so on. We can self-publish books, record music, make videos and upload them for others to appreciate. For many people this is great. However, if we decide to abandon everything to horizontal transmission then our young people might easily lose sight of, and abandon, the wisdom of their elders. They will then be more vulnerable to the impulses of the market, or the memes that are based on rumour, innuendo, and prejudice. To stop them being swept away on a wave of indiscriminating knowledge without roots, we need to ensure that education – whether at home, school, or other institutions – understands the duty it has to the continuing vertical transmission of knowledge; to exist alongside, and negotiate with, the horizontal.

The job of grammar in the 21st century is to make certain that we have a core, a place where valued authority, culture, knowledge, and skills in our society can reside. Grammar is our collective memory. However, it needs to be mature enough to recognize the degree to which it deals in uncertainty and is liable to change. It should be a modest art, reasonable and open to negotiation like all true *liberal* arts.

Chapter 9

Dialectic:
Logic, Dialectic, and *Logos*

'Logic!' said the Professor half to himself. 'Why don't they teach logic at these schools?'

C. S. Lewis, *The Lion, the Witch and the Wardrobe*

The relationship between dialectic and grammar is crucial: get it right and creativity flourishes; get it wrong and devastation follows. Like C. S. Peirce (see Chapter 6), I think it is useful to divide dialectic, or what he called 'critic', into a further triad. Peirce proposed *abductive, inductive,* and *deductive* logic; for me the three are *logic, dialectic,* and *logos*. Logic includes mathematical and scientific thinking, these are not the same but they can be considered complementary. Dialectic is understood as argument, debate, and dialogue, and also of mashing, mixing, and joining up ideas. *Logos* can be seen as a teleological pursuit of an end that might not be fully understood – the mystery of it all.

There is a lot to explore – what follows is just a beginning. In the trivium, dialectic has evolved over the years. Looking at the different facets of dialectic will help us understand how it has changed and why it is important for Trivium 21c.

Critical Thinking

In *Mastermind: How to Think Like Sherlock Holmes* (2013), Maria Konnikova explains how we could all improve our strategizing, problem solving, and creativity if we thought more like Sherlock Holmes. She outlines his methods, ostensibly called 'deduction', but points out that Holmes's thinking is more akin to what logicians would call 'induction' and 'abduction'. Konnikova also shows how Holmes's indulgences in pipe-smoking, walking, and playing the violin, have a strong relationship with his ability to think clearly.

Holmes's use of *logical* thinking, his *dialogues* with Watson, and his *enthusiasm* for playing the violin can, indeed, be a metaphor for the dialectical art: *logic, dialectic,* and *logos (enthusiasms)*. Summed up by some educationalists as critical thinking and creativity, my understanding of dialectic will ensure our students are able to use *logic* and develop an understanding of science, enter into a *dialectic* by learning to question, debate, discuss and argue, and also need to be given the opportunity to develop their own *enthusiasms* through authentic engagement with the creative arts, sport, vocational and other practical challenges.

In an open letter to his daughter, Juliet, the evolutionary biologist Richard Dawkins wrote, 'Next time somebody tells you something that sounds important, think to yourself, "Is this the kind of thing that people only believe because of tradition, authority, or revelation?" And next time somebody tells you that something is true, why not say to them, "What kind of evidence is there for that?"' (Dawkins, 2003: 248). In explanation he said, 'I was trying to tell her how to think about certain things; not what to think, but how to think' (Dawkins, 2012). This is a lovely explanation of how scientific method can challenge tradition and grammar. That is the job of logic, and it should be embraced. It can help take us on a journey towards truth. It can aid us in finding sufficient certainty for living in an uncertain world. Logic is a vital part of what we should teach our children. They should be able to straddle the arts and the sciences, knowing when and how to use methods of analysis, statistics, criticism, or logic and whether to apply deductive, inductive, or abductive reasoning.

Although scientific method is part of our pursuit of truth, it is by no means the only way. The American philosopher Thomas Nagel puts it like this, 'In every area of thought we must rely ultimately on our judgements, tested by reflection, subject to correction by the counterarguments of others, modified by the imagination and by comparison with alternatives' (Nagel, 2012: 103). In schools, and to a very large extent in education policy, this relationship has been reduced to a very narrow understanding of logic; a view that the philosopher of science, Karl Popper, believed began with Francis Bacon.

Popper thought of Bacon as a prophet of the new world of science, and that Bacon's view that 'knowledge is power' would lead, gradually, to the dominion of science over other modes of thinking. In *The Myth of the Framework* (1994), Popper likened these other modes to a 'rationalist church'. Bacon's modern, progressive thinking treated the world as a *tabula rasa*. Knowledge, tradition, and myth all bowed down before a harsh empiricism that observed nature as the start of the rationalist approach. To Popper, what to observe is not neutral; you approach the things you are interested in, and what you are interested in is not a process of the world opening itself to you – it is you making the world. According to Popper, if we dispense with doubt and imagination in our schools, we do so at our peril, because both are essential to scientific thinking, to the making and creating of art, and in the pursuit of knowledge itself. If, for Bacon, knowledge is power then, for us, knowledge should be the power to share, disagree, and grow strong bonds of community.

Critical Thinking about Critical Thinking

The current education and assessment system does not like doubt; it has its targets and assessment objectives. Teachers teach children what to think, what to write, and how to write it down for endless tests, which are intended to prove that they know what to think. Doubt is treated as an imposter; despite the language of opening minds, many are in fact being closed down.

In the run-up to the US presidential election in 2012, the Platform and Rules Committees of the Republican Party of Texas published the following two policy statements:

Controversial Theories – We support objective teaching and equal treatment of all sides of scientific theories. We believe theories such as life origins and environmental change should be taught as challengeable scientific theories subject to change as new data is produced. Teachers and students should be able to discuss the strengths and weaknesses of these theories openly and without fear of retribution or discrimination of any kind.

Knowledge-Based Education – We oppose the teaching of Higher Order Thinking Skills (HOTS) (values clarification), critical thinking skills and similar programs … which focus on behaviour modification and have the purpose of challenging the student's fixed beliefs and undermining parental authority. (Republican Party of Texas, 2012: 12)

A revealing dichotomy: critical thinking is OK when it challenges scientific assumptions that these Republicans question, but not when it challenges societal assumptions that Republicans hold dear. Clearly, critical thinking is an area of controversy; you could argue that that is part of its purpose.

Logic

There Is No Doubt That There Is Doubt

Everything is in flux.

Heraclitus

Logic is the art of reasoning. It is associated with a system of thinking that can lead to valid conclusions derived from a set of premises. This separates it from emotional responses and irrational feelings. The problem with logic is that, although it might seem to be a secure approach, it cannot cope logically with paradoxes such as, 'This statement is a lie'. Logic is an art used by philosophers, mathematicians, scientists, computer programmers, and lawyers, but we know for certain that it will never arrive at the whole truth.

If the main aim of education is to simply learn facts and then analyse them – as Susan Wise Bauer seems to suggest – then deductive logic takes centre stage. Deductive logic works but it is limited to certain types of argument; we can only arrive at sound conclusions if the premises the argument is based on are true. This means that when teaching deductive reasoning, we should be clear about how it works and where it works best.

In the real world, we tend to use inductive logic, which is less secure. A lot of the time, arguably, we use abductive logic, which is more akin to educated guesswork. When faced with arguments or evidence, children should be able to differentiate between what is being presented as 'fact' and what is more or less probable; between what has supporting evidence and what is just opinion. This is easier in simple cases, but far more difficult in complex examples.

To improve an individual's ability to make rational judgements, they will need all the tools of a logician's armoury. This will include more than just a technical knowledge of axioms and syllogisms, but also an understanding of the logical traps, fallacies, and paradoxes that beset our thinking. All this should be taught, preferably, in the context of various disciplines rather than as a separate subject. Some people think that deductive logic is the only 'real' logic, due to the doubt that surrounds abductive and inductive reasoning. Deductive logic is certainly far more secure, but it is only as safe as the original premise that it is set to analyse.

Measuring Truth

Science seems to be going from strength to strength, yet can we truly conceive of a time when scientific method will be our only approach to understanding? I talked to the writer Bryan Appleyard about this very problem. Appleyard has written a number of books including *Understanding the Present: Science and the Soul of Modern Man* (1992) and *The Brain is Wider than the Sky: Why Simple Solutions Don't Work in a Complex World* (2011). In the latter, he argues for the importance of art and literature and the depth of human experience, as opposed to the way in which science and technology, for example, are trying to reduce us to simple 'readable' products of our genes. In the former he puts forward a critique of how, as a society, we have become in awe of science. On the subject of science he said:

The idea that measurement and logic would eventually let us know everything, I think, is frankly, absurd. You need to teach scientists the history of philosophy, although they get very upset when you say this. Science was philosophy. It came out of philosophy and Renaissance magic, so I think the claim that the sciences and the humanities are somehow different is absurd. Whenever I see the scientific claim that everything is reducible to a single measurement, I know that it is wrong. Anything complex is not reducible to a single measurement. That's why it is a complex system. There is simplicity which is just stupid, and there is simplicity which is profound. I think part of the problem in education is that somehow we have arrived at the situation where we say, 'This is softer – the arts,' and 'This is harder – the sciences.' It just isn't true; it's interesting how often the assumptions of 'hard science' are completely overthrown. They should learn that science is as questionable a discipline as any other. It's not just something where you have to learn all the equations and then everything is true.

If we are to entertain doubt and uncertainty, we need to teach not with an idea of the 'two cultures' – softy arts and macho sciences – but in a way that shows 'truths' as complex and difficult things to get to. This is not anti-science; far from it. In fact, this stance can be found in the history of logical thinking and the scientific method. I believe that science itself is far more aware of its flaws than, perhaps, the rest of society. Sometimes wider society seems too much in awe of science. It has been so successful, and brought so much to our world, that those of us who are outside scientific culture can easily succumb to the illusion that it offers all-embracing answers for our increasingly complex lives.

The Whole Truth and Nothing but the Truth

The sense of reality is vital in logic.

Bertrand Russell

Rather than just accept my views about logic and scientific method, and its relationship to truth, it is useful to look into what logicians and scientists have said about their own methodology. Gottlob Frege (1848–1925) was responsible for taking logic away from empiricism and putting it firmly into the mathematical realm. Instead of logic being seen as a product of the human mind and the senses, and thereby derived from experience, he said that logic could be arrived at through mathematical principles and analytical truths. Influenced by Frege, Bertrand Russell (1872–1970) wanted logic to be used to understand the nature of external reality, and he brought to mathematics the idea of using objective, logical foundations. Russell discovered that Frege's logicism included inconsistencies, which caused Frege great distress. Russell had applied the techniques of logical analysis and found there were serious difficulties in arriving at truth and meaning. This led to the detailed analysis of language, concepts, and logic by groups of philosophers, mathematicians, and scientists. By the end of his life, Russell was troubled that logic had moved away from the pursuit of wisdom and had become over-concerned with analysis for its own sake.

The objectification of logic, and its link to mathematics, was criticized by Edmund Husserl (1859–1938). He thought that it was necessary to put logic and philosophy back in touch with the 'real' world of phenomena, empiricism, and pragmatism. In order to alleviate bias, his idea was to build knowledge by 'bracketing out' assumptions. By the end of his life Husserl, too, came to realize that his desire to put logic and science on a firmer footing had failed. Arguments persist to this day as to what logic is and whether it has any base in absolute certainty.

Russell's student, Ludwig Wittgenstein (1889–1951), was to downgrade all philosophical systems by following his own logic. He came to the conclusion that logic does not interpret our world. He was not against philosophy or logic, but he did say, 'Don't be afraid of talking nonsense … [but] you must keep an eye on your nonsense.' Wittgenstein wrote extensively about grammar and associated it with the styles and forms of life as lived – what I would call culture. His philosophy was playful, revealing the ridiculousness behind the games we all play. Whether one follows the idea of logic as expounded by Aristotle, Frege, or Husserl, it has proved to be a good method of thinking, but it is not infallible.

The philosopher Julian Baggini explained his thoughts on logic to me over a cup of coffee:

Russell's was the glorious failed project and that is the glorious history of philosophy. Whenever people have tried to find an absolutely secure basis, something on which the whole can sit entirely securely, it has always failed. Good that they've tried because we've learned stuff along the way. What we get by thinking about things rigorously, though, is generally greater clarity and greater coherence. On certain empirical matters we get, from a functional point of view, certainty, or as close to certainty as we need without anything being 100% certain. But on all the other important matters of living, it is just trying to understand things better.

Nagel talks about objectivity being a matter of degree, and relativity is the same. There is a sense in which, obviously, whether your coffee is delicious is relative because it is to do with taste buds. They vary. But, at the same time, to say it is completely subjective is not true because there are objective facts about coffee – there are reasons for saying some things are better quality than another. These reasons are related to subjective experience. They wouldn't make any sense unless human beings had general patterns of perception. But it makes perfect sense to say that some coffees are of a superior quality, and part of the reason for saying that is to do with the facts of human physiology.

Obviously it doesn't hold for Martians, but sometimes people try to make it too binary. If there isn't an objective fact about it, it's relative, it's subjective. What I think you rather need to ask is: what are the facts which inform these things, and how much room does that leave for relativism and a subjective judgement? And for every issue it will vary: with food, more so than with other things; with values, a certain amount but not completely; with how far Paris is from London, not at all.

Elementary, My Dear Peirce

Of course, my dear Baggini, but it also depends where you measure London and Paris from, which part, how you measure it, and what with – which is not straightforward on a spherical planet! Your answer will be pragmatic and subject to human error and inaccurate measuring devices.

The strength of the deductive method is that if the premise is true, you can be certain of the conclusions. The method fails should the premise be wrong, or vague, or unknowable. In other words, ask a silly question, get a silly answer. Is it possible to help my daughter to recognize a silly question when the answer might seem plausible? Induction, however, is looser and more likely to lead to probabilistic outcomes, but it can be more adaptable to circumstances. For example, you can ask questions in a looser way, 'If we are doing this, therefore, is it possible that ...?'

Here is Julian Baggini again:

> You start from two facts which are observations about the world and then you reach a deduction on the basis of these facts. You can make a deduction based on purely a posteriori evidence (for example, there are only two people in the room, one shot the other, the person who shot the other person is the person who wasn't shot). That's a deduction. There's nothing a priori about it. The only a priori thing is the fundamental principles of logic, the rule by which you work that out. You can even get too worried about that (that is, whether it's a priori).
>
> In ways we can't yet imagine, it may well be that we discover some facts about the world which contradict the basic laws of logic. What would that show? Well, to be honest, it would still show that in virtually every other case in the world the laws of logic hold. So, in a sense, the reason (man shoots man in room) is a robust deduction. It need not rely on any a priori claim that the laws of logic dictate that x, y, and z. It can be based on the empirical claim that 'this is what we observe'.
>
> From a practical purpose, there are always reasons for pursuing these things philosophically, almost for their own sake, but if you are interested in good reasoning the ultimate basis of it doesn't matter as much. Virtually everything we do is inductive, but it is highly constrained by logic. Logic doesn't get you from the observations to the conclusion, but the constraints of logic stop you getting from the evidence to a conclusion that is completely stupid or false.

Our conclusions can be as near-right as they can be, based on the evidence we are aware of. But the strength of our enquiry about who shot whom, based on all the evidence we can gather, must always entertain the possibility that the man shot himself or someone else shot him through the keyhole. Ouch.

Logic and the Fallible

The physicist David Deutsch writes, 'The real source of our knowledge is conjecture alternating with criticism. We create theories by rearranging, combining, altering and adding to existing ideas with the intention of improving upon them' (Deutsch, 2011: 32). He sees the importance of the 'tradition of criticism' and the search for 'good explanations' as a rationalization for progress since the Enlightenment. Deutsch, drawing on the work of Popper, believes in fallibilism: he sees the importance of doubt rather than certainty. This approach acknowledges that, in any field, the creative hunch or imaginative hypothesis will always leave the door open for disproof through experiment, dispute, dialectic, or discovery.

When knowledge is 'owned' by an authority or vested interest, it is even more important to open it up to scrutiny and questioning. Logical arguments can be shown to be true even if they are based on false premises. Conclusions reached are only as good as the information on which they are founded. If the data used is based on invalid assumptions, then it becomes difficult to ascribe genuine meaning to the answer. The particle physicist Lisa Randall puts it this way, 'Science generally settles issues with some degree of probability ... only infrequently can anyone absolutely settle an issue – scientific or otherwise – on the basis of evidence' (Randall, 2011: 202).

Scientific Progress as Paradigm Shifts

Popper's scientific narrative was a linear process by which changes happen in a smooth way while reaching towards greater truth. But, for some, this doesn't address why scientists can come up with completely novel hypotheses. The scientific philosopher Thomas Kuhn (1922–1996) saw that science, instead of being a linear narrative of progress moving ever closer to complete knowledge, moves instead in jumps that can contradict each other. He thought that science justified itself more than its method deserved, proving itself rather than subjecting itself to criticism (such as papering over any cracks that occur by overlooking contradictory results). However, when anomalies in proof accumulate to a critical point, a crisis follows, and this causes a paradigm shift: a new theoretical framework comes into play, with new hypotheses, and the process begins again.

Good Science and No Science

'It is wrong from beginning to end,' said the Caterpillar decidedly, and there was silence for some minutes.

Lewis Carroll, *Alice's Adventures in Wonderland*

We seem to be losing our hold on 'truth' and also on the means – logic and scientific method – for finding it. Imre Lakatos (1922–1974), a mathematician and scientific philosopher, brought Kuhn's and Popper's ideas together and argued for a rationalist view of science in which a 'meta-method' would evaluate the history of science and find out what was good science and what was bad or 'pseudo-science'. This would be based on the idea of 'testability'. That is to say, good science can be tested and be seen to be true or false, whereas bad science cannot.

Lakatos's friend, Paul Feyerabend (1924–1994), thought that science and myth had an intrinsic relationship and he went against the meta-method thesis and described how there is no such thing as scientific method at all. Feyerabend claimed that if there had been strict rules, science would not have progressed. Whenever we explore anything, or when we are told something is evidence-based, then we need to consider the following questions: Why was the area investigated? How was it being measured? How secure was the method used? How much doubt is there? Is the method used one that actually addresses the problem it purports to?

Analysis, which, in itself, can be a worthwhile process, is thus seen to be only as good as the context in which it operates. Logic is but one tool by which we reach for understanding. The idea that some studies/researches/investigations are unsuitable for a scientific approach – in other words, they aren't falsifiable – opens up the possibility that the arts and humanities have the potential to reach truths that science cannot. I want my daughter to explore a wide range of truths, not just scientific or analytical ones. I want her to develop the ability to reason, to be reasonable, and to develop and trust her intuition. I want her to have a sense of wonder and not be hoodwinked by charlatans. There is also a place for responding to the beauty or ugliness of the world with a developed sense of outrage or love.

Susan Wise Bauer's assertion that the trivium 'trains the mind in the art of learning' (Bauer, 2003: 20) is central to my thesis, but her idea that 'the logic stage' is about children analysing grammar, and deciding whether what they are looking at is right or wrong, is too black and white. Grey areas also matter. Parsing, analysing, and investigating are essential tools, but they are only part of the story of dialectic. Therefore, I would like to argue that this 'logical' art needs to do more than just analyse or reason; it needs to move beyond the realms of logic into the worlds of dialectic and *logos*, where it becomes more about the identity of the student and authentic engagement with their work.

Peirce's scientific method came from what he saw as the role of 'critic'. In his trivium it is abduction (creating hypotheses or conjectures) followed by deduction (clarifying the implications of the conjecture) and induction (testing). I discussed the importance of grammar in the previous chapter. It should be taught in a way that leaves it open to the critical art of dialectic. In Popper's version of the scientific method, it is almost as if the first two arts of the trivium are brought together: grammar as conjecture and dialectic as criticism. In Trivium 21c, I propose simply that we educate in a way that treats grammar as conjecture and opens it up to the criticism of dialectic. This criticism involves analysis, logic and scientific method. A student well versed in those critical skills should also learn to argue, debate, and think and work creatively.

Dialectic

In schools, dialectic is associated with debate, although it is more often called class discussion or dialogue. As Christopher Hitchens put it, 'When there is a basic grasp of narration and evolution and a corresponding grasp of the idea of differing views of the same story … [we have] the theory and practice of teaching by dialectics … [as practised by the Greeks]' (Hitchens, 2006: 277). This method of teaching requires students to have a knowledge of differing viewpoints; therefore, the learning of the 'grammar' of a subject needs to include alternative views to the 'traditional' in order to allow dialectic to work. Dialectic can include dialogic teaching, but it is not the same.

According to Peter Mack, in English schools in the 16th century, 'Rhetorical knowledge was reinforced by the comments pupils and students made on the texts they read. Dialectic was not taught at the grammar school but some of the grammar school textbooks drew on ideas from dialectic' (Mack, 2007: 99). This approach is not strictly dialectical; it is, however, an important part of the art. Mikhail Bakhtin (1895–1975) used the word 'dialogic' to describe a conversation that uses a process of exchange to listen and empathize with, but not necessarily agree. Dialectic, in the Hegelian sense, looks for synthesis and agreement, but Bakhtin did not believe this was necessary.

As Richard Sennett observes in *Together*, 'Dialectic and dialogic procedures offer two ways of practising a conversation, the one by a play of contraries leading to agreement, the other by bouncing off views and experiences in an open-ended way. In listening well, we can feel either sympathy or empathy; both are cooperative impulses' (Sennett, 2012: 24). In a school situation, it is desirable that some form of agreement is arrived at. Given the likelihood of disparate points of view, it becomes necessary to find out whether resolution is possible or not because of different frameworks of understanding. The thinking on both sides of the argument should always come from an appropriate evidence base, but how should the classroom teacher handle disagreement? How can we agree to differ? How might assessment lend itself to operate in a mature way that recognizes the possibility of difference?

Debate

Students need to engage in a critical process that engages the curious mind. A curriculum that drives the learner forward is absolutely essential. This is not about questioning simply in order to demolish an opponent without first considering their point of view. This is about questioning with an open mind, which allows for the possibility of changing one's own ideas. In this way lies wisdom. Here is Elizabeth Truss again:

I think I learn best when I'm challenged, I learn best when I'm debating things. The trouble is there is a strong tendency in parts of the education system not to be prepared to learn from history. I think we should stop being defensive. I spend a lot of my time proposing ideas about what to change about things. Sometimes the ideas might not be right, but partly why I'm suggesting them is to say, 'Let's not be satisfied – just because we've always done it like this doesn't mean it's the right thing to do.' You have to be prepared to constantly question, which is critical thinking. Some of the primary advocates of the critical thinking approach to education don't seem to be prepared to think critically about their own ideas.

Contrariwise

The importance to Holmes of his Moriarty is vital; without the evil genius where would he be? Perhaps we all need to develop an inner nemesis, or even a trusted friend, with whom to disagree – like Socrates searching for Glaucon, Holmes finding his Watson, or Kirk needing his Spock. The type of dialectic we have with another can be quite fruitful. The muscular version of dialectic that Abelard indulged in would, perhaps, most resemble the role a teacher assumes when they take on the role of devil's advocate.

During the Enlightenment, it was a dialectical impulse that brought about a rebellion against the whole authority of knowledge embedded in the Church and in tradition. In *A compendium of the art of logick and rhetorick in the English tongue* (1651), Petrus Ramus (*c.*1515–1572) writes that, 'Dialectica is the art of disputing well.' The right to say 'no' is fundamental. Natalie Haynes observed, 'The Socratic urge is partly to destroy the things you are presented with as perceived wisdom and partly what it means to be young. There is a reason why one of the things Socrates was executed for is corrupting the young.'

Dialectic, in this sense, has the protean impulse – to be versatile, to be able to adapt, but also to be the maverick, the radical, the dissident, the sceptic, to be naive and naughty. In *Letters to a Young Contrarian*, Christopher Hitchens writes, 'One should strive to combine the maximum of impatience with the maximum of scepticism, the maximum of hatred of injustice and irrationality with the maximum of ironic self-criticism. This would mean really deciding to learn from history rather than invoking or sloganising it' (Hitchens, 2001: 138). If we think of history as the tradition of a domain, indeed its grammar, then we can start to see how the opportunity to be contrarian to it is so vital.

This is the backbone of our constitution. Look at how the House of Commons is set up for confrontation: the government makes its thesis, the opposition presents its antithesis, and the process continues until an agreement (synthesis) is reached in which the majority view wins. How far a teacher would want to engage with this method is up to them, but the testing of the boundaries of knowledge is a very exciting way to engage students in the classroom. It makes young people see the possibilities of their responsibility: that they can take on the great traditions – and if that knowledge can be added to, then all the better. Can students be expected to enter into this form of dialectic if they are not 'experts' in the field? As teachers, we need to consider this carefully when it comes to implementing this method.

It might be rather rude to cast David Aaronovitch as our Moriarty, but, as the son of communists, the *Times* opinion columnist, broadcaster, and journalist was brought up with dialectic in his blood. When he appeared on *University Challenge* in 1975, he and his Manchester teammates challenged that bastion of the establishment with a protest, answering each question with the answers 'Che', 'Marx', 'Trotsky', or 'Lenin'. Later, he became president of the National Union of Students, wrote a number of books, including *Voodoo Histories* (2009) about conspiracy theories, and, for a man of the left, finds himself vilified (in much the same way as Christopher Hitchens) as a neoconservative for some of his views on Iraq and Tony Blair, and for working for Rupert Murdoch. If anyone understands the notion of being a contrarian, he should, as he told me when I spoke to him, 'If that's all you are doing [being a contrarian], in the end people will not respond to it, and why should they? "What is everybody thinking? I'll think the opposite." If they know that is what you are thinking, it ceases to have a value after a while.'

The comment sections of newspapers can serve various purposes. Some people read them to find out what they should think, some go to their favourite columnist to have their views or prejudices confirmed, but other journalists confound you, challenge you, irritate you, or surprise you. This is exactly what a teacher should do in the dialectic 'contrarian' phase. They should genuinely challenge the pupil to think in a different way, even though it might really annoy them … But it could also open up a new way of thinking that might only make sense in five, ten or twenty years' time as the misty-eyed alumni look back and say to themselves, 'Yes, now I see what they meant!'

A potential problem with dialectic is that the students might begin to question not only the authority of the knowledge, but the authority of the gatekeeper, the teacher. Should you teach kids to argue back? David Aaronovitch thinks we should:

My instinct is yes, but only in the context of what is valuable and what isn't. Just because it's an argument doesn't mean it's good, but it doesn't mean it's bad. I was taught in schools where having an argument with teachers was automatically bad. In the lower sixth we were discussing Henry IV, Part 1, *and we had this wonderful teacher – a gay guy, florid and big, bow-tied. I really liked him, but a bit on the melodramatic side. He was anxious to point out Shakespeare's disapproval of Falstaff but he overdid it, and I said, 'Actually, I think Shakespeare also liked Falstaff. He knows there are things about ourselves we are ashamed about but we enjoy picking at our scabs.' And he sent me out of the room. Now, what is the quality of the sending out at this moment? I can't speak for the manner in which I spoke, but did he send me out because he didn't like the idea? He could have quite easily said, 'That's interesting,' and if he'd said that he wouldn't have had to send me out. If he says, 'That's interesting,' what is the message everyone gets? It's not that his original statement is somehow negated. So yes, you want kids arguing.*

I mention David Starkey – a controversialist, historian, and bastion of conservatism – in the context of using argument as an emotional technique. Aaronovitch adds:

David Starkey is a perfect example of someone who actually loves arguing. If you don't argue with him he has nothing to argue about, but he can be quite offensive. Arguing is a risk but, by and large, if you put yourself in a position of constant dialogue you obviously like it. I obviously like it. I imagine most teachers like dialogue because one of the things that is happening when kids are arguing is kids are doing something. *The state I can't stand is indifference.*

Dissoi Logoi

It is possible to take dialectic one step further. Instead of looking for agreement and compromise, or disagreement and conflict, we can bring two things together that might, at first, seem to be complete opposites. This process uses the idea of dual thinking in a highly creative way.

Marshall McLuhan had this ability to think in a dual way; for example, he was both traditional and progressive at the same time and he used oxymoronic formulations, such as 'global village'. By putting the two words, global village, together, McLuhan presents us with a *dissoi logoi*, an ancient Greek term for a two-sided argument. *Dissoi logoi* is the art of seeing both sides in an argument as true, which calls for the ability to harmonize or understand opposing ideas. Instead of an argument being about one side being right and the other wrong, a *dissoi logoi* explores the possibility that both sides are right within their own context. Although one side may have a weaker argument than the other that might not always be so.

Whether through confrontation or accommodation, dialectic – when used against or with the stabilizing nature of grammar and in the context of tradition – becomes a creative force. Arguably, when tied with *logos*, it is the ultimate creative force. It is no accident that the trivium had a role to play in the education of some of the most creative names in history. Our mantra begins to come together ...

Logos

Plato and Aristotle: Skills, Work, and Wisdom

In *Plato's Earlier Dialectic*, Richard Robinson writes that Plato believes, 'Dialectic is a skill ... [and] Plato [regards the dialectician's work] as the alteration of his own personality in a fundamental way, as character building ... This character building is about altering oneself and "becoming wise"' (Robinson, 1953: 74). Aristotle altered the meaning of dialectic from Plato's 'highest intellectual activity' to one where, it could be argued, dialectic had a more utilitarian purpose with generic skills and was an end in itself. Plato intended these skills to serve a relationship with the highest form of knowledge – that of fundamental change in one's character.

At a time in our education system when factions on the left and the right are suggesting that we need to be educating young people to fill the gaps in labour-related skills, rather than encouraging education for and of itself, surely the idea of building character through learning and growth need to be in our minds more than ever.

Good Character

The word *logos* emphasizes a higher level of knowledge, skills, and experience. In other words, wisdom that has the capability to shape us, to make us who we are, or who we are capable of being. In essence, it is the essence of our character. In *Of Good Character* (2010), James Arthur seeks to distinguish between good acts, which good or bad people can do, and goodness. He writes about the ways in which the curriculum can present a reductive idea of skills that are 'marketable' for employers or 'convenient' for schools, yet he also points out that character education has an emphasis on high academic standards and a positive ethos. This is useful in an era when the challenges of a secular or multi-faith age may have undermined the grammar of virtue and morality. This is not about behaviour, punishment, and reward, which many people may reduce this to; moral education is not about control.

For Richard Sennett, in *Respect: The Formation of Character in an Age of Inequality* (2003), character is a process of curiosity, of 'turning outward'. For him, this involves character as well as an understanding through relationships with other people and 'shared symbols', practices, and artefacts, similar to the shared symbols of a religion. This dialogue with others creates a depth to communal experience: this might be attending a football match with your mates and wearing your team's colours, supping Chardonnay with your chums at Glyndebourne, or taking part in the London Marathon with 35,000 other runners. Sennett explains that, to turn outward, 'something has to happen deep within the individual.

"Turning outward" means the prisoner reforms rather than is reformed; he cannot simply be prescribed another, better set of social practices' (Sennett, 2003: 240).

Prisoner is an odd term for Sennett to use. If we see people who are classified as not having much 'character' (a dubious thought, but stay with it for the moment) as 'prisoners of the market' or 'uncritical consumers' – lacking the capacity and knowledge to make sense of the age in which they find themselves – then perhaps their imprisonment is more a matter of ignorance. This idea works in the light of Plato's Allegory of the Cave (which I explore later in this chapter). Character is not about the cult of personality; turning outward need not be the 'performing' act of the extrovert. It is the relationship between depth, discipline, and virtue, not between the shallow, ill-disciplined, and immoral. This character is about the journey rather than the destination, about doing things for their intrinsic value and not for some other reward. Of all the establishments in which young people may find themselves, schools can directly address the issue of 'good character'. They can do this, not through a few lessons reflecting on what a good character is, although that may help to contextualize the idea, but by opening up the possibility of experience. This means allowing the child to reform themselves by being challenged through authentic tasks and by rising to these tests.

Character Building

Our character is, paradoxically, only accessible through a distinctive attitude to work, craft, and the desire to create something or do something of importance in the physical world, but with 'beauty' or 'truth' as a transcendental aim. This is a journey towards deep understanding, a depth that gets to the essence of whatever form or domain in which we work. But this craft is not just about involvement with doing or making; it is about the essence of being, of presence, of being with a purpose. This comes from being able to engage with knowledge, not as a passive listener but as a doer. Even at times when we have to listen, we should do it attentively as an active listener, engaging with the process. The essence is not necessarily intrinsic to the form or domain; it is what we bring to them; it is our experience, our work, and our desire to appreciate their fundamental nature. This was summed up by the footballer, Danny Blanchflower (1926–1993), when he said, 'The great fallacy is that the game is first and last about winning. It's nothing of the kind. The game is about glory, it is about doing things in style and with a flourish, about going out and beating the lot, not waiting for them to die of boredom.'

Even in the role of spectator we have a part to play. A book is only 'great' if we read it, if we make that effort to engage with it. Only through the effort, engagement, and desire to energize the form or domain in a way that makes a difference can we arrive at a sense of the metaphysical; a oneness with the work, and with others who appreciate our work. This oneness is 'character building'; it is a sense of striving towards something. For some people this something is 'divine'. For those of a more secular persuasion we sense, instead of divinity, real achievement and wisdom. As Elizabeth Truss observed, 'It is about character.'

Striving

If God is dead, what are we left with? How do we cope with the idea of the metaphysical in a godless age? By rejecting Plato's idea of forms, the controversial philosopher, Martin Heidegger (1889–1976) moved from phenomenology (the study of consciousness) to existentialism (our individual existence in a meaningless universe) through the idea of nothing. Here, metaphysics is not 'something' but is arrived at by being 'present'. It is the search for authenticity in what we do, how we relate, and who we are. These essences are atop mountains and, like Sisyphus, we struggle to reach them – because every morning we find ourselves having to lug the rock and ourselves up the mountain again. Yet, by working hard we might, slowly, begin to understand, to feel, if not universal truths, then those truths to which our culture attaches importance.

In *The Case for Working With Your Hands*, Matthew Crawford writes, 'For the early Heidegger, "handiness" is the mode in which things in the world show up for us most originally, the nearest kind of association is not mere perceptual cognition, but, rather, a handling, using, and taking care of things which has its own kind of knowledge' (Crawford, 2009: 68–69). We are striving, as G. E. Lessing (1729–1781) observed, 'If God held enclosed in his right hand all truth, and in his left hand the ever-living striving for truth, although with the qualification that I must forever err, and said to me "choose," I should humbly choose the left hand and say "Father, give! Pure truth is for thee alone"' (quoted in McGilchrist, 2010: 461). It is the ever-living, ever-striving that is our purpose, and we either do it willingly or we turn our back on it.

Being Awake; Being Alive

The theatre practitioner Antonin Artaud (1896–1948) had the idea that an artist should be 'alive within the score'. For this, they had to 'submit to their necessity', 'be in harmony with their necessity', and be like someone 'burning at the stake, signaling through the flames'. By being aware of our mortality, doing what we do as though it could be our last breath, we achieve an intensity of purpose both in rehearsal and performance. It was this that Étienne Decroux (1898–1991), the teacher of Marcel Marceau, and a Marxist atheist, called the moment of having 'God within you'. The word 'enthusiasm' reflects this – it is drawn from the Greek *en theos*, meaning 'with God'. Enthusiasm is a necessary pursuit and should not be denigrated into meaning something lesser. Enthusiasm is the search for essence, that moment of 'flow', but also of intensity and work that is essential for high achievement. This is the idea of mastery: discipline, focus, work, beauty even in ugliness, truth, and the pursuit of in-depth knowledge. This is, perhaps, what Plato thought of as 'being awake'.

Mastery

For schools, mastery should imply that the journey is more important than the outcome. The quality of a life well lived, during schooling, is the richness that brings one far closer to truth than some grades written on a piece of paper. This is the search for wisdom and the good life, not utilitarian target setting and getting *x* number of exam passes and a job. As George Leonard writes in *Mastery: The Keys to Success and Long-Term Fulfillment*,

'How do you best move towards mastery? To put it simply, you practise diligently, but you practise for the sake of the practice itself. Rather than being frustrated while on the plateau, you learn to appreciate and enjoy it as much as you do the upward surges' (Leonard, 1991: 17). This equates to Mihalyi Csikszentmihalyi's theory of 'flow'. Flow can occur during difficult, risky journeys that challenge and stretch our capacities. These creative challenges may be hard to enjoy because of the elusive goal, but Csikszentmihalyi believes we create an unconscious awareness that understands the process. This 'muse' communicates 'through a glass darkly, as it were. It is a splendid arrangement, for if the artist were not tricked by the mystery, he or she might never venture into the unexplored territory' (Csikszentmihalyi, 1996: 115). Part of this mysterious trick of the muse is the less mystifying influence of the teacher.

This process represents the opening up of 'true knowledge' at the level of *logos* as expressed in Plato's Allegory of the Cave from *The Republic*. In this myth, Plato implies that the average person, without much education, would have very little relationship to truth; they would be staring at shadows cast onto the cave wall. Perhaps a modern-day equivalent would be staring at a flickering TV or computer screen. Yet, if they were led out of the cave, they would come into the sunlight of reason and dialectic – in other words, receive the education to qualify as a 'philosopher king'. This is exactly what schools should be doing: taking students on a journey towards the sunlight – with an emphasis on *towards*. In other words, schools help set a student up for the journey. Formal education can only be a staging post; there will always be more learning to do. Rather than philosopher kings, I like to think that when a child leaves school they are a like a *philosopher kid*, not fully formed but with the wherewithal to flourish in whatever they choose to do.

I asked Julian Baggini whether he thought we were on a journey from the cave. He replied: 'Ha, I think we're trying to understand the cave better.' Clearly a long way to go then! *Logos* is this journey; it represents the pursuit, the effort, and the striving. It is arrived at through the desire and pursuit of mastery.

The Allegory of the Cave, Re-Imagined

In my modern-day version, the cave is the journey from prisoner kids to philosopher kids. Prisoner kids are huddled in their caves tethered to machines that flicker with pictures, words, and sounds. Before them are the products of the 'knowledge age'; from screens and earphones they witness the shadows and sounds but they lack the education to understand. When education in its broadest sense intervenes, and their appetites and desires are honed and trained to reject instant gratification, they are on the journey to become philosopher kids – those who have mastery in a desire for learning and the ability to achieve. Now they admire wisdom and love pursuing it. At this point the child is ready to assume the mantle of the philosopher kid, but not quite yet, for there is one further act they need to perform. In order to achieve mastery and access fully the essence behind forms, the philosopher kids need to return to the cave as parents, teachers, coaches, or friends in order to lead other kids out and set them on their own journeys towards mastery.

The most important message for a school to pursue is the idea behind *logos*: students need *authentic* experiences – doing, making, creating, and being. This should run alongside the more abstract academic curriculum and take place within the school day as well as beyond. In these genuine experiences, and maybe in the rest of the curriculum too, the school will achieve something very special: the engagement of students' enthusiasms at a very profound level.

The Art of Dialectic

The art of dialectic therefore covers a very wide range of important activities in teaching and learning. In the context of whatever they are studying, students are taught the specific grammar that gives them structure and knowledge. This is taught in a way that also opens up the possibility of criticism, which in turn opens up the possibility for dialectic. Therefore, students should become well versed in being able to analyse and challenge, whether it be through logic, scientific method, or debate and discussion. Controversies should be welcomed and addressed. In classrooms, we should see the skills of deduction, induction, abduction, analysis, criticism, debate, argument, challenge, and dialogue. Added to this is the opportunity offered through *logos*: students should have quality time to develop their own enthusiasms and whether, like Sherlock Holmes, they like to play the violin, or whatever they decide to pursue, ways need to be found to ensure activities like these are recognized as being more than mere hobbies at the fringes of the curriculum.

Chapter 10

Rhetoric: Communication, Citizenship, and Community

Let Rhetoric be the power to observe the persuasiveness of which any particular matter admits.

Aristotle, *Art of Rhetoric*

What of our contemporary rhetoricians, are they still to be found in our schools? Yes, can you see them hanging around the staffroom? I think they might be disguised as the proponents of modern communication technology, encouraging the idea that the 'flipped' classroom is best, that you can learn lots from a computer, and 'Hey, get the kids to write their own blogs and put some stuff up on YouTube!' Other rhetoricians might be found defending the subject of citizenship or running school debating societies, honing those opening words to perfection. Failing that they might be in rather dustier schools getting students to perform memorized tracts of epic poems ...

The continuing struggle between the tradition of grammar and the modernist critique of dialectic needs to be resolved. Grammar (the transfer of knowledge and culture) submits itself to dialectic (the contemporary analysis, discussion, challenge, and debate), which can, in turn, bring about progress, creative tension, destruction, and change. But this is a cycle without end. In order to get out of the loop, something different has to happen. The way beyond this negative battle of wills can be found in the moment of pause and culmination provided by rhetoric. For example, by taking part in or reflecting on performance, by taking stock, or by testing things out, the debate can move to a bigger stage. It is these moments of performance that allow us to reflect. The performances can take place on a public stage or constitute a private entry in a personal diary. Rhetoric is a peroration, an art of summation, of evaluation. It has both an informal and formal role, embracing methods through which young people can become more confident citizens and communicate and celebrate what it is to feel, to think, to be eloquent – to grow into philosopher kids and maybe even philosopher kings and queens.

Alain de Botton believes that an emphasis on rhetoric in contemporary times is 'bizarre' and makes the point that '[it may have been] fine in ancient Rome, but do we need rhetoric nowadays? Hardly.' Is this true? Paradoxically, it takes an articulate man to draw our attention to it. Those of us who struggle with communication are less flippant about rhetoric. Perhaps it is only when you have been deprived of a voice that you realize its potential. In the stratified societies of Cicero, Quintilian, or Aristotle, rhetoric had a fixed role; it was reserved for speaking to a relatively small group from a limited *demos*. Demos referred to 'the people', but in practice it meant only those citizens who were able to take part in the assembly. This did not include women or slaves. Now, in our more inclusive age, we assume the idea of citizenship for all; but having a voice means knowing how to use that voice and how to use it effectively. Philosopher kings might need to know the art of rhetoric, but philosopher kids in philosopher crowds need to know more than just how to put together a PowerPoint presentation.

Nowadays, we are expected to be able to communicate in many ways, not just face to face but also using social media. In cyberspace, citizens of the world can meet together in a kind of virtual *agora*. In ancient Greek city-states, the agora was a kind of meeting place, which also served as a sporting arena, art gallery, market, place of worship, and even a venue for political meetings – a true civic square. The Oracle at Delphi, an agora par excellence, served as the centre, or 'belly button' as it was known, for the ancient world. I think of Twitter as a modern world equivalent of Delphi where the Oracle was inscribed with the aphorisms: 'Know Thyself' and 'Nothing in

Excess' – both handily communicating to the world in 140 characters or fewer.

People would come to Delphi from all around the ancient world to find answers, but also to perform, be seen and heard, show off, discuss, debate, think, feel, and reflect about themselves and their world – much the same as we do with Twitter, except we no longer have to travel physically. The town of Delphi grew up around the oracle and became a thriving community: the local people staged athletic games rivalling the Olympics, along with musical competitions and theatre. The growth of the institution of Delphi made the town more important and open – a place of cultural cohesion, a hub of the social network for classical times.

The social networks and gathering places of the 21st century are far more fluid. Although we can carry the rhetorical world around with us on a smartphone, the role of rhetoric is more difficult to define. There might still be a role for persuasive speech making that makes use of a repertoire of classical oratorical techniques, but in our more informal and instant messaging age, we also need to be able to move from the high style of grand oratory into what some would argue is a world of 'rhetoricality'. In the knowledge age, citizenship is about having the wherewithal to join in with the great conversations of our time as members of our neighbourhoods, networks, nations, and world.

The English comedian and writer, Natalie Haynes sees rhetoric as 'one of those things that some think is stupid and old fashioned':

So the only people who ever learn it are in schools that are fancy enough to have a debating society and then, oddly enough, those are the people who end up in government. The ability to clearly articulate your case is crucial in speech or in print. Whether you are at the very bottom of the work ladder trying to argue yourself a raise or whether you are at the very top of the pile trying to persuade people to vote for you to be President of the World, you need to be able to articulate your case. By keeping some children in a state where the very idea that they would need to be able to express themselves confidently and formally in public – that that's somehow 'for other people', that 'it's for toffs' – is just another way of keeping things the way they are now, where the powerful remain powerful and the powerless, quite literally, don't have a voice. The most depressing version is on a [TV] programme like The Apprentice, *where day-to-day you get candidates speaking almost literally gibberish and you realize it's because all they have to refer to is the modern vocabulary of business and there is absolutely nothing behind it.*

It is useful to look at the major ideas behind the formal art of rhetoric because, even in a tweet, we can improve not only how we communicate but also how our children might do so too.

Aristotelian Rhetoric and the Art of Communication: From the Grand Style to the Sound Bite

The basic ideas of rhetoric still resonate even in a world in which most of us have abandoned the grand style. Yet, through the knowledge of this ancient art young people can begin to create an articulate future. For Aristotle, rhetoric had three branches and five parts. The three branches were: deliberative, judicial, and epideictic (or panegyric). The five parts were: invention, arrangement, style, memory, and delivery. Each of these is relevant for the crafts of the classroom, whether you are working on your delivery technique or teaching children to communicate well.

Let's begin with the three branches of rhetoric:

1   **Deliberative**: *Associated with the future.* Getting people to do something either because it is the virtuous course or because it is in their best interests. If both, then all the better. This is best described as the political branch because the future is the stuff of all change makers, such as politicians, advertisers, teachers, and three-year-old children wanting a chocolate.

2   **Judicial**: *Associated with the past.* This is the forensic branch: trying to find out what happened and piecing together evidence from the material available. This is important for detectives, researchers, football managers, after-match commentators, and three-year-old children with faces covered in chocolate trying to deny they have eaten any chocolate.

3   **Epideictic**: *Associated with the present.* The display of 'now', the connective between past and future. This is important for news commentators, journalists, and three-year-olds who are caught in the act of taking a chocolate from the sweetie jar.

I interviewed Michael Lea, a speechwriter who has written material delivered by the British Prime Ministers David Cameron and Gordon Brown, President Barack Obama, Secretary of State Hillary Clinton, and ex-French President Nicolas Sarkozy, amongst many others, about his use of rhetoric in a modern context. I suggested that we are so inundated with the constant chatter from the world of modern communication that it is difficult to draw out elements of classical rhetoric from contemporary speeches and writing.

Lea first latched on to the notion of being genuine and having credibility, 'Although it's a cocktail, things don't work on their own. Let's use the "I have a dream" speech: the audience, the stage, context, all coming together to form "the moment".' This connects to the idea of presence, of being 'alive within the score', of 'signalling through the flames', which I explored in the previous chapter. The present tense is transitory, but in this fleeting moment we must learn to communicate in a way that is alive with possibility. We must *be* present. Being in the moment is about feeling and communicating in a way that energizes your audience. Because it is so immediate, it can be the most genuine. But as every con artist knows, it can also be the most manipulative. Advertising or stories that work really well can tap into our subconscious or emotional selves, exploiting our intuitive, immediate responses – 'you want this and you want it now' – and it soon goes viral.

So, if you are someone who is purposeful about what you want to go viral, how will the five parts of rhetoric be of use to you?

1   **Invention** (Proof): This is about constructing your argument and looking for what structure would be best for it, as well as what the counter-arguments might be. Again, your judgement of the audience is key. Invention, according to Aristotle, has two kinds of proof, inartificial proof or 'evidence' and artificial proof which is itself divided into three parts: *ethos, pathos,* and *logos.* Ethos means credibility: how you present yourself, your character, your disposition, and their appeal to others. Are you an honest kinda guy? Aristotle uses the word pathos to indicate a shared emotion: your own emotions and those you wish to evoke. Nowadays, seeing people cry in public is one of the most outward expressions of pathos. When a politician weeps we might warm to them, at first, but the moment needs to be right. At its best, pathos allows your audience to see you as credible. *Logos* (or logic) is the third element, which, in this context, is what Aristotle refers to as reason. Are you making a reasonable argument, one that seems based in a version of truth the audience can buy into?

2   **Arrangement or Shape**: Once you have your arguments and counter-arguments you need to consider the best way to present your claim. For this you also need to think about the third element
    …

3   **Style**: The three main types of style are low, medium, and grand. In our sound bite age, it has been argued that the grand style is on the wane, but I'm not so sure.

4   **Memory**: This was the part that most exercised the ancients, particularly with the arrival of the written word: would memory go into decline? By this they meant both the ability of the actor to memorize their part, but also the idea that memory is simply knowing your stuff and being able to recall it when you need to (perhaps for a tweet).

5   **Delivery**: Our performance, which includes voice, gesture, and pose. Perhaps teacher training courses wouldn't go far wrong if they concentrated on the workings of classical rhetoric and taught

teachers how to communicate and persuade their charges based on the above.

Aristotle's principles are not the only 'rules' of rhetoric that have been posited. For example, Cicero thought there were three parts to oratory: *docere* (to teach), *delectare* (to delight), and *movere* (to move). Any outstanding teacher should perhaps take this to heart, as long as docere is their main concern!

I asked Michael Lea if he had been trained in classical rhetoric. 'I learnt the art through the craft, by listening and reading other speeches,' he said. 'Most speeches are quite formulaic – there are two or three different formulas that great speeches seem to follow. Bear in mind that few people know the whole content of great speeches. Politicians work to a formula, and speechwriters need to be aware of the lines that will make the headline or be picked out for broadcast.' When working at Number 10, Michael particularly remembers the amount of time and care spent on identifying what sound bites would be singled out by the media, and making sure that they carried the intended message. These bite-sized chunks often work through repetition, such as in Martin Luther King's 'I have a dream' speech. This is what makes headlines. Lea often spent longer on crafting the sound bites than he did on the rest of the speech. Does anyone remember anything else about Tony Blair's speech in which he mentioned 'Education, education, education'? Unlikely. Instead, people remembered the sound bite and they got the message the government wanted to prioritize.

If we analyse newspapers it is clear how headlines and articles work. There is an art to telling the story in such a way that the reader gets the gist without having to read all of it. When Lea worked for the *Daily Mail* he recalls, 'We used "boxes" – fact files, mini-biographies, did you knows, and numbers of the day – to break up the text, so that the readers could have an understanding of the story by looking at the headlines and sub-headlines.'

The skill of journalists and speech makers becomes apparent to us when we go through a selective history of the sound bite and headline. There is a power in an aphorism which is able to conjure up so much more than just the bare words, 'We shall fight them on the beaches', 'They think it's all over', 'The lady's not for turning', 'Don't mention the war', 'Gotcha', 'Will the last person to leave Britain please turn out the lights', 'Annus horribilis', 'I may have the body of a weak and feeble woman', and the ultimate preamble of liberal values, 'We hold these truths to be self-evident, that all men are created equal, that they are endowed by their Creator with certain unalienable Rights, that among these are Life, Liberty and the pursuit of Happiness'. In this electronic age, we take the everyday rhetoricalities of our relationships into the wider space of the global village. Most of us enjoy at least the possibility, if not the practice, of instant communication with large numbers of people. You are only ever one tweet away from the rest of the world. We are all rhetoricians now, and all the world is our stage, whether we are aware of it or not. We must give our children practice and experience of performance and rhetoric to prepare them for the rhetoricality of cyberspace.

Rhetoric, Eloquence, Authority, and Science

When you are asked, 'How do you feel?' what sort of answer do you give? How can you best transfer what is in your mind to someone else? How can we communicate, for example, the metaphysical qualities of love? 'Shall I compare thee to a summer's day?' We need to converse in a way that reflects the beauty of our thoughts. It is difficult, if not impossible, and yet we must do the best we can to transfer knowledge, ideas, feelings, and thoughts (including half-thought-through impulses) to others, so that they can understand us. Given the imprecision of communication in all its forms, we must use every tool available to get across our message and our ideas as well as we can. In order for our audience to feel that they understand, we need to convey the things beyond words – the ideas that tap into our shared wisdom. A virtuous life doesn't just mean to be wise and live like a hermit with a vow of silence. Our community needs wisdom and it needs eloquence. Even when messages are starker or darker, we need a language for sharing and inspiring.

We also have to choose how we take part. Do we want to challenge or defend the cultural traditions in which we are embedded? Do we want to communicate with those who are the gatekeepers for those traditions, or those who want to smash down the barricades? In the recent past, trust and respect were automatically invested in those with authority. Superiority was associated with 'breeding' or, to a lesser extent, expertise. This distanced those in power from those without, and the gap was maintained because they could hide behind a rhetoric of patriarchal superiority, as if they were a race apart, passing on their edicts from on high. It seems that this is no longer possible. Authority figures can no longer automatically expect to be listened to or have their opinions taken on trust.

The same is true of science. There are many examples of fakery and self-aggrandizement: phrenology, recovered memory syndrome, Cyril Burt's falsified (or careless) research on the heritability of IQ, the exaggerated claims of various pedagogical fads such as Brain Gym and learning styles. In *The Rhetoric of Science*, Alan Gross writes, 'The sciences create bodies of knowledge so persuasive as to seem unrhetorical – to seem, simply, the way the world is. But however much scientists require the justification of realism, rhetoricians are realists only at their peril: for them, realism must remain an analytical target, a rhetorical construct like any other' (Gross, 1996: 206–207). In other words, beware any claim that insists that the world really is like this. The way in which we succumb to 'bad science' suggests that many of us are still in thrall to the white coat, even in an age when other authority figures struggle to be heard. Conversely, much 'good science' can be just as easily dismissed through the cynicism that accompanies the realization that it is rhetoric too. Look at how rumour and suspicion trumped science in the row about the MMR vaccine; at the root of the controversy was a scientist who was wrong, but people preferred his theory to those of the many other scientists who disagreed with him.

For some, the collapse of authority has its dangers as well as its benefits. Scientists and others need to be more open about the claims they make. However, there is danger that this has happened at the same time as the democratization of communication. As a result, there is no longer any degree of hierarchy of validity; every view is seen as carrying equal weight. We are encouraged to say what we think and that whatever we think is OK. It is our opinion, so it necessarily demands respect, regardless of how superficial or ill-informed it is. In a democratic electronic age the whistleblower is equal to the emperor. The philosopher king can rightly be challenged, but this may simply leave a void that we will try to fill as quickly as possible. The question is: how do we decide what to believe? How do we know whether what is being said is true if we are subjected to the wisdom of crowds rather than the wisdom of the wise? In times of cynicism, we can all point out naked emperors, even if they are fully clothed. This may end up with us regarding everyone in authority with suspicion. Their word is no longer to be trusted, their rhetoric a sham, and thus we are fools to believe them.

The art we need to inculcate in our young people is the discrimination of knowing who to listen to and recognizing when they are being conned. We need to understand the art of rhetoric if we are to realize the importance, or otherwise, of what we are being told. Then we will have the power to laugh at or expose falsehood, but not to abuse that power through inarticulate trolling, abuse, or lies. This learning begins at home and in the classroom: in how we use, listen, and develop our personal rhetoric, as well as in the ability to examine a debate objectively. In this way, children develop their own authority. This confidence should be based not just in the *what* but also in the *how*.

The Rhetorical Age

For Thomas Hobbes (1588–1679), rhetoric was the 'art of speaking finely'. In that word, 'finely', there is a core value for education. In other words, this is not just about communication, or effective communication, though that helps. Rather, it is about fine communication, which has elegance, excellence, wisdom, and virtue running through it. This qualitative argument is a palliative to relativism. It is not OK to communicate just as you see fit; we must remember that communication is a two-way process. We communicate with an audience in mind. We don't just speak, we don't want just to be heard; we want to make a difference to those we are communicating with. This is persuasion, not as a low form of skulduggery, but a higher form of art. This involves the desire and ability to do and say the right thing in the right way.

In *You Talkin' to Me? Rhetoric from Aristotle to Obama*, Sam Leith says that we have reached the most 'argumentative age of any in history … We may no longer study or teach rhetoric in anything like the way our ancestors did, but many of us rely much more heavily on it than ever before … Our commerce, our politics, our cultural and social lives are all rhetorical to an extraordinary extent' (Leith, 2011: 17).

Our lives are shaped by the memes that are passed on to us – culturally, institutionally, and technologically. Rather than through the high rhetoric of a great orator, we are surrounded by 'rhetoricality'. The marketization of society creates consumers of us all and we need to be aware of how easily we buy into something because of its surface appeal, which is made apparent to us through rhetoric.

In *Rhetoric* (2008), Jennifer Richards describes the move from rhetoric to rhetoricality. She argues that the schism caused by modernity ended rhetoric as it was then understood. She makes a case for a modern view of rhetoric that recognizes the importance of contrariness, of opening questions up rather than closing them down. It could be argued that much of what she says seems to belong more to the trivial art of dialectic, because she seems to place rhetoric in an interrogative place – a place that belongs to conversation rather than performance, and that makes use of philosopher crowds rather than the oratory of philosopher kings. Yes, there is crossover here, but rhetoricality should be more deliberate. Even in social media, where rhetoric is a two-way process, it is still public; silent followers will be aware of every tweet and even the smallest status update. This is where education comes in. We must teach young people how to take part as both audience and orators/performers. In this electronic age, we need to recognize our place in the philosopher crowd and in the agora, where we are playful but thoughtful too. We must also accept that, sometimes, we have to use the grand style.

The responsibility each of us has when we communicate using social media needs to be evaluated, and urgently. During the riots in England in August 2011, a young man, Jordan Blackshaw, used Facebook to incite an 'event' called 'Smash Down in Northwich Town'. The irony was that no rioters turned up, but the police did and they arrested him. Subsequently, Blackshaw was sentenced to four years in a young offender institution.

Each 'probe' we send out into the great conversation in the global village carries responsibility. On Twitter, it doesn't take long to find racist or homophobic abuse, grotesque sexism, and death threats. Attempts at humour can often go awry; 140 characters is a very small space in which to experiment with nuance and subtlety. Paul Chambers was charged under section 127 of the Communications Act 2003, even though the police thought his tweet about blowing up an airport in England was probably a joke. Chambers had to pay a £1,000 fine and legal costs and he lost his job. (His conviction was later quashed on appeal.) Joshua Cryer was given a two-year community sentence for the racial abuse of footballer Stan Collymore, and John Kerlan was convicted for inviting people to post excrement through a Bexley councillor's letterbox. The exposing of the name of a rape victim on Twitter, and on a variety of blogs, immediately led to three people being arrested. Hiding behind an apparent cloak of secrecy enables some people to think they are above the law, but if the crime is serious enough, that cloak won't save you. This is especially true when we consider the amount of personal information kept about us by internet providers. Social media takes us from the conversation in a pub onto a global stage, with the possibility that an unintended or badly worded utterance goes viral. In an age of rhetoric, schools would do well to help future citizens to be aware of how to use the art for their own ends, as well as understanding how the art uses us.

Effective Communication as Performance

All the world's a stage,
And all the men and women merely players:
They have their exits and their entrances;
And one man in his time plays many parts.

Shakespeare, As You Like It

The need to perform does not alienate us from ourselves; rather it is an expression of ourselves. I regard each school and classroom as a kind of Delphi – as a coming together of people who create a community, tell their own stories, ask questions, and thus achieve a sense of group belonging. Over time, the group members are shaped by a tradition and, in turn, shape it. In the process, they transform themselves – from Year 1 to Year 6 and from Year 7 to Year 13, my goodness, how they are changed! Knowing thyself seems as good a reason as any for education; a school or college becomes an institution that provides a communal space which enables its members to construct an identity collectively and individually. We should remember the Oracle at Delphi's advice to Chaerephon about his friend Socrates: he was the wisest because he understood how little he knew. Well, the greatest classrooms are paradoxical places that teach knowledge with the aim of wisdom but thrive with the hunger born of ignorance.

Schools should ensure that opportunities to perform and communicate are at the heart of what they do. Performance means making theatre, speech making, poetry readings, dance, sports events, community spectacles, art, and so on. Some schools run their own theatres, concerts, radio and TV stations, film companies, multimedia platforms, publishing houses, school newspapers, web pages, Twitter communities, blogs, computer programmer groups, art galleries, and workshops, with the philosopher kids developing their communicative skills through performance. This should be about creating content not capital. In order to do this, schools should use their partnerships with local communities, businesses, and individuals, as well as their heritage, history, and cultural institutions. Schools should encourage their alumni back into the cave and value the vertical transfer of knowledge through building their own history. One of the first impressions a new student should get when they enter a school should be the rhetoric of the tradition of that school – the institutional equivalent of 'know thyself'. In the classroom, teachers should also find ways of celebrating work through performances of all kinds, including writing, dance, speeches, and other kinds of performing that show off their students' learning to the critical community of their class and beyond.

In *How Language Works*, the linguist David Crystal writes:

> The modern academic view of rhetoric … deals with the whole study of creative discourse … modern rhetoric studies the basis of all forms of effective communication. (Crystal, 2006: 321)

This is the basis of citizenship. In order to take part in the big conversation, we need to take in as well as give out: to be an audience, to interpret, and to add to the debate, the argument, and the tradition. As Marshall McLuhan might have put it, we send out our probes (or our snippets, tweets, and fragments) in order to add to the mosaic of our world.

In a true democracy all citizens share responsibility for their community. We need to educate all young people to be philosopher kids, to be part of the philosopher crowds, finding their way through the global village. I want my daughter to be out in the global agora exchanging ideas, dialogue, argument, products, noises, and silences, in public and individual spaces, through dynamic, inter-personal and extra-personal communication, made possible by the technology of the electronic age, the architecture of our cities, and the maturity of our institutions and traditions. This is a bit more demanding than spending an afternoon learning how to use PowerPoint.

The Imperfect Trivium

If grammar is seen as authority, rules, and hierarchy of knowledge, dialectic as the challenge, analysis, and pursuit, and rhetoric as the expression and community of our disordered selves we can see that no art can have dominion over the other. In the past, the only way people have seen to accommodate this is either by imposing a truth on others or by being completely culturally relative. Neither is satisfactory. It is Hume (2007 [1748]) and others who point us towards a mitigated scepticism by which we can examine the cracks in our ideas, in our arts; for it is through their imperfections that the way can be found to bring them together:

- The crack in grammar is that despite its seeming solid and true, like a mighty oak, it is arbitrary and it changes, so no matter how hard it tries to be stable the wind keeps blowing it, time and the seasons keep changing it, and it is susceptible to other elements including the odd lightning strike. In a storm, it is not a good idea to shelter beneath it. Grammar offers stability that is not stable.

- The crack in dialectic is three-fold, in science and logic it has tried and failed to come up with a theory of everything, in dialectic it can argue to the point of destruction and in *logos* it cannot reach the point of truth. Dialectic is the criticism that is not fully realised.

- The crack in rhetoric is that in a rhetorical age, we are in a world where truths are contradicted as soon as they are uttered; where we belong by being adaptable and communicative in shifting conversations rather than in the senate with a more limited and enclosed audience. Rhetoric is communication and citizenry in a world of more than one language and more than one way of being.

Separately, the arts are unable to deal with the complexity of our world; together they can begin to educate our children properly through their contradictions. Just as a democratic Parliament governs through its disagreements we need to put our disagreements into the centre of the curriculum. We need to take the politics out of school policy and put it right bang in the centre of how we teach and learn most subjects. Instead of trying to bring up little grammarians, dialecticians, or rhetoricians we should be trying to raise children who have some understanding of all their fellow men and women, and have a polymathic hold on the world across the two or three cultures of the trivium.

When brought together, the three arts of the trivium are more than a sum of their parts. By teaching and learning through the trivium it is, perhaps, possible to see the development of a further art – whether this is called wisdom, virtue, or a good life. In the next chapter I will explore what this approach to education is for, and why it is needed, by looking at the Renaissance scholar and polymath Michel de Montaigne.

Chapter 11

We Have a Montaigne to Climb

This above all: to thine own self be true,
And it must follow, as the night the day,
Thou canst not then be false to any man.

Shakespeare, *Hamlet*

To Thine Own Self Be True:
Authenticity and Virtue

A child is likely to spend around 14 years of their life in education, not because they want to but because the state demands it. If parents don't want their child to go to school then they will have to provide an education for them instead. The success of a child's schooling, whatever form it has taken, will be summed up at the age of 16 with a bunch of qualifications and again at 18 (for some) with another bunch.

In order to become a more scholarly member of society, students are required to amass a certain number of academic qualifications, which are deemed the best sort to have. If any child fails in this task, then the horny-handed labours of vocational qualifications are laid before them. They are classified as 'non-academic'; although they are also the sort of people you could do with when you actually need something done! The remaining option is to find your own path, learning from the School of Hard Knocks or the University of Life, for which there are no exams or assessments.

Counting Counts

Schools today are awash with data. Teachers and schools are judged to be good or failing on the basis of how they perform on various measurements. Countries compare their education systems through data collected through organizations with acronyms … that's education in the 21st century: data and acronyms. But are we measuring the right things? Is being data-rich a good thing? Can we target and measure too much or too often? With more data might we make more dubious correlations? What would David Hume make of our obsessing over targets and test scores?

Somewhere along the line we seem to have forgotten something vital. By concentrating on counting and measuring we have neglected education. Consequently, the easily measurable and relatively late phenomenon, the exam, has taken the place of education. The lofty but fuzzy aims of 'a life well lived', 'wisdom', or 'a virtuous life' have been replaced by hard data. Meanwhile, the joy of learning has been displaced by a distorted, evidence-based view of education, which is not based on what works educationally, but on what it takes to get your pupils an ever higher number of ever higher exam passes and your school an 'outstanding' inspection outcome.

However, if the classroom teacher is more worried about whether a child gets a C or a D, or whether an inspector approves of their lesson plan, than whether they are educating children, then something, somewhere has gone very wrong. Hit me with your measuring stick! Where is the evidence-based education or inspection framework that proves our schools are producing wiser and more virtuous citizens who are living well-lived lives?

The challenge for the future of education is to develop a holistic approach based on the quality of education; the existing target-chasing quantitative approach does not serve today's students. This means that we need to take into account not just the exam results of the young people who leave our institutions, although that can be included, but we must also look at their character, their ability to take a full part in society, to live a rich and fulfilling 'good life', and influence those around them in positive ways. We all have a part to play in developing the richness of our society, but we need the maturity to realize it is not just the responsibility of our schools.

Creating this change will mean that we must re-realize that just because something is either difficult or impossible to measure, doesn't mean that it isn't important. This radical adjustment will involve challenges to society, to policy, to institutions, to schools, and also to what goes on in individual classrooms. We need to get away from the attitude that the primary role of schools is to deliver exam results, because if that is what we measure then you can bet your bottom dollar that is what they will try to do. If exams are mainly for the convenience of the school or the state, and cannot be shown to be of any practical use later in life, then a change in practice is necessary. But this implies we know what we are aiming for instead.

Philosopher Kid

So, let me try to articulate some kind of vision beyond that of accumulating exam passes, as currently envisaged. Let's start with a more detailed vision of the philosopher kid whom we met in the last chapter.

The idea of a philosopher kid is intended to help articulate the idea that both within and beyond our working lives, we have a responsibility to ourselves, our families, our friends, our neighbourhoods, our nations, and our planet. This is citizenship based on more than just a few lessons about the workings of parliament and how to vote. We have a duty to enter into dialogue in the present, with the past, in order to build a future. This discourse should be with those individuals we come into contact with through study, who we meet, and also, importantly, with ourselves. The philosopher kid understands the importance of becoming a rounded human being and is interested in seeking continual improvement in whatever they do. At a time when we need lofty ambitions for all our young people, the trivium offers a supporting structure for this kind of attitude. It won't work for everyone, but at least it has a pedigree and the possibility of making a real difference to children's lives. Now we need to explore how we can, with its help, realize these ambitions in a practical way.

For a start, we could revisit the idea of the Renaissance man and woman. The Renaissance person specializes but they also have an interest in a wide range of other pursuits. They are citizens who can comfortably range across C. P. Snow's two cultures of science and art (and more); they are truly multi-cultural polymaths. No one is an island any longer; we all are immersed in political and financial affairs; we are all exposed to influence from the media and advertising; we are all subject to taxes and financial planning. We learn, to a greater or lesser extent, how to keep fit, stand up for ourselves, protect our property, understand the law, look after our health, and so on. Over and above all of these mundane needs, we also wish to find our place in the world and meaning in our lives. We want to discover respect, love, and friendship, to share our happiness and pass on what we know. We want to challenge the traditions that no longer serve us and create a world that rejoices in its being.

We can learn some lessons for the future by looking at a genuine Renaissance man from the past. We can examine how his formative youthful years are reflected in his adult life by looking at what he passed on. This is the French writer and philosopher, Michel de Montaigne (1533–1592), whose upbringing was a mix of a traditional well-to-do 16th-century French education and some quite outlandish and progressive ideas. Montaigne's parents saw education as essential for young Michel's future success. As an adult, he enjoyed travelling and collecting ideas. He was curious, existing in a perpetual state of enquiry and with a good degree of scepticism central to his rational approach. In order to ascertain the influence of Montaigne's upbringing, it will be useful to look at both his own schooling and the education he wished for others. For Montaigne, education was a lifelong process.

Montaigne had a touch of the Socrates about him. His famous phrase, 'What do I know?' echoes Socrates and emphasizes how doubt and uncertainty are part of thinking and learning. To the American literary critic, Harold Bloom, Montaigne represents everyone 'who has the desire, ability, and opportunity to think and to read' (Bloom, 1995: 151). Here we have the epitome of the lifelong learner. It is clear from what Montaigne says about his education, and what can be gleaned from reading his works, that he did not seek out one guru, one method, or one teacher. He thought that universal theories were of no use in modern life. Consequently he was able to be both a man with strong opinions and open minded. A *dissoi logoi*?

Montaigne wrote two seminal essays on education, which will prove useful in our current discourse. Indeed, the very notion of the essay, so beloved of educators, was invented by Montaigne. The word *essai* means 'attempt', revealing that, for Montaigne, instead of achieving closure, there always remains the potential of finding another way of putting it, of beginning a new journey. There is always room for improvement. To emphasize that all is not black and white, Montaigne was to embrace the contradictory to the extent that he even argued with himself, often adding to his own essays and never seeing them as finished.

Montaigne believed that the task of the thinking person was to find ways to balance opinion, test it for truth or meaning through practice, and build up powers of judgement. This was a scientific approach; or rather, it was the way one lived one's life. His education, he thought, had helped him become a learner, someone who could learn independently, an autodidact or self-educator. His self-authorship comes out of the remarkable concatenation of tradition and progressivism, as becomes clear when his ideas on education are examined.

Michel came from a large family. His father, Pierre Montaigne, ran a successful wine business; he married Michel's mother when he was 33 and she was 'of age'. She was regarded as a very smart and able woman, but she had a difficult relationship with her son. Soon after he was born, Michel was sent to live with a peasant family in order to absorb their culture, quite literally, through the breast milk of a wet nurse. When he returned to his family, he was forced to speak Latin. A Dr Horst was taken on as his Latin tutor and neither would communicate except through Latin. Everyone else in the family, including the servants, had to learn some Latin in order to talk to them. Therefore, through the process of absorption, Montaigne had learned something of peasant life, and knew Latin grammar. Not for him the learning by rote beloved of 16th-century schoolmasters. Later, he learned Greek, but through games (his father was clearly on the progressive side) rather than textbooks. His father ensured that his son would have the key to the wisdom of the ancients and also a working knowledge of the language of the civil and legal services, which at that time was Latin. It was this early grounding, this wide-ranging cultural capital, that at once deprived him of what many would see as 'normal' or even important. However, Montaigne later reflected upon his upbringing as a quite pleasurable experience.

Every morning, Montaigne was woken by the playing of a lute or other musical instrument, and this gentleness suffused his upbringing. His early years were a strange mix of constraint and freedom. All this was to change at the age of six when Montaigne was sent to school. This twin approach of unusual upbringing and formal schooling was to foster an adult who would be independent and yet able to live within society. The school taught Latin by rote, but here Montaigne was at an advantage – he already knew his Latin. School would start early with the study of Cicero, Horace, and the like. The afternoons would be spent with abstract grammar, which almost destroyed any interest he had in reading, but his teachers kept his enthusiasm going by allowing him to read his own choice of books, and also by giving him some other well-chosen tomes on the quiet. These 'unsuitable' texts – which included Ovid's *Metamorphoses*, Virgil's *Aeneid*, and the works of Plautus, Tacitus, and Plutarch – would inspire him. Through these texts he learned that reading was exciting and, significantly, in the case of *Metamorphoses*, that things change. Later, his reading material would include more histories and biographies from which he learnt about man's diversity and complexity.

The evenings were about reading out loud, memorizing, chanting, and analysis. Montaigne 'conversed' with the ancients, joking with them in a friendly manner, reading and collecting: he would write fragments of texts and ideas he had collected in notebooks. In his teens he began studying philosophy, logic, and metaphysics. As he grew older, he and his fellow students took part in debates and rhetoric, all in Latin. In her book on Montaigne, *How to Live, or a Life of Montaigne in One Question and Twenty Attempts at an Answer*, Sarah Bakewell writes, 'From these, Montaigne picked up rhetorical skills and critical habits of thought which he would use all his life' (Bakewell, 2010: 61).

Many of his contemporaries learned classical rhetorical techniques, which consisted of memorizing hours of speeches, something that did not appeal greatly to Montaigne, although he did enjoy appearing in school plays – another outlet for rhetoric. Paradoxically, Montaigne wrote that he felt he must be slow witted. Maybe this was false modesty. He also thought, quite helpfully, that the slow way was the wise way. Montaigne argues that we are born to go on a quest for the truth and that the 'world is but a school of enquiry' (Montaigne, 2003 [1580]: 1051). When he left school Montaigne was well equipped to deal with the world of enquiry because, for him, his schooling continued.

Practising rhetoric is one thing, but arguments can also get out of control. Montaigne discovered this at close quarters through a shocking incident that would leave an indelible impression on him. In 1548 there were tax riots in Bordeaux. The school closed, and a 15-year-old Montaigne witnessed the murder of the local lieutenant general, Tristan de Moneins. Through these events, Montaigne began to appreciate the complexity and difficulties inherent in conflict.

Learning new things fascinated him; he would never stay still intellectually. Not satisfied with simply knowing, Montaigne was happier when learning, wondering, and musing, both outwardly and inwardly. He might come across as an anti-intellectual, yet he was highly educated, and even though he could be sceptical, education was his foundation.

Montaigne's influential *Essays*, first published in 1580, are like conversations with himself. They are open and playful, and are, arguably, about the process of thinking and learning itself. In 'On the Art of Conversation', he writes that the best way to improve the mind is through conversation, and that the more exposure we have to vigorous thinking, the more we will benefit. He is aware that, in debates, although we can learn to refute arguments, there is also a danger that we can end up refuting truth. He encourages a style of conversation that listens, learns, and questions – rather than disputes through which we simply try to get our point across. Montaigne didn't want to be *taught* by great minds; he wanted to *get to know them.* This gives a very different complexion to the idea of learning 'the best which has been thought or said'. He also takes logic to task, wondering whether it has ever enabled anyone to become 'intelligent'.

Two more of his essays concern us directly: in 'On Schoolmasters' Learning,' Montaigne complains about those who think they know it all, having learnt by rote, but are not wise in the way of a real philosopher, who, echoing Socrates, knows the limits of their knowledge; and in 'On Educating Children', he looks at the importance of enthusiasm in educational journeys towards learning and virtue. These essays reflect his thoughts on his own education and also give insights into how he felt children should be educated.

Montaigne writes about the contempt in which he thought teachers were held, quoting as an example how Plutarch uses the word 'scholar' as an insult. But why is it, he asks, that the most learned of people aren't the most 'alive'? He thought that just as a plant can suffer from too much water, our minds can atrophy from too much study: we 'aim only at furnishing our heads with knowledge: nobody talks about judgement or virtue. When someone passes by, try exclaiming, "Oh what a learned man!" Then, when another does, "Oh what a good man!" Our people will not fail to turn their gaze respectfully towards the first. There ought to be a third man crying, "Oh, what blockheads!"' (ibid.: 153). This refers to Seneca taking on the liberal arts of his time and prioritizing virtue.

Montaigne continues that schooling should not be about whether someone has learned a great deal but who has 'understood best' (ibid.: 154). Teachers should not just 'spew' out their learning; they should pursue understanding. Here, he argues, we should not just take on the ideas of others; we need to make them our own, obtain wisdom, and, importantly, enjoy it.

Montaigne, having a daughter rather than a son, dedicated 'On Educating Children' to his friend Diane de Foix, who was hoping for a son – a son who would expect to be educated rather better than a daughter. Ignoring the implied sexism of the age, I can easily think of it as an essay for my own daughter. Montaigne writes: 'We should always guide them towards the best and most rewarding goals' (ibid.: 168). These goals are not the pursuit of money or advantage but should be inward enrichment, character, and intelligence, which are more desirable than just knowledge. A child should be judged on what they have understood and made a part of them, not by just repeating material they have memorized. A child should have a range of ideas from which they can choose, or they can choose to remain in doubt. It is through their own reasoning that they should learn. The end product of a child's learning should be this: transforming 'borrowings' and coming up with their own judgement and end product. A child should be sparing about their personal accomplishments and not quick to criticize everything, even if it is not to their liking, although they don't have to agree with all they learn. Sometimes the lessons will be reading, sometimes discussions which are to be had with a happy face, sometimes work will be given to them, and sometimes the work will be a shared pursuit with the teacher. This transforming of borrowings is the essence of the trivium. You borrow the knowledge and wisdom of the past, transform it slightly or radically (with respect), add to it, even create it anew, and then lend it to your children.

Montaigne had it in for grammarians, such as Demetrius, observing that 'furrowed brows' are for them. He believed that virtue is found through control rather than through effort; through loving life, beauty, health and moderation – not in a life that is over-devoted to study; nor should virtue be ruined by the 'uncouthness and barbarity' of others. Montaigne said that our chief study should be philosophy, so as to form good judgement and character. We should be creating gentlemen, he asserted, rather than grammarians or logicians, who should not be overly concerned with the minutiae of rules of grammar and rhetoric, but should learn 'suppleness of voice and gesture' through performing. A good education should bring people together for games, sport, worship, and for community goodwill, 'There is nothing like tempting the boy to want to study and to love it: otherwise you simply produce donkeys laden with books. They are flogged into retaining a pannier of learning; but if it is to do any good, learning must not only lodge with us: we must marry her' (ibid.: 160).

For Montaigne, most of all, education should require us all to display virtue and pursue understanding, to obtain wisdom and enjoy it. Without this we remain no better than blockheads. Our current danger lies in moving even further away from Montaigne's ideal, failing even to value the knowledgeable person. Instead, we pursue the type of glory achieved by obtaining the greatest number of certificates; there has to be, indeed there is, more.

Chapter 12

The Professors

Although the theory of a dogmatic phase followed by a critical phase is too simple, it is true that *there can be no critical phase without a preceding dogmatic phase* ... All learning is a modification (it may be a refutation) of some prior knowledge.

Karl Popper, *Unended Quest*

I have my mantra – grammar, dialectic, and rhetoric – which gives rise to the idea of the philosopher kid, a free-thinking Renaissance citizen, with the ability to adapt, strive, and value both tradition and modernity, yet treat both with a certain degree of scepticism, because in each there is the possibility that 'there be dragons'. By valuing the pursuit of truth more than its ownership, a philosopher kid can take part in our common life, where the three arts meet. The philosopher kid will pursue wisdom through the arts and through their everyday life. Formal education should be seen not as an end in itself, but as a preliminary stage in life's journey. This is the education I want for my daughter. As a parent, I will help to provide it.

My daughter is currently obsessed with the idea of 'falling into a book'. I want her to put herself in our 'shared book', to build up an idea of who she is. She will also access knowledge through the school system, engage with it, make sense of it, argue with it, play with it, make connections, see contradictions, understand its fluidity, its importance, and its function. I want her to be given opportunities to express her growing relationship with knowledge by developing a sense of belonging. I want her to be able to criticize our common culture(s) in that shared place where we clash along with each other. I want her to trip across cultures, high, low, artistic, physical, philosophical, and scientific, and to be able to collaborate in order to restore, conserve, and remake the world as she sees fit. In this way, my hope is that she will become fully human, awake, and alive.

I want her to go to a school that will encourage all this. Am I dreaming? Is what I want so far from what there is that it will never happen? Am I being too radical?

The word 'radical' carries two traditions within it. It comes from the Latin *radicalis* meaning 'having roots' (from *radix* or 'root') and has come to mean anything that is fundamental to life. This meaning is retained in the worlds of mathematics, music, and botany and relates to the root of a number, chord, or plant. It is first recorded in English in 1562 as meaning 'inherent' or 'fundamental'; it wasn't until 1800 that it began to denote 'fundamental reform'. In the mid-19th century it came to mean extreme reform, and later in the 20th century it also meant unconventional. On the one hand, radical means a departure from a tradition, and on the other it means roots. In my argument for change, I am proposing change that is radical, in that it reflects progress and tradition, reform, and roots.

The Three-Legged Stool

Progress does not necessarily mean progress to a greater end; tradition does not necessarily mean that which came before endures because it is intrinsically better than that which came later. None of the arts of the trivium on its own holds the key to 'truth', knowledge, or wisdom. Each art – grammar, dialectic, rhetoric – is but part of the answer. We sit on a three-legged stool; take away a leg and we fall.

The most destructive conflict today is still between the grammarians and the dialecticians or, in current parlance, the traditionalists and the progressives. It is to both these groups that we need to reach out. The radical move of Trivium 21c is to get these two sides to accommodate each other and come together through the third art of rhetoric. I want to explore this possibility by looking at the arguments and ideas of three interested parties: academics, political thinkers, and teachers.

Firstly, I will appraise the thinking of two professors who seem to sum up this dichotomy. The first is Ken Robinson, who is often lauded by the progressives; the second is Daniel T. Willingham, who is acclaimed by the traditionalists.

Ken Robinson and the Creative Trivium

As one of the major proponents of creativity in education, Ken Robinson extols the virtues of the creative curriculum. Yet, when he does, he does so in a very traditional lecture format, which makes me wonder why that is.

Robinson argues that we need a new paradigm. In his TED talk from 2006, he talks about how schools kill creativity. Crucially, Robinson says that creativity usually emerges from an interaction of disciplines which encourage a different way of seeing. He draws from this that education needs to change, and to do so he wants us to mine our creative capacities. Robinson has said that he sees developing the creative mindset in children through schools to be as important as teaching literacy and numeracy.

In his later TED talk, 'Bring on the Learning Revolution' (2010), Robinson says many of us are wasting our talents, and that in numerous cases, education takes people away from their 'natural talents'. He argues against a 'tyranny of common sense' and to illustrate this thought he quotes Abraham Lincoln, 'The dogmas of the quiet past, are inadequate to the stormy present. The occasion is piled high with difficulty, and we must rise – with the occasion. As our case is new, so we must think anew, and act anew. We must disenthrall ourselves, and then we shall save our country.' Robinson takes from this that we need to 'disenthrall' ourselves from some of the old ways of thinking and doing things. He wants education to 'feed our spirit', which means to move away from the industrial model of education to an organic, agricultural archetype. He says this involves personalization; that is, making schools fit the children they teach. The technology that now surrounds us gives us the capability to do this. It is almost akin to Marshall McLuhan's view of how our electronic age can serve our 'pre-linear, pre-industrial' selves.

In his 2010 talk, 'Changing Paradigms', at the Royal Society of Arts, Robinson extols Benjamin Franklin as a polymath and a Renaissance figure, who wants the arts to be central to education. He believes that imagination is a unique capacity, which is systematically destroyed in children, although not deliberately. Robinson argues that the legacy of the Enlightenment is a breakdown in effective education because of a perceived need for economic utility, which has resulted in 'useful' and 'useless' subjects being studied. Public education, as developed during the Enlightenment, aimed to produce a broad base of manual workers, some administrative workers, a few professionals, and even fewer leaders. Deductive reasoning and knowledge of the classics were at the centre of this idea of intelligence, which benefited some people but not most. He sees the huge changes that are taking place in technology, population, globalization, and urbanization and fears that we are trying to do for the future what we did in the past: we are educating children for their economic capability and not their cultural identity.

The arts are a victim of this process. Robinson sees art as an aesthetic experience through which one becomes fully alive and in the moment, as opposed to an anaesthetic experience where one is deadened to being alive. He says we should be waking our children up: schools should not be places of 'utility, linearity, conformity, and standardization', but should be places of 'vitality, creativity, diversity, and customization'. He talks of the ascent of human nature being destroyed by education. Divergent thinking is an essential capacity for creativity; in order to foster this, we need to invest in human capacity, group learning, and collaboration.

Robinson says much with which I can agree. I recognize his neo-Platonist argument and I am completely at one with him in his opposition to the utilitarian, factory model of learning and his championing of the idea of the polymath. Where I fundamentally disagree, however, is with his prioritizing of creative thinking: in so doing, he is kicking away one of the legs of our three-legged stool. Robinson argues for creative, 'divergent' thinking, seemingly at the expense of the teaching of the knowledge and traditions that he wishes the creative mind could diverge from. But it can't diverge if it doesn't know!

Cultural identity is not something to be sniffed at. The classics, the great works, our tradition are all part of creativity. There might be a 'creative pre-born' desire within us (and there might not), but if we are always to pursue a new paradigm, or start a new tradition, then we are dislocated from our past and the conversation with it. The arts, in all their forms, are taught through the constraints of the rules and precepts laid down in the past and, in the main, this is the role of grammar; it is our collective wisdom, our common sense, our way of doing and seeing. By all means treat it with scepticism, but let's not dismiss it – because if it is abandoned, then creativity itself suffers. In the 1953 film, *The Wild One*, Marlon Brando's character Johnny is asked, 'What are you rebelling against?' to which he replies, 'What have you got?' This is not fruitful ground for the creative act; this is where the destructive act is sown. To rebel you need something to rebel against; you need a tradition.

Peter Murphy (2010), quoting research done by Charles Murray about fundamental creative discoveries in a range of disciplines in Europe and North America measured by per capita of population, comes up with the following 'most creative times in history'. In the visual arts this was the mid-1400s to mid-1500s, with a second peak in the mid-1600s. Music peaks in the early 1700s and continues to the mid-1800s. Literature peaks in the early 1600s and again in the mid-1800s. Science peaks in the late 1600s and then from the mid-1700s to late 1800s. High-level technology peaked in the early 1870s. Murphy argues that from the 1870s there has been a decline in the rate of creative achievement in the West, in mathematics, the visual arts, and literature, as well as in the number of outstanding creative individuals. There are some exceptions. There was a growth in the number of exceptional figures in literature, science, and the visual arts from 1900–1920 and some technologies advanced from 1920–1950. The film arts flourished during the 1940s and 1950s and recorded music from the mid-1960s to mid-1970s.

Murphy believes that, 'a society that can cope with opposition at the same time as it can function in an integrated manner is a society that is able to meld incongruous values into a rich and uncanny culture' (ibid.: 347). He cites the ancient and Renaissance city-states as examples. Murphy continues that in the act of creativity we need to be able to switch sides in our imaginations, 'This ability is indispensable to the scientist who is able thereby to imagine light as a wave and a particle simultaneously' (ibid.: 349). The ability to see things differently, and simultaneously pulling together seemingly incongruous ideas, is central to creativity. A sense of the past, of being different, and of communicating this to others is what drives many creative ventures.

Evidence: A Cognitive Psychologist Speaks

Daniel T. Willingham is professor of psychology at the University of Virginia and is the author of *Why Don't Students Like School?* (2009) and *When Can You Trust the Experts? How to Tell Good Science from Bad in Education* (2012). In a contact made possible by the technology of our rhetorical age (I contacted him via Twitter and he agreed to be interviewed over Skype), we had a very positive interview, during which I asked him about cognitive psychology:

I think of cognitive psychology as the latest set of assumptions and body of theory directed towards a scientific approach to understanding thought. There are people who have been trying to understand thought for quite a long time – the oldest recorded musings on how thought works are probably 2,500 years old. Scientific study of thought is, of course, much younger than that, probably 200 to 300 years old, and a really organized study, with all the trappings of academic departments and so forth, about a century. The cognitive approach is more like 50 years old, but there were other epistemologies in place prior to that.

Learning as a subset of cognitive psychology is one of the cognitive processes that we care about. We are at a very early stage in using this science, and we have to be careful about its use, especially bearing in mind how important a certain degree of scepticism is in our approach to 'truth'.

How true can scientific truth be?

I think my answer to the question is very much the same as most working scientists would give, which is: anything we know can't be regarded as absolute truth and has to be regarded as truth as we know it today – it's provisional. And there are different findings from the world of science and models of those phenomena in which we profess greater or lesser confidence, and always with the understanding of what that confidence means. I think of it in terms of time: I think this will last ten years before it gets knocked over. It's going to get knocked over at some point, right? So I think there is certainly a lot of phenomena from the world of cognitive psychology about learning that probably falls into that camp. The way we're thinking about them is probably not right, in terms of explanation, but in the practical terms of usefulness it will probably endure longer.

How about other ways to truth, say the arts and the humanities?

Arts and the humanities are able to tell us truths and, again, I consider myself a duffer on these matters. These are very deep questions – I haven't made a career out of thinking about them and reading about them – but I'll answer the question nevertheless. I'll never let a lack of expertise slow me down! Actually, I talk about this quite a bit in my new book When Can You Trust the Experts?, *about the limits of science and how scientists think about questions they can answer and questions they can't.*

In general, the prerequisites for application of the scientific method are that it needs to be something from the natural world; scientists seek to describe the natural world. And it needs to be something that you can measure in some way. You can't just execute scientific method in the absence of measurement, as that's not going to tell you whether your model is correctly predicting the world. So, in terms of education, lots of things fall outside the view of science.

For a start, education is not suitable subject matter for science. Education is an application. I think of scientific fields, like cognitive psychology, as being fields that theories of education can draw on. One way in which it is clear that education is different is that education is goal driven. In science you seek to describe the world as it is; in education and other applied fields you want to change the world. You are trying to make the world more like you think it ought to be, so it's similar in that sense to engineering, for example, or architecture, where you're trying to create something. You're trying to build a bridge or a skyscraper or, in the case of education, the thing that you're trying to change is not the landscape, you're trying to change children, and you've got a goal of what you want them to be like.

The definition of that, the specification of that goal, is completely outside the purview of science. It's a matter of one's values: what you think children should learn at school, what you think they should end up like when they're done with school. Once you've defined the goals, science might be able to help you achieve the goals.

I then gave Willingham a flavour of the thinking behind the Trivium 21c idea. He asked me: 'There is a little bit of a flavour of this which is like Bloom's taxonomy, right? Is it meant to be sequential? You initially have to gain the knowledge, before you begin to think critically, or is it the idea that these can run in parallel?' This is a crucial point. I explain that in the classic 'first instance' it is, indeed, that knowledge must come first before you can argue with it. However, I add the proviso that this becomes more flexible, and that my view is against the Dorothy L. Sayers approach in which there is a stage in learning when all you do is soak up knowledge before you can argue with it. Willingham responded:

I'm pretty sympathetic to that. I've written to that effect. I've softened a little bit in that I've found that the position is easy to caricature, and people do, with the idea that you're seeking to just fill their heads with knowledge and you're discouraging them from grappling with it in any way – asking questions and so forth. Of course, that's not what I really want at all.

A cognitive psychologist would tell you that if your goal is for kids to know things, a terrible thing to do is to give them a disjointed list of things to know and ask them to try to memorize it. You're always expecting and hoping they're going to be thinking about it. I guess what I'm fighting against is the idea that the main way to acquire knowledge is through posing questions for kids and expecting that they will come to discover this knowledge on their own. I think that it can happen, but it's incredibly difficult to pull off. I believe it can be done, but it puts an enormous burden on the teacher's skill.

First, you need to know the knowledge very deeply, so that if the child goes off in a direction you don't expect them to go off in, you need to know how to guide them back towards the goal, but to do it in a skilful manner so that you're not, essentially, bullying the child. The whole point is you're trying to let the child take the lead a little bit, or more than a little bit, so handling the interpersonal dynamics is very demanding. It's demanding doing it with one child, but doing it with a classroom full of children – I don't know how you manage it.

So, coming back to the question you initially posed, I think there is some sense in which you expect that you've got to have some foundational knowledge before you can engage with the dialectic processes. At the same time, and this is very speculative, one thing that we've really noticed in higher education in the United States is a huge influx of educators from China and India coming to the US trying to figure out what we're doing to make our kids creative. I've no idea the extent to which this is true, but what these educators are telling us is, 'All of our kids in China and India are full of knowledge but they're terrible at dialectic.' They don't put it that way, but using the terms we're using, that's what's going on.

So, you could imagine that these kids are the product of a system where dialectic is left until very late in the educational process and that, if you're not used to doing this over long periods of time, two things happen. One, you're obviously not very practised in it, but second, it may not really be a 'habit of mind'. American kids are certainly encouraged to question, and I think British kids are as well – it's viewed as a good thing if a kid asks a teacher a *question, for example. Challenging a teacher in the United States about content, respectfully, is viewed as a good thing. It's not clear that is always true in China, for example.*

I had a student from Korea who said that if you ask a question of the teacher then that implies that the presentation was incomplete, that there was something he didn't really tell you. I've heard from other students in China who say, 'No, no, it was fine to ask questions.' You know, obviously it's a huge, diverse country. I'm just using these as illustrations. Thinking about this question of grammar versus dialectic, we're in green fields here because I don't think there is enough known to do more than speculate. But doing something as you describe, as you have already disagreed with, of two years of knowledge and then you do dialectic – that would make me nervous.

I then suggested that some progressives believe that you can have critical thinking or creativity without needing much knowledge – the pursuit of dialectic at the expense of knowledge.

In my experience, when kids have a lot of dialectic, but not much knowledge, the dialectic is not very effectively deployed. They have great fun talking with one another, but they're really recreating the thinking of other people (their peers). It's useful in its way, but it might be more useful if they just read up a little bit and then they would have a more advanced starting point.

I moved onto rhetoric. Does writing an essay, or presenting your learning in some other format, focus and improve your thinking?

That's an interesting question. There is some data on this – there is not an enormous literature – but there is certainly some support for the idea. Loads of us have had this experience: when you're forced to write something it forces you to be more explicit about your own thinking. If you write a well-organized essay, it helps you to spot gaps in your own thinking because, as you're writing, you're thinking, 'Hmm, my argument is missing something here.' It's a bit like computer programming.

This is a very big advantage within cognitive psychology. Psychologists recognize that you may think you understand cognitive processes quite deeply, you think your theory is quite complete, but the ultimate test is actually writing a program. I can easily skip over a gap in my own knowledge and never notice it, but the computer is going to notice it, it's going to crash. So I think that is not a bad analogy for the value of communication.

If you're a good writer, and you are consistently able to produce well-ordered essays, then that is quite a test of your understanding of a subject: to write something about it. So, as I said, there is some data, and what there is, I think, supports this idea.

Finally, I wanted to explore my use of the word *logos* – whether the pursuit of something is important. Willingham asked: 'Do you mean how important it is in terms of motivation?' I agreed, but there is something more. I am trying to think about what it does to us, whether the opportunity to explore deliberate practice – the doing of something in an authentic way – can have a profound effect on who we are or how we experience who we are.

That's a great question, and honestly I hadn't thought of it from that angle. When I think about deliberate practice, I always consider what it means for the skill. There were a couple of decades of wonderful work by K. Anders Ericsson, which has been discovered by a lot of mainstream writers like Malcolm Gladwell and Dan Pink: the 10,000 hour rule – which actually Ericsson didn't coin, Herb Simon did. The idea of disciplined practice as being important to motivation, I'm sure there's something there. Just on the basis of my own experience, I think that most of us have the sense that that's tremendously important, that there's something about one's self-image that hard work and deliberate practice contribute to. You come to see yourself working hard, you become the kind of kid who works hard; it becomes part of your self-identity. And as you get older, of course, the image changes from

*student to whatever your profession is; it again becomes part of who you are.
I think this is a great idea, I think you're on to something.*

This interview with Willingham was extremely helpful. Later, on Twitter, he pointed me towards a piece of research in the *Journal of Research in Science Teaching* (Venville and Dawson, 2010) showing that if students are taught how to construct and use argumentation in their lessons, it improved both their ability to argue and their understanding of what they were studying.

Willingham demonstrates the importance of knowledge, and that it can work in the way that E. D. Hirsch describes as 'mental Velcro': once you have some, you can stick more to it. I would go along with this, but the things I want to attach to the Velcro are dialectical and they can connect through juxtaposition, criticism, or contrary viewpoints. It doesn't have to be a clean attachment of what is already known or approved. The importance of dialectic, as Willingham points out, is that it can improve understanding and, to my mind, create new understandings as well. This is the essence of creativity.

Ken Robinson's neo-Platonist idea – that we are born creative and have it driven out by our schooling, and that we need schools to help us 'find' our métier – needs further exploration. Whether someone is born a dancer or a musician, like the vegetation in Death Valley, as Robinson argues, they await the nourishing rain to enable them to reach their potential. If instead they are more of a *tabula rasa* and, through nurture, find themselves becoming a great dancer or a musician, in the great scheme of things, this doesn't matter. Schools should enable us to work towards something, over time, in an authentic way. This should be part of a broad curriculum that enables children to explore possibilities and this is where *logos* is understood. I disagree with Robinson that in order to do this we must 'disenthrall' ourselves from tradition. In my view, we engage with common sense. We don't treat it as the enemy of progress, but as part of the highly creative meeting place of the three arts of the trivium.

Chapter 13

The Grammarians vs the Dialecticians

All political arguments need to begin with an appreciation of our relationship not only to dreams of future betterment, but also to past achievements: our own and those of our predecessors.

Tony Judt, *Ill Fares the Land*

Think tanks and parliaments echo to the sound of the great education debate, which also reflects the schism between traditionalists and progressives. The education we want for our children in the 21st century is highly political. As parents we are faced with choices that question our principles. We negotiate with our own thoughts and those of our partners, our children, and other parents who congregate outside the school gates waiting to pick up their offspring.

The education that my wife and I want for our daughter is also an emotional decision based on how we feel about what is available. The schools on offer are either progressive or traditional – the state ones veering towards the former, the independent ones towards the latter. To select a school for our child we are faced with the great class divide. England has one of the most socially divisive education systems in the world. This division is not just about how schools are funded or organized, but extends to what and how children are taught and assessed.

In *The Righteous Mind* (2012), the moral psychologist Jonathan Haidt writes about how our intrinsic morality divides 'liberals' and 'conservatives'. If a progressive teacher sees a classroom of rows of children passively absorbing knowledge from teacher talk, they react as emotionally as a traditionalist teacher might if faced with the advice that they might be a better educator if they tried more group-work. Haidt's work echoes the ideas of the philosopher David Hume. Where Hume saw reason as the slave to emotion, Haidt sees the relationship as an elephant and its rider. The elephant of our emotion reacts to a situation, to an argument, by moving one way or another; this lurch affects our conscious self, the rider. Haidt believes our intrinsic moral 'taste' receptors drive our elephant in a conservative, liberal, or libertarian direction; then we use our capacity to reason to justify the way we have turned.

If our moral taste receptors incline us towards one of the three arts of the trivium, then the case that I make in this book – that conservative thinking tends towards traditional grammarian ideas, and liberal thinking towards the progressive dialectical – suggests that what we do is based on an emotional reaction rather than on reason. This means that accommodating both traditions, rather than defeating one side or the other, cannot be achieved through reason alone.

For this book, I wanted to talk to individuals who considered themselves to be either progressive or conservative to see if it was possible to ascertain how they feel, as well as reason, about how to achieve a conscious coming together of the three arts. For this to happen, conservatives or traditionalists will need to be persuaded to accept the merits of dialectic; liberals or progressives will need to see the necessity of the tradition of grammar. If I can do this, I will have succeeded.

In Chapter 2, I discussed Ferdinand Mount and his notion that the progressive versus traditionalist argument in education was exemplified in the proffering of the hemlock cup to Socrates. Mount is known as a one-nation Conservative. He is a baronet, although he does not use his title, and is related to Prime Minister David Cameron. He wrote the 1983 Conservative manifesto for Margaret Thatcher, for whom he was head of the Number 10 policy unit from 1982–1984. He has more recently written a couple of highly eloquent books, *Mind the Gap* (2010) and *The New Few* (2012), which look at rising inequality and the increasing gap between 'them' and 'us'. Some people assert that this trend began during the very government for which he worked, but I am more interested in the fact that this conservative thinker is sensitive to issues that might be construed as being the concerns of progressives. Mount was also one of the few people who had heard of the trivium. He had this to say:

> *'Bring back the Trivium' is a slogan that warms my heart. There is indeed a false opposition between the critical and the absorptive school of education. One cannot function without the other. It is impossible to make proper critical judgements without a secure base of knowledge. But it is also impossible for that base to be secure if we have not brought a critical intelligence to bear on the information being thrown at us. We have to assess its reliability, its relative importance, and its relation to other facts. It is when you are listening and learning that you should be thinking hardest.*

This is a thoughtful description of what the trivium does, and his comment about the order in which grammar and dialectic are introduced is important. Can our critical faculties be developed in such a way that we can dispense with the need to know first, and can just retrieve it whenever or wherever through our 24/7 access to technology, as some have argued? Mount was emphatic:

> *First, what I think very strongly is that knowledge must precede criticism, scepticism, contemplation, and all the other desirable stances. Without information, such stances are merely shallow posing. The [global] warmists point to melting glaciers and icebergs in the Arctic; the sceptics point out the relatively modest changes in global temperatures and thickening ice in much of the Antarctic. The enriching of knowledge is an essential preliminary to questioning received wisdoms. Thus comparative religion is not intrinsically*

a diversion from, or a challenge to, faith. Many great theologians have found it inspirational. Ditto multiculturalism.

So, when should the process of questioning perceived wisdom begin?

As for how we improve theories and paradigms by refining, testing, and arguing, all this seems to me not irrelevant to teaching children how to think. But to pretend that such epistemological questions can constitute the central activity of the Lower Fifth [i.e. pre-16] is, I think, premature. The golden years of maximum brain activity should be spent principally in absorbing, in reading and listening to every conceivable source of knowledge. And rote learning, in all its forms, is an essential discipline in acquiring intellectual muscle.

Mount's argument here is, essentially, a strong grammarian one; although he sees the absolute need for critical thought, he says that it should arrive later than most schooling, in sixth form and university. This is not my view, but I do take his point that knowledge needs to be the absolute beginning of argument. I am disappointed that he does not see that dialectic has a role far earlier in education. It seems that the traditionalist elephant might be very difficult to steer. My quest might be more difficult than I hoped. How about the progressive elephants – how easy are they to steer?

I thought I would ask Matthew Taylor, chief executive of the Royal Society of Arts (RSA) and previously chief advisor to former Prime Minister Tony Blair. The RSA has a long history of involvement in education in Britain – it runs a chain of academy schools and promotes the RSA Opening Minds competency-based curriculum. Taylor sent his children to state comprehensive schools. As such, he is well placed to have a view on the progressive agenda in education. I asked him if he thought the debate between the progressives and the traditionalists had been damaging to education. His reply was heartening:

I think there has been an unhelpful, lazy dichotomy which puts facts and traditional didactic teaching on the one hand, and then puts concepts, skills, competencies, and engaging, project-based teaching on the other. So, what one understands a lot of the time is that you should teach facts and grammar, and it should be taught in a fairly traditional way, versus a caricature of competencies, in which children work on projects where there is a much greater emphasis on engagement and the development of skills, competencies, and insights, rather than an emphasis on subject and fact.

Now, of course, neither side would accept that account. I do think facts are important and it is essential to learning that you learn some of the facts, because facts are the basis for building up conceptual knowledge. I'd like to get out of that dichotomy though; because I think what's interesting is the possibility of teaching facts in engaging ways. So, I'm drawn to video games and video technology and reward systems as ways of getting kids to learn facts.

This sounds as though there is the possibility that, on the progressive side at least, there is a way to accommodate the traditionalist's view of the importance of knowledge. The rub might come when I question the validity of a history curriculum, for instance, that is heavily based on our island story, kings and queens, and heroes and heroines of our past:

It seems to me there are real problems about that because it requires us to give a highly partial account, and I wonder who has the right to say that children should learn a particular history of our 'great island nation'. I'm not suggesting for a moment that one needs to feel shame about Britain's past. But the suggestion that Britain's past is great, in the face of national decline? Some of the effects of the Empire which continue right up to this day … You're basically saying you should learn history as ideology.

If content is a problem, what about the reason for that content? Can it act as a kind of cultural glue for our country?

I support the idea that it is good for young people to learn similar things, so there are things they have in common that they can talk about, but that's where I get confused. Why are people saying all we are learning about is the Tudors and the Nazis? Because, if we are all learning about Nazis, at least children can talk to each other about the Nazis. I don't quite get what this argument is.

If it is that people should learn the chronology of kings and queens, I'm not actually opposed to that, because it's like the times tables. It's saying that the foundation for history is the understanding of chronology. Fine. But I would be guided by historians about whether or not that is the factual base necessary for deeper conceptual understanding. It seems to me ludicrous not to be guided by the subject experts.

It's exactly the same with the sciences. I have a predisposition about science as somebody who didn't like science at school, and regrets it deeply, because I think science should start with the big, exciting, amazing, Brysonesque 'Isn't science crazy?' stuff and then work back. Primary schoolchildren should be told things like, 'Do you know that atoms are so small that if an apple had been created on the day that the universe was created, and we took one atom from that apple for every second since the Big Bang, we'd still have half the apple left!' We should start with wonder and when kids start to say, 'That's amazing,' you say, 'Well, OK, but do you want to understand why and how?'

Taylor sees knowledge as vital and he recognizes the importance of fundamental subject knowledge and skills. There might be a way for him to accommodate much of the traditionalist agenda, if it were to come from 'experts'. He does have an issue, though, with how topics are taught. As he suggests, it's the old 'grammar is boring' conundrum: 'Could progressives recognize the importance of facts, but then could the traditionalists recognize the importance of getting children to learn facts in really innovative, engaging, funny, and fun ways?'

I explored this further with Phillip Blond, the director of the centre-right think tank ResPublica. He is a conservative political thinker with a background in philosophy and theology. I wondered what he thought the correct balance should be between grammar and dialectic, between being told what to learn and having a degree of autonomy to criticize or become an independent learner:

For myself, I was only able to learn in my mid-20s – there is a point in the education cycle where you do start reading for yourself. But I think the reason that the goal of the self-authoring self or of educational autonomy is rubbish is because, to paraphrase Newton, we all stand on the shoulders of giants. We only make progress because others have made progress before us, and really the key is to learn the tradition before you can innovate or before you can build on it. It's this idea of perpetual autonomy that has produced such poor educational results. There's nothing progressive about this so-called progressive method because, I think, it might apply to talented people earlier in life, their early teens, and less talented people later in life, but even the most talented people learn from others.

I'm going to find this more difficult than perhaps I thought. Do you draw out the ability from the child or put it in?

There is something to be brought out of children and that is particular inclinations or talents. They are somewhat innate, but they are also switched on by the environment. But, by the same token, part of education is

increasing your peripheral awareness, deepening and broadening yourself.
You are able to drill deeper if you have a wider base to support you.

I ask Blond to reflect on whether this base should just be traditional 'knowledge' or include the idea, beloved of progressives, of competencies and skills:

The point is we need a new level of intellectual, cultural capital. We need a
new hardware – people who can do maths, computing, design – and we
also need a new software – interpersonal skills, the ability to learn, human
kindness, trust, responsibility. All of these soft skills are absolutely a
prerequisite for utilizing the hard skills, and, of course, vice versa.

So, I ask him, by way of summing up, whether education policy is just a battle between the old and the new:

I tend to think this is all about being a human being. It's very simple. Human
beings are progressive creatures, in the sense that they proceed on the
achievements of others. Otherwise, we would be static beings still living in
caves. Therefore, we have to learn what others have given us; we then create
a legacy for our future.

Nick Pearce is the director of the left-leaning think tank, the Institute for Public Policy Research (IPPR). Before that he ran the Downing Street Policy Unit and was also a special advisor to David Blunkett when he was the education secretary. He co-wrote *Wasted Youth* (Pearce and Hillman, 1998) and has co-edited several books, including *Politics for a New Generation* (Pearce and Margo, 2007) and *Tomorrow's Citizens* (Pearce and Hallgarten, 2000). I asked Pearce how the progressive left would deal with, for example, selecting knowledge or facts based on the canon:

Things are much more fluid, open, and contested than they used to be. I think that critical reflection does require you to have been inside 'something' and does require that constant process of engagement. It isn't something that you can either arrive at, never having been taught it in the first place, or be taught a 'shriveled' version of, or taught skills that don't enable you to reflect on it because they are specious, thin, or vacuous.

This means that you need to be taught the 'great tradition' in order to criticize it, and you need critical faculties that are sufficiently developed in order to make any criticism, whether to attack or to defend:

Some Conservatives would say we've been forcibly cut off from our history by the left and, I suppose, in response to that you'd say to them that history has always been much more contested than you ever give it credit for. There are plenty of other voices in that history and if it weren't for, for example, feminists and others, it would never be brought to light.

This is exactly my point: for progressives it should be a debate, it should be contested. What does modernity lose from tradition if the progressives have a year-zero approach? Can the left embrace ideas about the ground they have abandoned (such as ideas around civilization)? Has this ground been completely abandoned to people like Roger Scruton?

Scruton is interesting because I think his book, England: An Elegy, *is beautifully written, and you learn some very deep things from it. The ability of Conservatives like Scruton to connect you to an account of the historical past that is rich and real, when trying to think about your national identity, contrasts very sharply with people on the left who try to connect with national identity and end up saying, 'Let's have a St George's Day Bank Holiday and wave the flag a bit more.' It ends up being very thin because they can't connect. They don't have, as Scruton's book has, 'the Law, the Church, and the land'.*

Now what would be your left equivalent? You end up with a Tony Benn, 'Yes, I know about English history and I'll bring you the Diggers, Winstanley, and things like that.' They're meaningless to lots of people today. Billy Bragg has a much more modern sensibility, but he tries to turn it into a set of dispositions and values. It tends to be a love of England because it's a bit spiky, and you get lists of people's favourite composers or authors. Conservatives, though, are able to rest on these big building blocks of tradition.

Can these big building blocks of tradition be thought of as high culture or are they simply a bourgeois construct?

I've always resisted the post-modern claim that 'high' and 'low' is an artificial construct, that popular culture is every bit as valuable as anything that the bourgeoisie have philosophically called 'high culture'. After all, there must be some inherent properties of art or beauty that are not simply a function of how they are received by human beings in any particular social configuration. If you deny people their own cultural expression and the validity of anything they experience in their own cultural lives, then you're in the business of exclusion and oppression. But if you simply validate everything people do in their own daily lives, if you say 'culture' is simply anything that you consume and produce, anything that people in advertising and marketing departments are able to put down your throat, then you're into the endorsement of things that have less value than they should in our civilization.

This is a real breakthrough. It seems that there is the possibility that some progressives can see and, importantly, feel the importance of cultural tradition. Similarly, that there is substance in a tradition that can act, in its own way, as a critique on the modernity driven by the market.

Sam Freedman was one of the senior policy advisors in the Department for Education from 2010–2013. Formerly of the highly influential think tank Policy Exchange, Freedman helped devise the Conservative Party's free school policy. I asked Freedman whether there was a need to teach the canon (i.e. grammar) at an early age, especially now that he has young children himself. Is teaching it somehow lacking in variety or being uncreative?

I think you can have the same canon of material given to kids and they'll treat it in very different ways with their teachers. They'll bounce off it in different ways. If you look at the creative industries in this country, they are dominated by people who went to very traditional public schools, partly because their parents could afford to indulge their interest, but also because being able to bounce off the canon is a very good starting point for moving into a creative industry.

Is the canon a product of our class system? The values of the bourgeois persist. So is a certain type of cultural capital always going to be out of the hands of those who can't afford to indulge their children?

A fairly obvious point about cultural capital is that people, like me, make sure that their children have lots of books, which is why you have the gap starting very, very early. This is why we're throwing so much money at sending two-year-olds to nurseries.

To take them away from their parents?

There are two models of schools that are really good at closing the gap between rich and poor kids. There is one with massive parental engagement: spending a huge amount of time with the parents, helping them to read as well as their kids. And then there's the other one which says, 'Sorry, parents out! We'll lock the door and you can come and get them at 6 o'clock. We've been with them all day, we've 'cultured' them, given them social norms and culture. In fact, we'll send them to a boarding school in another county to get them away from this environment.' And actually they both work.

And is there a moral equivalence?

I think so, as long as there's consent, definitely. Probably the first is more sustainable because it's cheaper and easier than just creating fortresses all over the place. But I think they both work, which is quite interesting. Whether the second model works when the kid leaves the school is a very interesting question. They can get the social norms, they can get the culture, but when they're sent back out into the community, can they cope?

So, is cultural capital more important than poverty in determining a child's future?

What would I cite? Chinese families: although the Chinese sample in this country is fairly small, it is very stark. The same is true of lots of smaller ethnic groups: Indian families, Ghanaian and West African families, Jewish families, even very poor Jewish families. The only groups where there is a big gap are white – both boys and girls, but especially boys – as well as Afro-Caribbean boys and the Pakistani community. What are the similarities between those three groups? They don't have 'cultural capital' in their societies, whereas your middle-class Ghanaian, Indian, and Chinese, even if they're poor here, do have that cultural capital.

I ask Freedman about his experience of schools, such as KIPP and charter schools, in the United States, and whether he can explain to me the job title, Director of Culture:

What I discovered when I was in New Orleans is that a lot of schools had someone whose job it was to make sure that the school's particular set of values are in every part of the curriculum and in every lesson – completely consistent throughout the school. Every teacher is reinforcing them. A lot of it is to do with behaviour.

So, is there any space for eccentricity and difference if the system is overly rigidified?

A good system will say, 'Here are the values and norms we are promoting as a school, here is the literacy model we are using', etc., but will still give plenty of scope. One of the most interesting lessons I went into when I was in New Orleans was in one of the KIPP schools. It was a brilliant history lesson about war. The teacher was comparing the American Civil War with the Iraq War and how war had changed over time, and whether it was morally different if you had fewer people dying. The pupils must have been about 11. At the same time he was also reinforcing the school's set of values, he was focusing on literacy, etc. It doesn't mean you can't do a really interesting lesson, if it's done right. But it's a difficult thing to do, obviously, or education would be easy.

Here is another breakthrough: a lesson that goes beyond teaching just the chronological facts but also one that highlights dialectic and difficulty. I continue my questions: does Freedman have any thoughts about the movement to include behaviours and competencies in the curriculum – creativity, global awareness, teamwork, and so on?

Those sorts of things are not something that a curriculum can do. It's the wrong place to try and get that stuff to happen. The curriculum is the place where you say, 'We think you should know this stuff and be able to do these things.' On top of that, the school then has to work out the values – they have to come from the school. We are saying that a curriculum that says that kids should be creative is of no use to anybody. That has to come from the school. A curriculum is a document, it's simply a guide to where kids should be at each age in terms of what they should know and be able to do and as a basis for assessment. If you are going to have national assessment you need a basis for national assessment.

This issue about the distinction between knowledge and skills also came up when I asked Nick Pearce what he thought about the skills-based curriculum and why it was part of the 'progressive' agenda in education. Pearce said:

In the 1980s you had the introduction of competence-based qualifications: NVQs. This came from the right, not the left. It was explicitly based on behaviourism, which said, 'You don't need to understand what goes on in their head. You don't need to look for depth, knowledge, and understanding. You just need to know whether someone is competent at doing a task.' This concept of skills came to be associated with a very narrow and thin understanding of critical faculties. Essentially, skills came to be associated with a quite 'bureaucratized' and limited understanding of competence and performance and that had, I think, deleterious consequences for vocational education. It also had deleterious consequences for liberal thinking about education too, because people took the view that subject knowledge didn't matter; that what mattered was the ability to reflect on yourself, learn about yourself, etc. I find that a very thin, unsatisfactory, and ultimately wrong approach and I also think it does a huge disservice to the liberal education tradition.

Melissa Benn is a passionate advocate for state comprehensive education. She is co-founder of the Local Schools Network and is author of *School Wars* (2012), in which she argues for a fair, non-selective education based on the idea of 'universal excellence'. I asked her about the familiar battle between high and low culture and what should be taught in our schools. She responded with a simple distinction: 'One of the things that I think is very important is difficulty. Learning, to me, is about how much you engage with difficulty. Bob Dylan is difficult, it's popular culture, but it's difficult.' I ask her about the teaching of knowledge and cultural capital and she was very clear:

When I hear people in debates say that there is no need to teach knowledge because you can just look it up on Google, I think that is profoundly wrong. Knowledge has to have roots. You have to feel it matters and to know why it matters, to know why knowledge is important. I don't think the Google paradigm does that at all. It's not about simply accessing something. It's about it being part of the beginning of your understanding of the world. You inhabit it. You interrogate it. You reject bits of it and then create your own traditions. When you grow up in a tradition, you tend to take it for granted, you don't see it; but that's cultural capital, isn't it? The more you know the more you want to know, and the more you know the more you can argue about what you know, and it all becomes very interesting. Whereas if you don't have any basic knowledge, you're into a very different kind of thing, living in a moment that has no meaning, has no passion, and goes nowhere.

Benn goes on to talk about her own experience at one of Britain's first state comprehensive schools, of which she has fond memories. It was, in the main, a positive experience. However:

I loved my schooling – but I have gaps in my education, particularly in science. Partly adolescent inattention, partly down to the more laid-back approach of the seventies where teaching was more dependent on the individual quality of the teacher, nowadays education is much more efficient. My elder daughter has 11 GCSEs at A and A* but at times I would have wished for more engagement with learning. I think there is a generation that has been totally switched off literature and criticism, because mostly it's just box ticking.

This word 'efficient' set me thinking: Should education be efficient?

Progressivism, for me, is about quality in education and freedom of exploration. I believe in school autonomy – we do need a national curriculum with a broad and balanced entitlement but with autonomy of delivery. I think with that, along with high teacher quality and certain other changes like smaller classes, you could begin to bring in a richer, less efficient, and more progressive model in schools.

The trouble with the [traditional] private schools and the grammar schools is that they create the philosopher kings – literally, socially, and intellectually. By definition they make everyone else supermarket oiks.

This is very tricky. If we aim high will we always be disappointed?

In my own experience, school set me up to know and to like to learn, to have an appetite for learning. I can remember coming out of the London School of Economics and all I came out with is a list of what I didn't know, which was positive. Interaction is a hugely important part of education, as Stefan

Collini said, 'To be stimulated by someone, to be amused by someone, even to be frightened by someone you're learning from, is a very important part of the education experience.' And that was so true. When I was at school there were inspiring teachers – and I see that with my girls. If they are interested in someone it will inspire them in terms of the subject.

That happened to me at university. My personal tutor was David Starkey, the historian. No point of interest or common ground, but the fact that he was such a brilliant lecturer, the fact that if I wanted to argue with him I'd better know my stuff, all of that was an important, small part of my education. It was more important than meeting a boring left-wing person I might agree with.

This brings me to dialectic. It seems that progressives can accept the value of teaching tradition as part of a rounded education. Where there is more of a problem, perhaps, is whether traditionalists can see the point of teaching tradition in a way that opens it up to criticism, and whether it can be added to or changed as history moves.

Dialectic

I put Alain de Botton's point that modern society does not want a questioning population to Phillip Blond. Do the powers that be really want a self-conscious citizenry?

I disagree with the great man, because modern capitalist society does want everyone to question everything; therefore they believe in nothing, therefore you can do whatever you want with them. The opposite is true. The nihilist questions everything and then they die. Only people who believe in things can create, construct, work with others, and build from there.

If creating and constructing things is only possible without criticism, we should not teach children to criticize then?

I always used to forbid my students from disagreeing with me, because they didn't have minds which they could make up yet because they weren't tutored. You need to know first before you can disagree with what you know. Whereas, at the moment, we disagree that we know, even though we claim we are knowing something, precisely because we are disagreeing that we don't know it! It's a mutually contradictory position. A lot of debate is interminable relativist nonsense; until we have teleological education we can't get proper disagreement. What I mean by teleological is education towards an end – that could be an educated man or woman, and an account of what that might be. The point is, at the moment, what passes for disagreement is laughable, 'It's OK to eat people; it's not OK to eat people.'

So, disagreement has its place: criticism can be part of education if we can forge some sort of agreement about what the ultimate aim for education should be. If that aim is positive and constructive then the act of criticism is contextualized; it is not just an aim in itself. Perhaps it is about enriching the process of learning?

Max Wind-Cowie works under the auspices of the centre-left think tank Demos and heads their Progressive Conservatism Project. If anyone can pull traditionalism and progressivism together it should be him! In his pamphlet, *A Place for Pride* (2011), Max and his co-author, Thomas Gregory, come to the conclusion that education is central to the task of community cohesion, generating pride in one's country, and promoting social networks and social engagement – the proper foundation of a real Big Society.

So, does he agree with Alain de Botton's point that for the 'powers that be' questioning citizens are not wanted?

Well, I don't agree, but I don't want to raise generations of people who respond to everything and everyone with cynicism – I think that is the danger. The problem with critical thinking is that it doesn't encourage children to distinguish between areas where scepticism and cynicism are warranted and areas where they are not. As a Conservative, I would say that the areas where scepticism and cynicism are less warranted – the institutions that are established as part of civic life, that have a history and a tradition behind them, and have a role in our civic life – are not things that you should be spending as much time questioning as, for example, websites you find on the internet. I believe that there are institutions that we should be raising children to a large degree to accept as benign. Then there is a plethora of other sources of information, guidance, and convictions that we should be teaching children to be deeply sceptical about.

Does the British tradition not include dissent?

It is the 'dough' effect: the way you make the British loaf is that you keep kneading it, rolling it, and incorporating, but it doesn't crush dissent, crush questioning, or crush reform. It incorporates just enough of it; that is the strength of all British institutions. It's why they have been strong. But your dissent from an institution is only justified if you have participated in it. Those institutions can only incorporate your dissent, your reform, your call to action, if you're part of them. Otherwise, what you are doing – it's the difference between questioning and being cynical – is standing outside of those institutions and criticizing, which makes you (I can't think of a nice way to say this) no better than a foreigner in the purest sense of that word. What I mean is that, rather than participating as a virtuous citizen, you are non-participating.

But in most cases the outsider is kept outside, they are not invited in. They are excluded by the prejudices that have accrued over time, not being born in the right family or in the right place. Is it any wonder that some people stand outside and hurl rocks, it's not through choice is it?

I do think that is right, but I would also make a plea for the paradox of British institutions. We have cultivated a set of institutions which sit outside the state, which enable you to participate in civic institutions while opposing them, which I think is an almost unique part of British civic life. The throwing rocks thing is an interesting one; for instance, when we look at the way in which the London riots took off. These are, presumably, exactly the sort of people who feel like they are not part of any institution, and we have failed to incorporate them, like air, into the dough.

One of the reasons we have failed is that we have not, in education, made an effort to explain to young people that there is a difference between 'being an individual' and individualization. There is a difference between saying, 'I have a set of opinions and I want to bring those opinions to the public square and I want to win an argument about this,' and saying, 'I have a set of opinions – you can't tell me I'm wrong because they're my opinion, and therefore there is nothing for us to discuss.'

Education has adopted the latter model to far too great a degree. It respects the individual's right to an opinion, respects the individual's right to question, all of which is good. But it then says that there's no need for deliberation to reach agreement or compromise, because I've respected your right to an opinion, you've respected my right to mine, and we'll leave it at that. The phrase 'We'll agree to disagree' is the most hateful phrase in the English Language. You can't just agree to disagree if you are going to be part of a social group.

Is this the difference between dialogue and dialectic?

I would say that dialogue that doesn't go anywhere, that doesn't aim at a conclusion, leads to people throwing rocks. Encouraging young people to participate in debate is a really good thing, but debate for debate's sake –

that all you need to do is have an opinion and that your opinion is somehow sacred and that is what defines you – this is encouraging a profound alienation.

This is a crucial difference coming through from the right. Self-directed learning is not, of itself, a good thing because it can be so destructive to society. There is a difference between the self-authored self and the need to develop agency and independence whilst existing within society. This is the difference that is expressed in cultural theory as the distinction between the horizontal and vertical transfer of knowledge. There is a danger in a skills-oriented curriculum, or when teaching critical thinking, that the vertical transfer of values and knowledge is destroyed or dismissed in a way that causes the destruction of society itself. The traditionalists can accept the importance of criticism if the overall aim of schooling is clear – that this is criticism with a purpose. The purpose is framed by the aims but also through the focus provided by the third art of the trivium, rhetoric.

I ask Wind-Cowie about the aims of education:

Fundamentally it's about character. I think it's important to move away from purely individual-based assessment, not because it's somehow appalling how some people do better than others, but because we shouldn't believe that what we achieve is purely down to us in every sphere of our lives. Rather, it's about the interplay of you and the other people around you. The important thing about being in a class is that you are part of a social institution. You are, in your own little way, a town square, and that is important.

Can there be a really diverse social make-up to that square?

I obviously do believe that schools are there to socially engineer and I think that schools that have a mixture of backgrounds are better than schools that have an incredibly homogenous intake. Schools are important to this, but we can't just rely on schools.

Many schools run breakfast clubs and after-school clubs, and they are heavily involved in childcare. Some would argue that is their most important role: keeping kids off the streets. Does Wind-Cowie approve of this, of wrap-around care?

This is quite wrong. The school shouldn't be the whole of your identity. It is paradoxical that you want schools to be forging identities and to be strong institutions that help protect children from ever-increasing circles of ignorance. But what you don't want is schools to be the only institution in children's lives, which is one of the dangers of the obsession for turning schools into parenting institutions.

I then move on to the idea of rhetoric, and the opportunities that students have to show their learning. Nowadays, for most students, this is the exam, but aren't there other ways we should be encouraging students to show their learning and different ways of assessing it? I ask Wind-Cowie whether participation should be a formal part of what is taught and, ultimately, assessed:

It's appropriate that we test children because we need some way of ordering children on their way out. I would like to see assessment take account of both knowledge and skills, in a way that it does in some areas of the curriculum incredibly well. But I would also like assessment to take account of the degree to which young people have exposed themselves to participation, have involved themselves in strengthening and facilitating the institution they've been part of.

How to approach assessment and what it is for is another area of contention. Matthew Taylor of the RSA pointed out:

> Policy makers have been trying for 25 years to say that all children should reach a certain academic threshold. That was never the case before. This is a new mission. It was the case, until 30 years ago, that we accepted that quite a lot of young people would reach a very low level academic threshold. We weren't that worried that they couldn't read or add up very much because they would go and work in factories. These jobs don't exist anymore. Even low-paid jobs now require you to be able to communicate and have different kinds of skills. So let's compare like with like.
>
> I've heard people deride higher education and say it's been devalued by people doing degrees in golf management, but there's no evidence at all that that's impacted on the elite. It's like arguing that the more children there are playing football on a Sunday, the more that damages Wayne Rooney's performance. We have systematically expanded higher education and, yes, there are people who are less academically adept who are going into higher education, but we are trying to get more pupils to achieve an academic threshold than we did in the past.

Making it easier for children to pass exams by bringing in modular learning and some 'easier' vocational qualifications has become a battleground. Taylor responded to the accusations from some Conservatives that education has been dumbed down:

> Because we have set it as a social goal that we want all children to attain a certain level, and to stay on now until 18, we're having to resort to a different set of methods and techniques, such as modular learning, BTECs, and all these types of things. But what's the point in having a system of learning and accreditation where 60% of the kids are going to fail? The evidence is that attainment has risen, but it hasn't risen as fast as accreditation, so we have deliberately made it easier for more children to reach the standards that we set at 16 and also to go to university.

That hasn't lowered standards. It's just that we have the deliberate policy of social engineering. The number of children staying on throughout education has risen far faster than the underlying increase in IQs and attainment. I don't see what's wrong with that. Meanwhile, the evidence suggests that, in relation to the worst secondary schools, there has been a major step forward in the last 10 or 15 years. There are very few disastrously failing schools now.

Taylor admits that standards have been made easier in order to socially engineer an increase in the number of students attending university. But what effect has this undoubted improvement in numbers passing exams had on the quality of education? Here is Phillip Blond again:

Modern schools are often utilitarian factories that fail to produce either individual happiness or general happiness. They teach to an end that isn't actually an end, because most students don't even come out with excellent exam results, but then follow a course in life that is predicated on the exams that they do. I think that schools have to be more than that, and that means a broader and more – I hesitate to use the word – 'liberal' curriculum, with a less formal account of what success is. Exams and academic excellence have to be a part of it – success in exams shows something – but our exam system is manipulation. It is rote learning. It has no critical elements in it. It doesn't give you any indication of critical or intellectual imagination or capacity. I don't really have any faith in exams. An 'A' at A level – who knows what that means?

Now we seem to be getting somewhere: a call for a broader curriculum, exams with more critical and imaginative elements, and an appeal for the importance of less formal experiences to be given a higher importance –

what I refer to as 'the authentic curriculum'. I asked Blond whether, if exams are manipulative, the idea of targets exacerbates this problem:

> *It's the general perversion of targets. The more you use a proxy to stand in for the real thing, then the more you measure things by a proxy and the more you tend to realize the proxy over the real thing. I think you should set objective standards that are richer (beyond just the exam results), but you also become entirely indifferent to how those standards are realized. You are entirely free and happy to pursue excellence, a broad account of excellence, but you don't centralize, you don't standardize, and you don't determine. You're free with regard to how you fulfil, as long as you fulfil. But the matrix that you fulfil has to be a richer one than the current paradigms.*
>
> *I believe in principles and outcomes. I believe in teleological education and I think that, almost from the beginning, as a child, what you really need is a vision as to what you should become. You copy an ideal you want to fulfil and direct your life that way – and that's what's lacking from education at the moment.*

Part of learning to disagree properly is to practise it; it is part of the journey towards wisdom. So, what would be a worthwhile goal for education – the pursuit of wisdom or a good life?

> *They are both teleological. I prefer the good life. I believe in virtue ethics and [Alasdair] MacIntyre and colleagues. I believe in flourishing as a model, and I think there are objective needs for human flourishing.*

Criteria-led marking has become part of our exam system. Students are told what they need to write in order to get a grade. This is not something that lets them develop their critical faculties and nor does it encourage unique viewpoints or arguments. It transpires that Nick Pearce had something to do with this while in government. He said:

> *It's very hard for people in power to spend their time going through qualifications. When I was an advisor to David Blunkett, I worked quite closely with Tessa Blackstone on 14–18 qualifications. The centralization of the English state has meant that we literally sat in meetings deciding whether there should be a Critical Thinking AS/A level. Now, that is ridiculous! This should not be the responsibility of ministers. Power should be configured in our society so that the people who are responsible for those things are professionally equipped. You now have children told, 'In this paragraph you've got to make two points; in that paragraph you've got to make two points; your essay on Shakespeare is not complete unless it has this structure and says these things at each stage.' That is an absurdity.*

This is important stuff. The exam system is part of the problem, and part of that problem lies in the accountability of the exam system. If we are teaching kids how to answer questions 'properly', when they haven't got the slightest idea what they are talking about, then there is a real crisis. Exams should recognize the role of a well-structured and thought through argument, a dialectic that can sit outside the expected criteria. This is different from teaching children that there is a predetermined way to answer a question, and if you don't conform, you fail. The unexpected should be valued, not destroyed by assessment objectives which tell you what you should think. The art of dialectic is not served well in much of the current exam system; we should assess quality of argument as well as content.

How can we cultivate an education system that develops the whole person? Matthew Taylor again:

> *Schools are complex institutions that not only have to address the needs of society, but also the desires of children and their parents. They are trying to do three things: they are trying to give children the knowledge they need; they are trying to give children the broader set of competencies and life skills and*

predispositions which are important to their success; and they're trying to find children's enthusiasms and grow those enthusiasms, because if children feel enthusiastic about a subject or an activity, then that is the foundation from which much can grow. I think that schools should understand themselves to be places that are always wrestling with these three competing priorities – knowledge, competence, and enthusiasm. But it will never be resolved because these three things are complex. If I were critical of schools, primarily it would be their inability to integrate these things and create a more holistic development.

I argued earlier that the relationship of knowledge to character is essential for a 21st-century trivium, so I am interested in what Taylor means by 'holistic development':

Schools, as a whole, aren't nearly systematic enough at discovering children's enthusiasms. I think that is where the science has slightly changed things. Now, we know the 10,000 hour stuff, that if children spend enough time at something they will become very good at something. There is also Carol Dweck's work on the importance of effort and young people understanding that effort pays off – that success is not about innate ability, it's about effort. I think this reinforces the point about enthusiasms, because if you can find things that young people want to do, want to be good at, want to be adept at – whether it's football, painting, language, or whatever it might be – you can harness that enthusiasm and get them into the habit of recognizing that if you work hard at something, become good at it, then that is a bedrock for an attitude of mind and a theory of learning which is really empowering to young people.

Bearing in mind that enthusiasm comes from the Greek word 'with God', as well as my ideas based on *logos* (when someone pursuing a discipline through authentic experience and engagement has a profound learning experience), I asked Taylor whether *any* enthusiasm is reasonable to pursue, even an interest in appearing on *The X Factor*, for example:

I don't think the problem is low aspirations. I think it is narrow aspirations. To get young people to think much more openly, and in a much more informed way, about the range of things they could choose as enthusiasms, and then support them in that, is a really big new task for schools. It's not about careers advice. Getting young people to reflect on what they want in life is an important role now for schools. I think Eton would lay open a lot of possibilities for things that you could do if you decided to make an effort, whether it was sport, medicine, or law. There would be lots of careers where children would know from their parents and their contacts that, if I work away at that, if I'm enthusiastic about that, I can reach this level. I think in working-class communities there are far fewer routes. It looks as though the only things you can get good at by working hard in them are The X Factor *and football.*

This, to me, seems to be about developing the capacities for a 'life well lived' or 'the good life'. It is certainly a far wider aspiration than just utilitarian skills for a working life. An important part of Trivium 21c is the idea of citizenship, but an authentic citizenship – one built from the study of authentic thoughts, ideas, and practices, experiencing and engaging with those ideas and practices, making them your own, and communicating or performing them. This, I suggest, is something far more useful for helping young people become engaged in our society than discrete lessons in citizenship. Taylor responds:

I think we have to re-socialize public services. We need to blur the boundary between the public sector and civil society. We need to re-conceptualize many public services as being co-productions in which public servants work with service users and citizens to generate the shared social outcome. In the case of schools, I believe very strongly that schools need, for want of a better phrase, 'a new deal'. That deal is this: schools recognize that their role is not simply to educate children between 8.45 a.m. and 3.15 p.m.; their role is to be beacons for a culture of learning in the wider community. The wider community, by the same token, needs to recognize its responsibility to be participants in the broad task of the socialization of young people.

So, we need to see that the job of the socialization of young people is a job that belongs to all of us. We are all involved. And that ripples down in all sorts of ways – mentoring, the way we interact with young people on the street, the role employers play with young people, the expectation that many more of us will support the work of schools in one way or another, and a much richer engagement of parents. Educating young people is the responsibility of the whole village, as it were. Schools that lead on that are going to have to throw themselves open. The RSA has been doing a project called the Area Based Curriculum Initiative in Peterborough, getting institutions – heritage and third-sector institutions – to genuinely work with schools on the co-creation of a local curriculum, one embedded in local institutions and local knowledge.

This engagement between young people and the cultural heritage and traditions of local and national institutions and global concerns is essentially the work of citizenship. Citizenship is about authentic dialogue and rhetorical interactions based on a respect for tradition, as well as engaging with people who are radical, entrepreneurial, or challenge the status quo in some way. I asked Max Wind-Cowie whether marketization is working against compromise and just forming individuals who want to get what they can get:

If we have an education system that is constructed on individual attainment and individual opinion then we're never going to be pushing children to form the kind of institutions that we want them to form, or to join the kinds of institutions that we want them to join. We have to start by recognizing that the individual within education is not the most important thing. It might be that the strengthening of the individual is the thing we're aiming for – after all, a virtuous citizen is a strong citizen – but the individual is not the most important thing in the practice of education. The practice of education should be about groups and should be about encouraging people to do things together that makes things, solves things, or answers things in a way that encourages people to participate with one another. And that's not what we do.

This is a surprise. I wasn't expecting to hear a defence of group work in schools from a traditionalist!

Groups offer routes to socialization, to – let's be properly Marxist about this – collectivization, within schools, within education. The reason I think it's important to identify the group as being more important than the individual within the classroom and within the curriculum is not necessarily because I want that group to form its own institution, but because I want the individuals within that group to learn how to be in institutions, to learn how to adapt and bend that aspect of their will to institutions.

Does this include the groups that come together through technology, social media, Twitter, and so on? Are these institutions suitably hierarchical or are they more anarchic?

The internet can encourage the participant not to participate, it can encourage you to self-select, it can encourage you to bring groups together over which you have instant and ongoing consent, but you've got no particular obligation to it. The ease of the opt-out, the ease of self-selection are problematic things. But, having said that, there are, of course, opportunities for pre-existing institutions to use the internet in order to ensure that the role they have in people's lives is extended into this important sphere that is increasingly central to people's existence.

There is also a crucial thing here – the internet allows you to persist in ever more eloquent ignorance. You can use the internet to exclude debate from your inner intellectual core, and that kind of fragmentation of learning (which is the aim of self-directed learning – learning that it is fragmented and autonomous) is profoundly dangerous.

Is this where we might find more agreement between progressives and traditionalists? The notion of the common life seems to echo what Matthew Taylor described in relation to the RSA's idea of the Area Based Curriculum. It is a theme that seems to be important to the left. Nick Pearce again:

Democratic, mass, high-standard education is what we are aspiring to. Are you educating children together? Do your schools embody some notion of common life? How do you break down segregation into its different dimensions? You want your schools to be integral to the wider community, so that the sense of where the culture resides in the community and the responsibilities we have to our schools as adults – as well as parents and as members of the community – remains incredibly important. The function of schools of being integrated in the community and serving the community is not just about their intake and what they do, but also about their interconnections within that community. We have to re-establish some notion that education is a common enterprise. What is really important is equipping our children not just for their own success but for a common endeavour.

Pearce praises the work of the Scandinavian children's centres, staffed by trained professionals, which serve to offset the disadvantages of the home environment:

These centres build common life between us. They are not just a place where you can dump the kid; it's much more powerful than that. They are also building the social capital that comes with common life. For example, friendships are made across social classes and by parents as well as children.

It is in this spirit that we can see education as a space that builds a common life, the common trivial place where the three roads meet. This is where grammar – the impulse to conserve the authority of tradition, our place of rules, precepts, and control – meets the critical, radical questioning of dialectic. It is also where we need the authenticity of *logos* and the analysis of logic. It is where modernity meets tradition. It is here that we have the community, the conversation, the performance of our interactive lives, as well as the more formal aspects of performance that help build our character as individuals and as communities. To take a full part we are but philosopher kids in the pursuit of the good life.

The way to do this, to make the kind of school I would like to send my daughter to, is to listen to both the conservative and liberal impulses. So, here is my list of criteria for teaching in our schools:

- Cultural capital should come from the teaching of knowledge and reflect the best that has been thought or said. This should involve complexity and difficulty, so there should be space for students to criticize, to think, and to develop their own character, as well as develop their own enthusiasms.

- Schools should develop a curriculum that responds to change, as well as being rooted in a sensitive awareness of our traditions and how they are evolving. It should seek out academic, cultural, social, artistic, and physical challenges that are authentic, that stretch each child, and give them experiences they would not otherwise get.

- Schools should teach the importance of a sceptical approach to both tradition and modernity. Children should be encouraged to be curious, to question and debate, but alongside the idea that the institution in which the debate takes place deserves its place in our civic society because it provides the space for that debate.

Schools should not serve the grammarian over the dialectician or the progressive over the traditionalist. Like parliament, the school is a fundamental institution in which debate takes place. The school I want for my daughter will enable her to leave with a wide range of interests and excitement about the continuing pursuit of wisdom.

We started this chapter with a one-nation Conservative, Ferdinand Mount. Let's end it with what the British Labour Party are attempting to do with the notion of one-nation politics. In his introduction to the pamphlet *One Nation Labour: Debating the Future* (2013), Jon Cruddas MP writes about his vision for progressive politics, which is 'a politics that is both radical and conservative'. He believes that where there is 'a sense of belonging' and where there is 'the agreement of a common ground reached between different groups and interests' this is 'the outcome of deliberation'. That is, crucially, 'a democratic process that is never completed and always contingent'. He sees the potential for 'a politics of togetherness' and 'a way of talking about the "we" while holding to the uniqueness of each individual'. Cruddas writes, 'The Conservative tradition has been a powerful national force … it gave many people meaning, value and a sense of belonging … But for all its good … [it] relied on deference to secure its power.' It is therefore a democratic aspiration rather than an authoritative one to join tradition and how to marry it to the 'best in modernity' through the right to sit at the 'common table' and the obligations inherent in that role.

Education has a role to play, and the metaphor of sitting at the common table is akin to the common meeting place where the three roads meet. Cruddas is ascribing to One Nation Labour the same arguments that I have adduced for the trivium: the three roads – tradition, modernity, and the obligations to our shared community – meet and make common cause in a process that is always contingent and never complete.

Chapter 14

The Contemporary Trivium

What did you learn in the morning?

How much did you know in the afternoon?

Were you content in the evening?

Did they teach you how to question when you were at the school?

Did the factory help you grow; were you the maker or the tool?

Did the place where you were living

Enrich your life and then

Did you reach some understanding of all your fellow men?

Ewan MacColl, 'Ballad of Accounting'

The Magic Formula

In August 2012, the think tank IPPR published an essay by Michael Barber, Katelyn Donnelly, and Saad Rizvi called *Oceans of Innovation: The Atlantic, the Pacific, Global Leadership and the Future of Education*. Michael Barber is the chief education advisor to Pearson, the largest education company in the world. Previously he was head of Tony Blair's Delivery Unit (2001–2005). In the essay, they call for a radical 'whole system revolution' to meet the needs of the 21st century. The work is based on research about current international needs, especially economic ones, and how education needs to drive innovation, economic power, and leadership. They argue that the most successful education systems in the world need to rethink what they teach and how they teach it. The authors believe that innovation and entrepreneurship should be central to the education offer. They sum up their argument as to what that offer should be in an equation:

Well-educated = E(K+T+L)

where E = Ethics, K = Knowledge, T = Thought, and L = Leadership. Ethics is the way of being and doing exemplified by the institution and its relationships. By Knowledge they mean the type of knowledge to be taught in schools which is 'significant'. Thought is the type of (critical) thinking that goes back to Plato – it should be part of lessons rather than a separate subject. Leadership means communication, collaboration, and community.

This, then, is E(K+T+L). The contention here is not just that a curriculum of this kind would better prepare students for the 21st-century lives they will lead; it is also that the explicit combination of knowledge plus thinking plus leadership underpinned by ethics is the combination most likely to unleash in young people the qualities which will enable them to be innovative in their work and life and constructive in their engagement with communities at every level from the local to the global …

[C]ollectively we don't know yet how to achieve E(K+T+L) for every student. (Barber et al, 2012: 57, 60–61)

With this formula, it would appear that the wheel is being reinvented: at first sight it seems to be nothing more or less than the trivium as argued for in this book; clearly, it is a remarkably similar mantra. Not yet knowing how to achieve E(K+T+L) is perhaps due to the fact that the authors are looking only to the future and not to the past. How to achieve what Barber and his colleagues are calling for involves radical change – change that is rooted in the history of the trivium. It is to this that they should attend.

The Spine

I am, therefore, agreeing with Michael Barber when I state that a great education is one that balances the three roads of the trivium and gives education a spine on which to build. There might be a chasm between progressive and traditionalist thinkers, but in many classrooms I have a suspicion that a more pragmatic approach occurs already. Teachers are probably adept at pulling together both traditions in practical ways. It is teachers, in the main, to whom I address this chapter.

In my drama teaching, I found a key for unlocking the students' creative abilities: the mantra. Once they had the mantra in place, they became independent learners. It was by using this mantra that students made art happen, independent of their teacher. In the process, understanding was delayed. We lived with uncertainty for as long as possible, in an unresolved fluid reality that allowed us to explore a variety of emotional and intellectual responses, individually and in groups. We cogitated, played, analysed and experimented. With discipline and focus we explored the rules and the precepts. Finally, we began practising the art. The imposed limitations had led to a creative freedom. This was revealed in a wide variety of ways of seeing, reconstructing, and representing and communicating experience. This was learning as an art form. The process had begun with constraints, rules and precepts; the end was independent children capable of open and free expression.

This is how art works. At its heart, the trivium is a creative process. And it has led me to propose that the trivium is a mantra which can have wider application in all branches of education. It suggests how education could work in the 21st century. But it needs firm foundations. In order to be critical and creative, kids need to know stuff, to have a good grasp of the basics, the grammar of a topic. Only then can they become creative, critical citizens fully engaged in the complexities of our communication age, yet also responsive to and knowledgeable of our rich and varied history and culture.

What follows are some ideas about what Trivium 21c, as a spine for schooling, might look like. This is not 'the method': it is intended as a starting point. The suggestions are drawn from across the great education divide and the wide spectrum of theories and practices. It is not exhaustive and you might have better ideas. These are but fragments of the whole, drawing together ideas in a way that works more formally than a pick-and-mix pedagogy. Although there is a good degree of crossover between the three arts of the trivium, there may well be disagreement about where to place some of the components.

If I were to give the movement a title it would have to be a *dissoi logoi*: Progressive Traditionalism. Trivium 21c encompasses the following aspects:

- **Outcome**: The philosopher kid. Wisdom and the ability to live a good life. A respect for the best that has been thought or said, yet with the confidence to test it out, with the good grace to bow to acceptance, or cultivate doubt – sometimes anger – and a desire to add to or change, honouring progress as an equal to tradition yet able to question both. Importantly, an ability to take part in the great conversation and make a contribution towards our common life.

- **Ethics**: With its roots in *logos* and rhetoric, an ethical education points towards human flourishing: developing agency, enthusiasm, independence, leadership, and mastery; guided by principle, character, virtue, and ethical awareness; underpinned by questions about moral purpose. This gives rise to the philosopher kid, the Renaissance man or woman, the polymath.

- **Trivium**: Taking on both the traditional and the progressive and valuing them both as important in education. Focusing on the need to communicate well in a variety of forms, such as speech, writing, arts, and crafts; enhanced through scepticism, engagement, and realization of the creative tension; cultivating dialogue and curiosity, mastery of learning.

- **Grammar**: Knowledge, skills, tradition, authority, discipline, hierarchy, and cohesive cultural identity (including vertical transmission of knowledge), cultural and social capital, conjecture, 'finding out', connecting, treated with a degree of scepticism.

- **Dialectic, logic, and *logos***: Analysis, critical thinking, philosophical enquiry, thought, discipline, deductive, inductive, and abductive reasoning, creative, scientific, and mathematical thinking, sorting out, criticism, dialogue, argument, questioning, individual identity, wit, humour, play, progress, modernity (including horizontal transmission of knowledge), debate, *dissoi logoi*, wondering, argument, effort and challenge, pursuit of truth, beauty, essence, character, emotional engagement, journey, self-discipline, resilience, reflection, virtue, authentic experience, wonder, enthusiasms and their pursuit, being alive.

- **Rhetoric**: Turning outwards, persuasion, communication, conversation, ethics, performance, community, relationships, citizenship, social capital, leadership, telling and showing about … responsibility.

The Goals of Schooling

A great education is defined by its goals. If we are to make changes to schooling, we must first ask, 'What are our goals?' In order to ensure they are clearly defined, we need to make certain we understand what we mean by goals. Are our goals *teleological, deontological,* or *eudemonic*?

Teleological means the process of being directed towards an end or goal, and can lead to the idea that 'the ends justify the means'. It comes from *telos* which means 'final purpose'. It looks for an end result. Deontological is more about denying, sacrificing, or changing what we want to do in order to do the 'right thing'. It is about sticking to rules and codes. Eudemonia is a lifelong pursuit founded on wisdom, practice, and excellence. It is about human happiness or the rather more useful term, human flourishing. All three can be brought together: we have aims, we have responsibilities, and we have a need to flourish in the every day. Sometimes the right thing to do is to sacrifice our immediate happiness and learn the importance of delayed gratification for future fulfilment.

Do we want goals that are about ends, or about the journey? Should the journey be one where children, instead of following their own dreams and desires, deny or sacrifice their lives in order to serve the greater good, perhaps the nation state? If we need more engineers, for example, then despite what the individual wants, we might ensure young people become engineers for the greater good of our country. Or perhaps we want individuals to be happy and follow their dreams, even if that doesn't seem to serve the greater good? These choices will make a lot of difference to the types of goals we set in our schools.

Trivium 21c: Define your Goals

In schools, the journey should be towards wisdom and the need for knowledge via wonder and curiosity. This should be a journey that builds enthusiasm and a hunger to know more, and which develops the habits of mind, adaptability, and creativity that have enabled educated people to make real contributions to the great conversations of their time, by making, engaging, and sharing in their communities and the wider world. It is a journey that will enable the philosopher kid to learn the best that has been thought or said, to engage with it, adapt, change and add to it, and learn a way to approach established knowledge and create new knowledge in a world that offers many chances and challenges. The goal of education should not be about work, but about life. Life includes work, but it is clearly so much more: education for its own sake includes life, the universe, and everything!

At the heart of this idea is that in your school, your class, or your domain, you help to nurture citizens with a curiosity in, and an ability to use, knowledge and foster an expertise in communicating and learning. Learning is a lifelong pursuit; when students cease to study with you, they should be further along the journey but still exploring towards these ends. While in your classroom, students should be imbued with knowledge, enthused by the subject, contributing to the school and wider community, and engaging deeply with it all. Above all, the students should be able to perform to a level that transcends their own expectations. We should all have dreams; schools should go further in making them happen. This can be expressed through the school motto and its aims.

Trivium 21c: The School Motto

I approached the leaders of three very different types of school to see if there were any similarities in approach, across the sectors, that are drawn from ideas from the trivium. Until she finally retired in 2013, Dr Irene Bishop CBE was the head teacher of St Saviour's and St Olave's School in the London Borough of Southwark, an 'outstanding' inner-city girls' comprehensive school, near the Elephant and Castle. As an institution, the school goes back a long way. Dr Bishop said, 'Tradition is very important to us; our school motto, which is also our mission statement, is "Heirs of the Past, Children of the Present, Makers of the Future".' It evokes the trivium, the tradition of grammar, the dialectic of the now, and the rhetoricality of making the future.

Jonathan Simons is the chair of governors from the Greenwich Free School, again in inner London. He said, 'We have a very clear set of values that run through the school, which we call "Growth, Fellowship, Scholarship" – which comes from our acronym. We are unapologetic about saying these are the values that we want to instil in our pupils, and not just through the curriculum but through everything they do.' This is essential; there is no point in having values unless they are seen to be central to the school's ethos. A new school can't fall back on its past, but it can lay the foundation stones for a good future.

Dr Anthony Seldon is the master of Wellington College, a public school in Berkshire, which also sponsors a state academy school. He said:

I think there is a common ethos that is important to have in all institutions, which are time honoured, and which were defined in ancient Greek philosophy, around virtues. It's clear that young people pick up values not from learning the names and being taught what they are, but from seeing them being modelled by adults and out in the community. There's no point in telling them that integrity is a core value if they don't see the school acting with integrity. As for our academy, I don't think you can bludgeon a core set of values into each institution – it is too much of an imposition. Values should be partly organic, partly generic; the prioritization will substantially come from each academy. So, the values we have at Wellington are worked out by the whole community, by the kids and by the adults.

Trivium 21c: Ensuring Your Goals are Articulated in Your School Motto

The school motto should offer an eloquent expression of the three roads of the trivium. Schools should make certain that the motto gives an idea of what the school ethos is, as well as what they wish their students to aspire to. The three areas of focus as defined by the trivium – grammar, dialectic, and rhetoric – could also be stated as means to achieve the aim of turning out well-educated philosopher kids. Clearly, the ethos is something that should unite everyone in common aims and be discussed accordingly. These 'time-honoured values' also need to be open to review. The motto and the aims are an expression of the spine for a school, and should be active in your community of learning.

Trivium 21c: The Only Way Is Ethics

Ethics might be open to challenge at any time, so a school should be sufficiently sure of itself to understand how virtue and morality can be contested. Also, the institution should be mature enough to debate openly and balance the competing impulses of tradition and modernity. Ethics include the moral principles, knowledge, behaviours, and customs that hold a society, culture, or subculture together. In this context, ethical codes and conventions include an idea of right and wrong, and can also define moral character, even if that behaviour is formed through the ethical codes of gangs or even terrorist groups. Usually, though, ethical behaviour would be perceived as moral behaviour. The ethical code of an institution should therefore bring about the expectations and cultural and social capital that enable individuals, through their own agency, to behave in a virtuous way, either by reflecting or rejecting the ethical codes that are expected of them.

Dr Irene Bishop reflects on the pressures that surround her school, 'I do think there are some things wrong in society where people feel that there is no point in being part of society, because they've got their own society which gives them what they need, through gangs or whatever. They've got their own code of ethics, they've got their own rules, their own uniforms, and also they've got their own hierarchy, an unpleasant hierarchy.' At Greenwich Free School, deputy head teacher Sarah Jones believes that 'active citizenship' should be encouraged to counteract other pressures:

In active citizenship, they bring any issue – from the news, from school, from their local communities – and they can consider how they can campaign on that issue. This enables kids to be empowered to make a difference; it gives them the tools to make a difference. That's the kind of thing that your middle-class kid gets modelled at home all the time. We want kids to understand that they can get involved, that they can physically change their local environment for the better.

Citizenship is an active process. It should be authentic rather than abstract. It should be imbued with a sense of social and cultural capital; a human becoming is a human belonging.

Trivium 21c: Virtue and Virtuosity

Virtue is a standard of excellence or morality; a means to an end or the end in itself. It will guide us but at times we will fail to achieve it. Virtue includes moral strength, good qualities, and righteousness. Sharing the same root as virtue, we also have 'virtuoso', meaning someone who is skilled, learned, or even an expert. Training in being a virtuoso opens up the world of excellence; excellence, in turn, is virtuous. Virtue could be seen an active idea, rather than an abstract otherworldly one. It is a tendency, a disposition, or habit. This habit could be result of our own agency, and/or the habits of mind that are formed and internalized through our relationships with each other and our institutions.

An important job of the school is to promote an ethical framework that enables us to choose, if we wish, to develop a virtuous character. Such a framework should guide and develop character, virtue, and virtuosity through active authentic engagements and relationships. Schools should exploit their local communities to engage fully in this process. This also means that the activities that are in danger of falling away, not only into extra-curricular provision but disappearing from there too, should be brought back as a central concern of the curriculum itself. This could be called an 'authentic curriculum'.

Trivium 21c: The Relationship between the Three Arts

In *Teach Like a Champion* (2010), Doug Lemov recommends, amongst other things, that a teacher:

- Stops day-to-day lesson planning.

- Plans with the idea that you are leading to mastery.

- Begins with the end in mind.

- Starts 'unit' planning.

I would concur with this. The whole process of teaching through Trivium 21c demands that you develop learning along with knowledge, and change the process of teaching and learning as you go; therefore, it is essential that the whole picture is acknowledged rather than just the day-to-day. You will teach differently as the course proceeds, whether it is by day, week, month, year, or course. Naturally, adjustments will need to be made, but if you are absolutely focused on the knowledge and skills you are imparting, and on them being digested and not regurgitated, then you will aid the process of digestion subtly, yet remorselessly.

In *Visible Learning*, John Hattie cites a report that states, 'Effective teachers have high expectations and increase the academic demands on their students … Effective teachers communicate high expectations for students to self-regulate and take charge of their behaviour and academic engagement'

(Hattie, 2008: 259). This is mastery in academic engagement and in learning.

Trivium 21c is a journey towards mastery and wisdom. It asks for:

- Progression in quality and quantity of knowledge.

- Increasing challenge.

- Developing enthusiasm and complexity.

- Increasing skills.

- Building resilience.

- Looking for beauty and/or truth, profundity, and doubt.

- Celebrating performance.

- Taking part in the great conversation.

And it is possibly:

- Transferable and self-reflective through the idea of the mantra being part of a whole-school approach.

It has been argued many times over the centuries that the trivium:

- Enables learning to learn.

- Develops positive habits of mind.

And it asks the questions:

- How should we ensure students progress?

- How should we adjust our teaching?

- Do students learn differently as they progress?

The answer lies in the idea that we teach in order to let go. Alongside the acquisition of knowledge and skills is the idea of learning, playing with, and honing knowledge for our own ends. This improvement might be about becoming more knowledgeable, more skilled, or both. Whether this journey is about a whole discipline or focuses on each moment along the way, or both (it is for the teacher to decide), it should be based, loosely, on the precepts of independence, grammar, dialectic, and rhetoric.

Trivium 21c: Teaching from Dependence to Independence

The classroom journey has been described in a variety of ways in pedagogical books on teaching, such as:

- **Directive (directed practice)**: This is the domain of the teacher – 'I'. The teacher has authority as does the subject or discipline.

- **Guided discovery (guided practice)**: Shared between the teacher and the student – 'we'. The teacher guides the student in the acquisition of the subject or discipline, encourages engagement, critical awareness, and enthusiasm.

- **Receptive – exploratory (independent practice)**: The domain has moved to that of the student – 'you'. The teacher ensures that ownership moves from the authority of the teacher to the authority of the student within the discipline or even against the discipline.

Or as Doug Lemov puts it: I – We – You:

I	We	You
(grammar)	(dialectic)	(rhetoric)

You could almost think of this as going from the traditional to the progressive:

Teacher Centred	Teacher and Student Centred	Student Centred

226

Grammar

Schools should ensure that the curriculum they provide reflects the greatest that culture has to offer. Grammar is the key to unlocking doors, the key to understanding the human condition, the examined life. When teachers have the choice, they must not choose knowledge by how accessible it is, but by how important it is; they should then use their professionalism to make it accessible. Anthony Seldon advises, 'One should look at those aspects that are proven by time to be enduring rather than the ephemeral. Given that time is limited in the curriculum, it's better to study those things that are major rather than those things that are minor.' Jonathan Simons agrees, 'If you don't have a basic corpus of knowledge, and the critical skills about how to progress your own knowledge, you can't do anything.' Each subject has its grammar, the history of how it became itself, the wisdom (and the mistakes) of the past, which make it ready to be altered in the present.

In *Mastery* (1991), George Leonard describes how we start the journey of teaching and learning with small incremental steps and that we should clearly reveal the process. Doug Lemov (2010) explains how to break down complexity into simple pieces and build knowledge systematically. The skill of a great teacher is to make the start of the journey, the grammar, fun, engaging, or necessary; sometimes all three.

Trivium 21c: Grammar

Grammar represents the building blocks, the foundational knowledge, the facts, opinions, works, ideas, and thoughts of real value; which are all, probably, contestable. In order to access knowledge the teacher can help by:

- Building from bite-size pieces of knowledge.

- Teaching about and modelling research skills.

- Talking about the process of getting ideas and mastering the fundamentals of the discipline or subject.

This process can be made more motivating and palatable if, at the start, teachers ensure that they:

- Introduce relevant concepts, rules, facts, and fundamentals of the subject.

- Only set short homework tasks, if any, at the beginning.

- Provide resources that can be accessed by students at their own speed and are open ended.

- Provide notes, or minimize note taking, then teach memorization or other ways of absorbing knowledge and skills.

- Start simply.

- Introduce deliberate practice – even repetition, rote, and ritual.

- Plan and teach through the trivium (make it explicit).

- Increase capacity by building on previous knowledge – make larger pieces connect through 'mental Velcro'.

- Gradually increase knowledge load and complexity.

- Teach research skills and take delight in connecting ideas.

- Use analogy.

- Tell stories about the knowledge you are teaching and emphasize narrative(s).

- Talk about the people behind the knowledge – whose shoulders?

- Begin to introduce arguments against the knowledge, where relevant. Show how it is contested and open up this space ready for the next stage. Encourage a degree of scepticism.

Trivium 21c: Dialectic/Logic/*Logos*

Try teaching logic in the context of your subject. Show how to approach subject-specific thought and reasoning and how it links to other subjects and their approaches. Greenwich Free School's Sarah Jones considers this process to be essential in education, 'If you are equipped with thinking and reasoning, you can make choices for yourself. The thing about a great education is we teach kids it's OK to challenge, it's great to think about things, and to ask difficult questions.' It is also central to the ethos at St Olave's. Dr Irene Bishop observes, 'I think it is our job as educationists to give children the tools to be able to find their own way in the world. That means giving them the opportunity to develop their own ideas. I don't think it's to inculcate them with something that they never question, because as soon as that child gets to the point when they realize that there are questions, how do they cope?'

This means that questioning, thinking, and debating should be a substantial part of teaching and learning. Anthony Seldon agrees, 'All young people should learn how to debate, construct an argument, know what a good argument is, and how to avoid personal comments that can destroy reason.' In schools there are various ways of doing this. A debating society is clearly a good idea, as are classes in the theory and history of thought and knowledge. At Wellington College they have a Philosopher in Residence – something that might be worth pursuing in other schools, whether through the idea of a philosophy cafe or team teaching lessons where underlying philosophical enquiry can be brought in, as a way of linking learning with wider issues from the history of thought. At Greenwich Free School, they now use philosophical enquiry both in tutorials and also in the body of lessons. The school sets aside time for debating as a pure skill, arguing for the other side, thinking about logic and argument creation. Here is Sarah Jones again, 'We get all our teachers to build on these skills in lessons, so when they're teaching English, they are thinking whether a debate or more creative, imaginary stuff like P4C [Philosophy for Children] is suitable. And in maths, teachers are asking, is it a logical sequence?'

The teacher needs to bring in enquiry so that it becomes a part of the school ethos rather than just an add-on. The children need to grapple with knowledge that is rich, so that an atmosphere of curiosity and criticism is created. The theory of knowledge component in the International Baccalaureate (IB) might serve as inspiration. Perhaps this component could be extended into a course on the theory and history of thought, which could take the place of religious education in all secular schools (although religious thought would still play a major role). In faith schools, however, this could be taught in the first instance from within their religious tradition.

More muscular argument is also necessary and passionate disagreement should be part of the classroom experience. Anthony Seldon says:

Argument is fundamental. We are too often frightened of disagreement, so we suppress disagreement and we get a kind of unsatisfactory soup. The best and the most creative ideas have come out of quite strong and tough argument. If you have strong disagreement based on grounded arguments, that can make for great learning, great spectacle, and great opportunities in education. I'm not certain that when I was 11 I really did know what I felt about literature. At my age today, I still don't really know what I think about most things. But, of course, it's important and valuable to argue and debate.

Children do not always 'know' what they are saying, they are not always right; but they need the opportunity to express themselves, whether they are right or wrong, in a framework that allows them to engage. It is essential that this is tied together with knowledge; they should develop an awareness of how 'sure' they are and why.

Lessons are generally enlivened by dialectic: it can inform the story, it can be a narrative force by introducing the 'baddy', it can enlist the passions through argument and conflict, and it can drive the learning forward as students engage more fully with the learning. This stage is highly active and engaging as it uses practical experiment, exploration, dialogue, debate, and/ or argument. Our schools must resound to the sound of debate.

For Carol Dweck (2006), the 'growth mindset' sees students engage in the process of difficulty and working at things; this mindset is encouraged by understanding that performance is enhanced by practice rather than innate ability. The classroom needs to be a place of progress, not just arrival. Performances along the way can celebrate progress, by sharing work and ideas that are half-formed rather than complete. An expectation of self and peer criticism, as well as from the teacher, should be encouraged, especially if children pursue perfection in the knowledge that they will rarely arrive at it.

The idea of elite performance – and the belief that we mainly err – is completely different from the continual award of merits and gold stars for good work. This path to wisdom involves developing self-discipline, practising deliberately, and gradually increasing complexity. This can create the 'flow factor' that relies not on instant gratification but on increasingly complex tasks.

According to Mihaly Csikszentmihalyi, 'Complexity is the result of the fruitful interaction between … two opposing tendencies …' (Csikszentmihalyi, 1996: 363) the two tendencies are the cultural traditions of a domain and the individual's ability to respect, respond and to be in conflict with it if necessary. In the classroom, the teacher in the dialectic phase will ensure children:

- Analyse and explore.

- Try out deductive, inductive, and abductive thinking.

- Make connections and justify thoughts.

- Ask and answer questions by finding out answers, possible answers, ideas, and opinions.

- Test out and argue.

- Use logical thinking, syllogisms, fallacies, and other ways of arguing.

- Experiment and play.

- Make sense of ideas.

- Are creative, critical, resilient, and enthused.

To bring this about, the teacher should use, among many others, the following methods:

- Introduce alternative views on topics and teach about enquiry and judgement.

- Model connecting and making sense within the subject and beyond, encouraging thinking and drawing it out.

- Introduce and increase complexity – provide scaffolds where needed.

- Explore thought and how thinking has changed in the subject.

- Gradually increase homework load, note taking, and evaluative work.

- Open up dialogue through questioning.

- Introduce debate and the habits of discussion.

- Argument – be provocative, play the devil's advocate.

- Point out ethical issues which allow for wider engagement than just with the topic under discussion.

- Do less *for* the student and do more *with* the student; be a critical friend whilst retaining the authority of expertise.

- Encourage a culture of criticism.

Rhetoric

Rhetoric is the expression of our learning, enabling us to take part in, and be a part of, the great conversation. Here, identity is forged as we remake ourselves, in the society and communities into which we are born, how we affect them and why, and the traditions that we pass on. This can constitute performance in an exam or in other walks of life, taking part in the great conversation, producing something. Whether it is a piece of art, an essay, a craft, a sport, a science, a blog, or climbing a mountain, rhetoric is a form of communication, the culmination of a period of preparation. Rhetoric is where we strive to take part in the best that has been thought, said, and done.

Trivium 21c: Rhetoric – The Expression of Your Learning

We begin with the idea of persuasion. Can the student persuade people that they know what they are talking about? This can be done through the written word or through speech. It can also be expressed in a wide range of skills, performances, and materials. This art can include, amongst others, artistic and sporting performance. As a teacher, how do you judge, in the widest terms, the performative aspects of your subject? However you do this, in the context of rhetoric, these are the skills your students should become familiar with:

- Expressing and listening to opinions.

- Arguing and articulating ideas elegantly.

- Teaching, lecturing, communicating, and leading.

- Appreciating beauty and aesthetics.

- Understanding complexity whilst attempting to communicate simply.

- Expressing evidence-based ideas and opinions.

- Performing and understanding performativity.

- Generating rather than just resolving questions.

- Acknowledging the importance of audience, communication, and citizenship.

- Appreciating ethical concerns.

- Being aware of the community of which they are a part.

- Being able to perform confidently in different situations.

- Helping establish and strengthen communities.

- Knowing how to express dissent effectively.

- Knowing how to make changes.

- Being responsible for their own work.

In order to strengthen the rhetoric phase the teacher should also:

- Ask the students to present the 'big picture' in a variety of media, checking the students' understanding and what they have brought to it.

- Encourage opportunities for performance.

- Realize that additional support for expert learners does more harm than good; by not 'letting go' you produce students who are ever reliant on the teacher.

- Produce open-ended homework tasks and allow the students to set their own homework tasks.

- Let the students follow their own enthusiasms in the framework of the discipline (as it allows).

- Let go.

- Challenge and be a critical friend, with authority but also with grace, allowing space for failure and the possibility for great success.

Assessment

Along with the journey of education, assessment also has to change. Just as demanding a dissertation at the grammar phase is probably unfair, learning a poem and reciting it is not. It would be bizarre to end a PhD course with a fifteen-minute multiple-choice test, just as it would be odd to expect a course with debate at its core not to involve some sort of discussion in its assessment.

The same is true for day-to-day classroom assessment. There are many ways of assessing – for example, no hands up (where students are encouraged to answer questions or share their ideas at the behest of their teacher rather than putting their hands up) – but no technique should be used exclusively. Teachers should have flexibility in what they do, and in so doing, provide an example for the children.

Trivium 21c: Assessment

In this table is a suggested assessment journey that supports the idea of progression as previously outlined. In it I am using assessment ideas that have been shown to be effective, and I am matching them to the trivium, using assessment in a particular rather than in a blanket way. How we assess should be sensitive to the journey the student is engaged with.

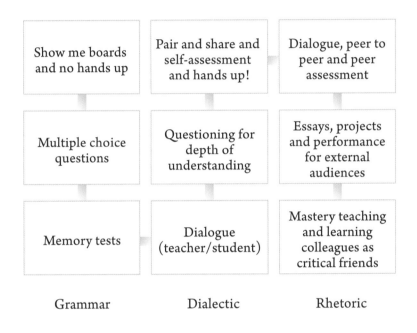

Show me boards and no hands up	Pair and share and self-assessment and hands up!	Dialogue, peer to peer and peer assessment
Multiple choice questions	Questioning for depth of understanding	Essays, projects and performance for external audiences
Memory tests	Dialogue (teacher/student)	Mastery teaching and learning colleagues as critical friends
Grammar	Dialectic	Rhetoric

Not all of these ideas will be suitable for every subject, but in them there is the concept of progression that I would highly recommend. In other words, effective assessment will vary for different parts of the journey. Note that peer assessment is relevant, but only when a certain amount of expertise has been gained.

| Teaching styles | | |
Grammar	Dialectic (Logic/ *Logos*)	Rhetoric
Directive	Guided discovery	Coaching
Building blocks	Logic	Lecturing
Piecing	Questioning	Challenging
Incremental steps	Seminar	Seminars
Reveal process	Debate	Tutorials
Share concepts, rules, facts, and fundamentals	Argue	Demand eloquence
Standing on the shoulders of giants	Progression	Self-reflection
Provide resources	Analysis/synthesis	Open up new questions
Teach note taking	Talk	Express and listen to opinions
Simplicity	Building	Let go
Repetition	Exploration	Set open-ended problems and tasks
Ritual	Play	Give space
Increase capacity incrementally	Introduce and increase complexity	
Scaffolding	Habits of discussion	
Connecting	Structured controversy	
	Do less *for* the student; do more *with* the student	
	Increase homework load, note taking, and evaluative work	
	Inspire, advise, critique	

Grammar	Learning methods Dialectic (Logic/ Logos)	Rhetoric
Memorizing	Application of knowledge	Presentations
Build knowledge systematically	Exploring context	Performance
Research	Guided practice	Show off skills
Note taking	Critical thinking	Express opinions
Reading	Analysis	Appreciate beauty
Viewing	Discovering	Understand complexity
Get facts	Connecting	Express simply
Access information	Asking questions	Elegant argument
Connect knowledge	Testing out	Judgements
Delay gratification	Making sense	Positing questions
Learn to deal with not understanding	Justify thoughts	Listening to opinions
Expect frustration	Experiment	Appreciating elegance and beauty
Learn to delay criticism	Ask questions	Leading
Acquire skills	Practise skills	Lecturing
	Train	Generating questions
	Play	Teaching
	Self-discipline	Connect with other institutions and expertise
	Work hard	
	Compete/support	
	Arguing	
	Enjoy elusive nature of learning	
	Enthusiasm	

Grammar	Assessment Dialectic (Logic/ *Logos*)	Rhetoric
Show-me boards No hands up Memory tests Multiple choice Short answer Precis Repetition Recall	Dialogue: teacher–student Pair and share Argument Essays that show argument between two or more viewpoints Self-assessment Questioning for depth of understanding Dialogue: peer to peer to teacher Peer assessment Viva voce Essays that start to bring in the students' own opinions, backed up with evidence	Essays Projects Performances Mastery tutorials Student-led seminars with peer and teacher critiques Dissertations Pieces of art Assess use of skills in context of the domain Assess originality

Begin with the end in mind, stop day-to-day lesson planning and start planning 'units'. Stretch and challenge. Build mastery through engagement with the 'trivial' arts. From 'show and tell' in a primary school to a university dissertation, the trivium is central to the educative process.

The central message is that teachers should not teach and assess every lesson in the same way.

Trivium21c: Examinations

Instead of being purely the tail that wags the dog, exams should assess the curriculum as experienced. Formal assessment at a national level should include recognition of the three roads: grammar, dialectic, and rhetoric. A series of school-level qualifications and experiences should include the following:

- **Multiple choice and short answer tests**. These have a part to play in showing basic knowledge, but other types of knowledge would need to be explored in more detail in order to reveal depth of understanding within and across subjects.

- **Essays showing how ideas have been drawn from research and made into thoughtful argument**. These essays should be of a standard such that instead of students just showing they know the tradition, they should also be able to demonstrate how and why they challenge or accept the tradition.

- **Exams in the form of viva voces, debates, speeches, blogs, longer pieces of work, artefacts, and performance**. Whatever works best for the particular academic domain should be included, but should be carefully overseen to make sure that there is a level of parity between disciplines.

By drawing distinctive types of exam from the arts of the trivium, as relevant to different subjects, breadth and depth of assessment would be assured.

The examination and curriculum system that most closely assesses the values as expressed in the trivium is the International Baccalaureate and the Middle Years Programme, so here would be a good place for schools to start when adapting current practice. The international element of the IB is about ethos, not availability. In order to safeguard the idea of cultural capital, perhaps we could envisage a British (Isles) Baccalaureate, where our shared traditions could be enriched, as well as our relationships with Europe, the Commonwealth, the English-speaking nations, and the rest of the world.

Trivium 21c: Authentic Curriculum

All students should experience a balance between academic and authentic learning. The authentic curriculum should take up around 40% of formal curriculum time, as well as a large chunk of the extended school provision. The authentic curriculum should be varied and adaptable to the individual child. Although breadth of experience is more important early on, depth is also essential – the opportunity to specialize should be open to all. There should be an opportunity for group activities, such as music, art, sport, dance, drama, debating, crafts, apprenticeships, career opportunities and work experience, singing in a choir, performing in a school play, going on theatre trips, foreign travel, researching local history, producing a school magazine/newspaper/website, making films and TV programmes, writing and reciting poetry, circus skills, accountancy, writing a novel, composing a symphony, inventing a product, discovering a new planet, making a break-through in science, climbing a mountain, unearthing a Viking tomb, translating something from the original Anglo-Saxon … You name it, the authenticity is in the pursuit and the engagement, and for its own sake.

The authentic curriculum should be monitored and any notable successes – which might be in the form of the experience itself or suitable exams that the domain already operates, such as music exams or apprenticeships – should be tracked, but not thought of as exam equivalents. Instead, they should be valued in their own right. A Gold Duke of Edinburgh's Award should be just that; it shouldn't need academic, gold-standard equivalence to be thought of as a good thing.

Community forming is an essential part of much of the authentic curriculum. It is through the active pursuit, perhaps in a group climbing a mountain, where the flourishing of students and their peers relies on the virtue of each other working through an agreed ethical framework. This experience should not be cheapened by making it the equivalent of half a GCSE. Elizabeth Truss observes:

> *I think there's nothing worse than fake authenticity, which is where it's claimed 'this is what's going on', but really it's just a paying lip service type of exercise, an ersatz experience, the sort of thing you do on a corporate away day. If it's genuine, it's useful. Joining the Scouts is authentic. The core purpose of a school is that the student leaves having learnt something and knowing how to learn, and also wanting to achieve things, to aspire. I think that our whole philosophy of education has to be about ensuring our children fulfil their potential.*

Part of the authentic curriculum is the idea that children should engage with the local community, its history and heritage. Local and national companies and cultural organizations should offer inreach and outreach, which would enable their employees and volunteers to come into schools and schoolchildren to work off-site with them. These organizations could include artists, banks, service industries, retail, and industry as well as institutions like the Scouts, Girl Guides, the military, churches, the National Trust, zoos, hospitals, care homes, theatres, orchestras, recording studios, or computer and electronics companies. They could offer 'real' experiential learning during the school day and at after-school opportunities, residential weekends, holiday learning experiences, and even gap years.

Why does Dr Irene Bishop ensure her girls have so many authentic experiences?

> *Because we're an inner-city school, where lots of children come from deprived backgrounds, and we feel we should make a difference. One of the ways of making a difference is to give them all the things that I would give my own children. So we take them to the ballet, we take them to the theatre, we teach them to play a musical instrument, we allow them to go to concerts, we take them abroad, we have school journeys where they have challenges like Outward Bound.*

Any middle-class parent would do that for their child, so why should our kids not have exactly the same opportunities? It actually makes them more rounded, and it helps them learn more. Without all this 'stuff' they don't become truly human. They are all building blocks that make that person able to go out into the world and be a maker of the future. You could come into school and just do work to pass exams and so on. In this school, one of the reasons we are 'outstanding' is because we do this.

To enrich, stretch, and challenge students, it is a great idea to invite in-residence artists, writers, philosophers, and scientists to the school. You can then offer non-timetabled opportunities for small group sessions or 'events'. There is a huge amount of untapped potential out there, so rather than seeing education 'done over there in that imposing building', these activities bring our learning communities back together. The Extended Project Qualification (EPQ) is an excellent qualification that more schools could introduce. It enables students to study independently or interdependently. They can explore a topic of interest to them, in performance, writing, research, design, and so on. The Creativity, Action, Service (CAS) program from the IB also offers a model of how this idea could work. Students are encouraged to take part in, amongst others, arts activities, expeditions, sports, projects, and community service, and are asked to reflect on how their participation affected them and the people with whom they worked.

Does the School Educate Well?

Let us educate first and then measure what occurs. Students can take exams, contribute to school life, engage with other institutions, take part in the arts, in physical activity, voluntary work, or community action, have an authentic experience of work, or do a thousand other things – and all this could be included in what we value. The problem with assessment, according to Anthony Seldon, is that:

With any assessment you look for the quantitative, and in schools these are exam results, they are turnover, they are numbers. None of those are particularly good ways of assessing schools. How do you know if you are running a good family? You know it when you see it. You know what bad families look like; it's very hard to just write it down.

An inspection is a pretty limited and limiting process. There's something better and greater. How do you know what a great human being is? You know when you're in the company of greatness, just like you know when you're in the company of someone who is a negative force, but it's very hard to have a checklist with a clipboard and go down it. It's actually rather demeaning to human beings to do that.

Schools should judge themselves by how they fulfil their aims in the day-to-day and in their long-term outcomes. In the case of state schools, the government should share in helping to formulate some of those goals in partnership. When inspecting the school, they should then assess them on those terms, not on a strictly centralized idea of what the criteria should be. It is the ethos of the school as part of a community that should be rich and varied, and this should be judged on its own terms. Does the day-to-day curriculum and teaching reflect that ethos? What are the real outcomes? Elizabeth Truss says: 'I think schools should be judged on how well pupils achieve, the destinations of those students, as well as the more intangible things like the ethos the school creates.'

Alumni programme

Schools should operate an alumni programme, which would collate information about immediate and longer-term destinations for ex-students. It could also act as a catalyst for bringing the philosopher kids back to the cave, to help them lead and inspire other students. Information about longer-term destinations would also be of interest to prospective pupils and parents; and this data should include more than just what jobs people have and where they studied. This information would be about more than just the school. Alumni programmes also provide an example of the positive ethos of the school as part of a journey – the philosopher kids becoming philosopher adults.

Sarah Jones from the Greenwich Free School describes how this is partly achieved in KIPP schools in the United States:

They track their kids through college, and their kids know that they can ring their school and they'll talk to them still, care about them still. It's not just about gathering data about who leaves and where they go; it's about maintaining that relationship because they love them. They're still their kids and they still want to support them. Lots of benefits come from that: knowing what they're doing, being able to bring them back to inspire younger kids. If kids just think all I'm telling them is how to pass an exam, they lose their desire to learn.

Any school that chose not to have an alumni programme would, in itself, be making quite a negative statement about its ambition.

Be In Charge of the Development and Assessment of Teaching

Elizabeth Truss observes, 'At the moment exams have two purposes: one is assessing the students and one is assessing the school. I think those two purposes need to be separated.' In order to assess teachers each institution should define, again through negotiation, what sort of teachers it wants. These expectations should be expressed simply, perhaps as Ten Commandments (as below), and should focus on the quality of teaching the school wants its students to experience.

In an issue of the *New York Times Magazine*, from December 1951, as part of an article entitled 'The Best Answer to Fanaticism: Liberalism', Bertrand Russell wrote what he called the Liberal Decalogue which consisted of ten commandments for a teacher to 'promulgate'. At number one was:

1   Do not feel absolutely certain of anything.

And at number eight:

8   Find more pleasure in intelligent dissent than in passive
     agreement, for, if you value intelligence, as you should, the
     former implies a deeper agreement than the latter.

These two suggestions seem highly pertinent to the trivium and I think it would be useful for schools to write a short mission statement about teachers and their relationship to knowledge via the trivium: how do we want our teachers to 'be' in the classroom? We want teachers to allow sufficient space for individuality, both for the discipline they teach and also for their own style, which would give a distinctive flavour to the education offer in a school. Rather than a centralized attempt to dictate this by government bureaucracy, we need a more localized feel which is representative of the surrounding community.

If only my daughter could be formally educated through a contemporary interpretation of the trivium, she would be able to access the ancient rhythms of learning by knowing a simple mantra – grammar, dialectic, rhetoric – and using it as the key to access any subject matter. Should any topic become difficult, she could take a step back and ask herself: What is missing here? Have I explored the grammar fully? Have I analysed or looked at the arguments in enough detail? Have I practised enough? Have I tried to communicate my thinking about this topic to someone? This, in a nutshell, is how the trivium can become a tool for the autodidact. Simple.

Trivium for the 21st Century: Encore

A century is an arbitrary concept. As we moved from 1999 to the year 2000 a sudden change did not occur, education did not suddenly come face to face with the need for a new paradigm. Time moves on, and things do change but instead of revolution imposed by politicians, a highly stressed workforce in schools should re-realize their historic inheritance and absorb the political into their everyday practice not by pursuing one or other agenda but by bringing different ways of seeing the world into their schools and classrooms.

The tension between traditional and progressive educationalists can be resolved. The future of education can be a reinvigorated trivium; it is, as we have seen, infinitely adaptable, for the 21st century, indeed for any century. The trivium can satisfy the cries from across the political divide: traditionalists profess the need for high standards and the importance of knowledge as vital components of a good education with the teacher as 'sage on the stage'. Progressives have a desire to foster critical thinking skills, soft skills like creativity, empathy, and teamwork, vocational skills and with the teacher as 'guide on the side'. Both these approaches are made possible if schools adopt a trivium for the 21st century and encompass both the traditional and the progressive in their ethos and pedagogy.

This idea is drawn from the arts, and from the practise of all arts. Art education begins with rules and precepts, teaching the art form, and develops new ways of seeing, new art forms, new relationships and new ways of communicating. This is also true of the three arts of the trivium where the three arts meet. The art of grammar highlights the importance of skills, rules, and knowledge drawn from an, albeit contested, tradition. The art of dialectic covers critical thinking, analysis, questioning, arguing, discussing, developing enthusiasms, and the need for grit. The art of rhetoric encourages free expression, citizenship, community, and communication. More than the sum of its parts the trivium develops the transferable skills that enable individuals and groups to begin to realize their potential: the ideal of the 'philosopher kid'. The teacher learns to, gradually, 'let go', and the trivium helps develop free-thinking, independent learners with a sense of responsibility to others. Yet this is nothing new, we get there through ancient traditions to build the knowledge and skills necessary for the future.

Where the three arts 'clash along' creativity flourishes. That should be of no surprise. The trivium is, if you like, the art of arts. Why am I, a teacher of drama, drawn towards it? Perhaps it could be because at the heart of theatre is a process very much like the trivium. We have our grammar, the script. We use critical skills to examine, analyse, and develop our thinking, we play, argue, question, workshop, and rehearse with the desire to uncover great truths and beauty; in other words we use logic, dialectic, and the never-ending pursuit inherent in *logos*. Finally, the art rhetoric: we perform, together, to an audience where we commune and share, listening to the response. We adapt, we change, and we remain open and are ready to begin the whole process again.

A Bit of Trivia

When browsing on the internet I came across the following quote by the poet William Cory:

At school you are engaged not so much in acquiring knowledge as in making mental efforts under criticism ... you go to a great school not so much for knowledge as for arts and habits; for the habit of attention, for the art of expression, for the art of assuming at a moment's notice a new intellectual position, for the art of entering quickly into another person's thoughts, for the habit of submitting to censure and refutation, for the art of indicating assent or dissent in graduated terms, for the habit of regarding minute points of accuracy, for the art of working out what is possible in a given time, for taste, for discrimination, for mental courage, and for mental soberness.

That's it! That's the school I want my daughter to go to, I thought. Then I looked more closely. Oh dear, this is from the website of a very expensive boys' public school: Eton. Not a place for my daughter, clearly; gender and class stand in her way.

She is awake *now*, so awake, inquisitive, thoughtful, and fun loving. Why is there no school for her?

Acknowledgements

This has been an extraordinary experience for me and it has only been possible through the kindness, help, and support of many. Firstly, Ian Gilbert, for taking the initial risk and for his belief and encouragement, Caroline Lenton for backing up Ian's initial punt with the resources of Crown House, and Peter Young, for his support when I needed it most. Peter's reading and rereading of my draft manuscripts, his criticisms, and his ability to guide me through the fog have helped me realise the final shape of this book. My personal and deepest thanks go to Kerry, my wife, and Lotte, my daughter, for living with me and supporting me through this experience; both of you will never know how important a contribution that was. I am also indebted to my mother for her belief and the encouragement of other members of my family and my friends. I would also like to pay special thanks to those who have given of their time by being interviewed for this book especially as I was unknown to them, their generosity of spirit has been truly heartwarming: I have been inordinately lucky that so many busy and influential people took an interest in this project and made contributions that were at once thoughtful, challenging, and enlightening. Thanks especially to David Aaronovitch for taking me to White Hart Lane to see the mighty Spurs, an act of kindness I will not forget.

I would also like to thank all those I have worked with over the years, both staff and students, and also those who engage with me on Twitter; you have all helped me think this book through.

Last, and least, thank you to my schooling, without which this book would not have been possible.

Shall we forever make new books, as apothecaries make new mixtures, by pouring only out of one vessel into another?

Laurence Sterne,
The Life and Opinions of Tristram Shandy, Gentleman

Bibliography and Reading List

Aaronovitch, David (2009) *Voodoo Histories: How Conspiracy Theory Has Shaped Modern History.* London: Vintage.

Ackroyd, Peter (2002) *Albion: The Origins of the English Imagination.* London: Chatto and Windus.

Adams, Douglas (1979) *The Hitchhiker's Guide to the Galaxy.* London: Pan Books.

Adler, Mortimer J. (1952) *The Great Ideas: A Lexicon of Western Thought.* New York: Macmillan.

Adler, Mortimer J. (1984) *The Paideia Programme: An Educational Syllabus. Essays by the Paideia Group.* New York: Macmillan.

Alexander, Robin (2004) *Towards Dialogic Teaching: Rethinking Classroom Talk.* Cambridge: Dialogos.

Appleyard, Bryan (1992) *Understanding the Present: Science and the Soul of Modern Man.* New York: Pan Macmillan.

Appleyard, Bryan (2011) *The Brain is Wider Than the Sky: Why Simple Solutions Don't Work in a Complex World.* London: Weidenfeld & Nicolson.

Araya, Daniel and **Peters, Michael A.** (eds) (2010) *Education in the Creative Economy: Knowledge and Learning in the Age of Innovation.* New York: Peter Lang.

Aristotle (1991) *The Art of Rhetoric,* tr. H. C. Lawson-Tancred. London: Penguin.

Aristotle (1995) *Aristotle*, tr. David Ross (6th edn). Oxford: Oxford University Press.

Aristotle (1996) *Poetics*, tr. Michael Heath. London. Penguin.

Armstrong, John (2010) *In Search of Civilisation: Remaking a Tarnished Idea*. London: Penguin.

Arnold, Matthew (1986) *The Oxford Authors: Matthew Arnold*, ed. Miriam Allott and Robert H. Super. Oxford: Oxford University Press.

Artaud, Antonin (1993 [1970]) *The Theatre and Its Double*, tr. Victor Corti. London: Calder Publications.

Arthur, James (2010) *Of Good Character: Exploration of Virtues and Values in 3–25 Year Olds*. Exeter: Imprint Academic.

Bacon, Francis (2002) *The Major Works*, ed. Brian Vickers. Oxford: Oxford University Press.

Baggini, Julian (2012) *Philosophy: All That Matters*. London: Hodder Education.

Baggini, Julian and Fosl, Peter S. (2010) *The Philosopher's Toolkit: A Compendium of Philosophical Concepts and Methods*. Oxford: Wiley-Blackwell.

Bakewell, Sarah (2010) *How to Live, or a Life of Montaigne in One Question and Twenty Attempts at an Answer*. London: Vintage.

Barber, Michael, Donnelly, Katelyn, and Rizvi, Saad (2012) *Oceans of Innovation: The Atlantic, the Pacific, Global Leadership and the Future of Education*. London: IPPR.

Barnhart, Robert K. (ed.) (1988) *Chambers Dictionary of Etymology*. London: Chambers.

Bauer, Susan Wise (2003) *The Well-Educated Mind: A Guide to the Classical Education You Never Had*. London: W. W. Norton & Co.

Bauer, Susan Wise and Wise, Jessie (2009) *The Well-Trained Mind: A Guide to Classical Education at Home* (3rd rev. edn). London: W. W. Norton & Co.

Benn, Melissa (2012) *School Wars: The Battle for Britain's Education*. London: Verso.

Berkeley, George (1996) *Principles of Human Knowledge and Three Dialogues*, ed. Howard Robinson. Oxford: Oxford University Press.

Blackburn, Simon (2006) *Plato's Republic: A Biography*. London: Atlantic Books.

Blackburn, Simon (2008) *How to Read Hume*. London: Granta.

Bloom, Allan (1987) *The Closing of the American Mind*. New York: Simon & Schuster.

Bloom, Harold (1995) *The Western Canon: The Books and School of the Ages.* London: Papermac.

Bohm, David (1996) *On Dialogue.* London: Routledge.

Boucher, David and **Kelly, Paul** (eds) (2003) *Political Thinkers: From Socrates to the Present.* Oxford: Oxford University Press.

Bourdieu, Pierre (1979) *Distinction: A Social Critique of the Judgement of Taste,* tr. Richard Nice. London: Routledge.

Büchner, Georg (1971) *The Plays of Georg Büchner: Danton's Death, Leonce and Lena, Woyzeck,* tr. Victor Price. Oxford: Oxford University Press.

Cicero (1971) *On the Good Life,* tr. Michael Grant. London: Penguin.

Cicero (2000) *On Obligations,* tr. P. G. Walsh. Oxford: Oxford University Press.

Collini, Stefan (1998) 'Introduction', in C. P. Snow, *The Two Cultures.* Cambridge: Cambridge University Press.

Conley, Thomas M. (1993) *Rhetoric in the European Tradition.* Chicago, IL: University of Chicago Press.

Conway, David (2010) *Liberal Education and the National Curriculum.* London: Civitas.

Corrigan, Kevin and **Glazov-Corrigan, Elena** (2004) *Plato's Dialectic at Play: Argument, Structure, and Myth in the Symposium.* University Park, PA: Pennsylvania State University Press.

Crawford, Matthew (2009) *The Case for Working With Your Hands or Why Office Work Is Bad for Us and Fixing Things Feels Good.* London: Viking.

Cruddas, Jon (ed.) (2013) *One Nation Labour: Debating the Future.* London: LabourList.

Crystal, David (2006) *How Language Works.* London: Penguin.

Crystal, David (2012) *Spell It Out: The Singular Story of English Spelling.* London: Profile Books.

Csikszentmihalyi, Mihaly (1996) *Creativity: Flow and the Psychology of Discovery and Invention.* New York: Harper Perennial.

Dawkins, Richard (1989) *The Selfish Gene.* Oxford: Oxford University Press.

Dawkins, Richard (2003) 'Good and Bad Reasons for Believing', in *A Devil's Chaplain: Reflections on Hope, Lies, Science, and Love.* Boston, MA: Houghton Mifflin.

Dawkins, Richard (2012) *Beautiful Minds* [TV programme] BBC Four, 1 May 2012.

Deutsch, David (2011) *The Beginning of Infinity: Explanations that Transform the World.* London: Penguin.

Dweck, Carol (2006) *Mindset: The New Psychology of Success.* New York: Ballantine Books.

Everett, Daniel (2012) *Language: The Cultural Tool.* London: Profile Books.

Ferguson, Niall (2011) *Civilization: The West and the Rest.* London: Allen Lane.

Fletcher, John (2011) *A Pocket Philosophical Dictionary.* Oxford: Oxford University Press.

Freeman, Charles (2003) *The Closing of the Western Mind: The Rise and Fall of Faith and Reason.* London: Pimlico.

Freire, Paulo (1970) *Pedagogy of the Oppressed.* London: Penguin.

Gardener, Howard (2011) *Truth, Beauty, and Goodness Reframed.* New York: Basic Books.

Gleick, James (2012) *The Information.* London: Fourth Estate.

Gordon, W. Terrence (2010) *McLuhan: A Guide for the Perplexed.* London: Continuum.

Grafton, Anthony, Most, Glenn W., and **Settis, Salvatore** (eds) (2010) *The Classical Tradition.* Cambridge, MA; London: Belknap Press of Harvard University Press.

Gramsci, Antonio (1971) *Selections from the Prison Notebooks,* ed. and tr. Quintin Hoare and Geoffrey Nowell Smith. London: Lawrence and Wishart.

Gross, Alan G. (1990) *The Rhetoric of Science.* London: Harvard University Press.

Haidt, Jonathan (2012) *The Righteous Mind: Why Good People are Divided by Politics and Religion.* London: Allen Lane.

Hart, Randall D. (2006) *Increasing Academic Achievement with the Trivium of Classical Education: Its Historical Development, Decline in the Last Century, and Resurgence in Recent Decades.* New York: iUniverse.

Hattie, John (2008) *Visible Learning: A Synthesis of Over 800 Meta-Analyses Relating to Achievement.* London: Routledge.

Haynes, Natalie (2010) *The Ancient Guide to Modern Life.* London: Profile Books.

Hirsch, Jr, E. D. (1988) *Cultural Literacy: What Every American Needs To Know.* New York: Vintage.

Hirsch, Jr, E. D. (2006) *The Knowledge Deficit: Closing the Shocking Education Gap for American Children.* New York: Houghton Mifflin.

Hitchens, Christopher (2001) *Letters to a Young Contrarian.* Oxford: Perseus.

Hitchens, Christopher (2006) *Love, Poverty and War.* London: Atlantic Books.

Hitchens, Christopher (2012) *Arguably*. London: Atlantic Books.

Hitchings, Henry (2011) *The Language Wars: A History of Proper English*. London: John Murray.

Hobbes, Thomas (1681) *The Art of Rhetoric with a Discourse of the Laws of England*. London: For William Crooke.

Hughes, Bettany (2010) *The Hemlock Cup: Socrates, Athens and the Search for the Good Life*. London: Jonathan Cape.

Hughes, Jonnie (2012) *On the Origin of Tepees: Why Some Ideas Spread While Others Go Extinct*. Oxford: One World Publications.

Hume, David (1985 [1739]) *A Treatise of Human Nature*. London: Penguin Classics.

Hume, David (2007 [1748]) *An Enquiry Concerning Human Understanding*, ed. Peter Millican. Oxford: Oxford University Press.

James, C. L. R. (2005) *Beyond a Boundary*. London: Yellow Jersey Press.

Johnson, Christopher (2011) *Microstyle: The Art of Writing Little*. New York: W. W. Norton & Co.

Johnson, Samuel (1755) *A Dictionary of the English Language*. London: Printed by W. Strahan.

Joseph, Sister Miriam (2002 [1937]) *The Trivium: The Liberal Arts of Logic, Grammar, and Rhetoric*, ed. Marguerite McGlinn. Philadelphia, PA: Paul Dry Books.

Joseph, Sister Miriam (2005 [1947]) *Shakespeare's Use of the Arts of Language*. Philadelphia, PA: Paul Dry Books.

Judt, Tony (2010) *Ill Fares the Land*. London: Penguin.

Judt, Tony, with Snyder, Timothy (2012) *Thinking the Twentieth Century*. London: William Heinemann.

Kant, Immanuel (2007 [1790]) *Critique of Judgement*, tr. John H. Bernard. New York: Cosimo Classics.

Kant, Immanuel (2007 [1781])]) *Critique of Pure Reason*, tr. Marcus Weigelt. London: Penguin Classics.

Kenny, Anthony (1998) *An Illustrated Brief History of Western Philosophy*. Oxford: Blackwell.

Kimball, Roger (2000) *Experiments against Reality: The Fate of Culture in the Postmodern Age*. Chicago, IL: Ivan R. Dee.

Konnikova, Maria (2013) *Mastermind: How to Think Like Sherlock Holmes*. Edinburgh: Canongate.

Landau, Cecile, Szudek, Andrew, and **Tomley, Sarah** (eds) (2011) *The Philosophy Book.* London: Dorling Kindersley.

Lanham, Richard A. (1991) *A Handlist of Rhetorical Terms.* Berkeley, CA: University of California Press.

Lawton, Denis and **Gordon, Peter** (2002) *A History of Western Educational Ideas.* London: Woburn Press.

Leith, Sam (2011) *You Talkin' to Me? Rhetoric from Aristotle to Obama.* London: Profile Books.

Lemov, Doug (2010) *Teach Like a Champion: 49 Techniques That Put Students on the Path to College.* San Francisco, CA: Jossey-Bass/Wiley.

Leonard, George (1991) *Mastery: The Keys to Success and Long-Term Fulfillment.* New York: Plume.

Littlejohn, Robert and **Evans, Charles T.** (2006) *Wisdom and Eloquence.* Wheaton, IL: Crossway.

Lockman, Diane B. (2008) *Trivium Mastery: The Intersection of the Three Roads, Classical Education from Birth to Tween.* Denver, CO: Outskirts Press.

MacCabe, Colin (1982) *Towards a Modern Trivium.* Strathclyde: University of Strathclyde.

Mack, Peter (2007) 'Rhetoric and Dialectic in the Renaissance', in Jonathan Powell (ed.), *Rational Argument in Ancient Rhetoric: BICS Supplement 96.* London: Institute of Classical Studies, pp. 91–103.

Magee, Bryan (2010) *The Story of Philosophy.* London: Dorling Kindersley.

McGilchrist, Iain (2010) *The Master and His Emissary.* London: Yale University Press.

McLuhan, Marshall (1962) *The Gutenberg Galaxy: The Making of Typographic Man.* Toronto: University of Toronto Press.

McLuhan, Marshall (2005 [1943]) *The Classical Trivium: The Place of Thomas Nashe in the Learning of his Time,* ed. W. Terrence Gordon. Corte Madera, CA: Gingko Press.

McLuhan, Marshall and **Fiore, Quentin** (1996 [1967]) *The Medium is the Massage: An Inventory of Effects,* coordinated by Jerome Agel. London: Penguin.

McNeely, Ian F. and **Wolverton, Lisa** (2009) *Reinventing Knowledge: From Alexandria to the Internet.* London: W. W. Norton & Co.

Marshall, H. E. (2005 [1905]) *Our Island Story.* London: Civitas.

Montaigne, Michel de (2003 [1580]) *The Complete Essays,* ed. and tr. M. A. Screech. London: Penguin.

Mount, Ferdinand (2010) *Full Circle: How the Classical World Came Back to Us.* London: Simon & Schuster.

Mount, Ferdinand (2010) *Mind the Gap: The New Class Divide in Britain.* London: Short Books.

Mount, Ferdinand (2012) *The New Few, or a Very British Oligarchy.* London: Simon & Schuster.

Murphy, Peter (2010) 'Creative Economies and Research Universities', in Daniel Araya and Michael A. Peters (eds), *Education in the Creative Economy: Knowledge and Learning in the Age of Innovation.* New York: Peter Lang, pp. 331–359.

Nagel, Thomas (2012) *Mind and Cosmos: Why the Materialist Neo-Darwinian Conception of Nature Is Almost Certainly False.* Oxford: Oxford University Press.

O'Hear, Anthony and **Sidwell, Marc** (2009) *The School of Freedom: A Liberal Education Reader from Plato to the Present Day.* Exeter: Imprint Academic.

Pearce, Nick and **Hallgarten, Joe** (eds) (2000) *Tomorrow's Citizens: Critical Debates in Citizenship and Education.* London: Institute for Public Policy Research.

Pearce, Nick and **Hillman, Josh** (1998) *Wasted Youth: Raising Achievement and Tackling Social Exclusion.* London: Institute for Public Policy Research.

Pearce, Nick and **Margo, Julia** (eds) (2007) *Politics for a New Generation: The Progressive Moment.* Basingstoke: Palgrave Macmillan.

Plato (2007 [1955]) *The Republic,* tr. Desmond Lee. London: Penguin Classics.

Popper, Karl (1994) *The Myth of the Framework: In Defence of Science and Rationality,* ed. M. A. Notturno. Abingdon, Oxon: Routledge.

Popper, Karl (2002 [1974]) *Unended Quest: An Intellectual Autobiography.* London: Routledge.

Ramus, Petrus (1651) *A compendium of the art of logick and rhetorick in the English tongue. Containing all that Peter Ramus, Aristotle, and others have writ thereon: with plaine directions for the more easie understanding and practice of the same.* London: Printed by Thomas Maxey.

Randall, Lisa (2011) *Knocking on Heaven's Door: How Physics and Scientific Thinking Illuminate the Universe and the Modern World.* London: Bodley Head.

Redpath, Peter A. (1998) *Masquerade of the Dream Walkers: Prophetic Theology from the Cartesians to Hegel.* Amsterdam and Atlanta, GA: Editions Rodopi, B. V.

Richards, Jennifer (2008) *Rhetoric.* London: Routledge.

Robinson, Ken (1999) *All Our Futures: Creativity, Culture and Education.* London: National Advisory Committee and Cultural Education.

Robinson, Ken, with **Aronica, Lou** (2009) *The Element: How Finding Your Passion Changes Everything.* London: Allen Lane.

Robinson, Richard (1953) *Plato's Earlier Dialectic.* Oxford: Clarendon Press.

Ruskin, John (2004 [1859]) *On Art and Life* (rev. edn). London: Penguin.

Russell, Bertrand (1951) 'The Best Answer to Fanaticism: Liberalism', *New York Times Magazine*, 16 December 1951. Reproduced (1969) as 'The Liberal Decalogue', in *The Autobiography of Bertrand Russell*, vol. 3. London: George Allen & Unwin, pp. 71–72.

Salisbury, John of (2009) *The Metalogicon: A Twelfth Century Defense of the Verbal and Logical Arts of the Trivium,* tr. Daniel D. McGarry. Philadelphia, PA: Paul Dry Books.

Sandel, Michael J. (2012) *What Money Can't Buy: The Moral Limits of Markets.* London: Allen Lane.

Scruton, Roger (1998) *Modern Culture.* London: Continuum.

Scruton, Roger (2000) *England: An Elegy.* London: Chatto and Windus.

Scruton, Roger (2007) *Culture Counts.* New York: Encounter Books.

Sennett, Richard (2003) *Respect: The Formation of Character in an Age of Inequality.* London: Allen Lane.

Sennett, Richard (2008) *The Craftsman.* London: Penguin Books.

Sennett, Richard (2012) *Together: The Rituals, Pleasures and Politics of Cooperation.* London: Allen Lane.

Shakespeare, William (2007) *The RSC Shakespeare: Complete Works,* ed. Jonathan Bate and Eric Rasmussen. Basingstoke: Macmillan.

Snow, C. P. (1998 [1959]) *The Two Cultures.* Cambridge: Cambridge University Press.

Starkey, David. 'Losing Our Identity'. Sunday Times Festival of Education. Wellington College. 23 June 2012.

Tarnas, Richard (1991) *The Passion of the Western Mind.* London: Pimlico.

Tawney, R. H. (1914) 'An Experiment in Democratic Education', *The Political Quarterly*, 2: 62–84.

Todorov, Tzvetan (2009) *In Defence of the Enlightenment,* tr. Gila Walker. London: Atlantic Books.

Toulmin, Stephen (2003) *Return to Reason.* Cambridge, MA: Harvard University Press.

Trombley, Stephen (2011) *A Short History of Western Thought.* London: Atlantic Books.

Venville, Grady J. and **Dawson, Vaille M.** (2010) 'The impact of a classroom intervention on grade 10 students' augmentation skills, informal reasoning, and conceptual understanding of science', *Journal of Research in Science Teaching*, 47(8): 952–977.

Vermes, Geza (2012) *Christian Beginnings: From Nazareth to Nicaea, AD 30–325*. London: Allen Lane.

Voltaire (2011) *A Pocket Philosophical Dictionary*, tr. John Fletcher. Oxford: Oxford University Press.

Williams, Raymond (1958) *Culture and Society: Coleridge to Orwell*. London: Hogarth Press.

Willingham, Daniel T. (2009) *Why Don't Students Like School? A Cognitive Scientist Answers Questions About How the Mind Works and What It Means for the Classroom*. San Francisco, CA: Jossey-Bass/Wiley.

Willingham, Daniel T. (2012) *When Can You Trust the Experts? How to Tell Good Science from Bad in Education*. San Francisco, CA: Jossey-Bass/Wiley.

Wilson, Douglas (1991) *Recovering the Lost Tools of Learning: An Approach to Distinctively Christian Education*. Wheaton, IL: Crossway Books.

Wind-Cowie, Max and **Gregory, Thomas** (2011) *A Place for Pride*. London: Demos.

Webography

Eton College (2012) 'William Cory.' Available at: www.etoncollege.com/william_cory.aspx/.

Gray, John (2012) 'A Point of View: The Enduring Appeal of Sherlock Holmes.' Available at: www.bbc.co.uk/news/magazine-19268563/.

Hobbes, Thomas (1839) *The Art Of Rhetoric Plainly Set Forth. With Pertinent Examples for the More Easy Understanding and Practice of the Same. The English Works, vol. VI (Dialogue, Behemoth, Rhetoric)*. Available at: oll.libertyfund.org/?option=com_staticxt&staticfile=show.php%3Ftitle=770&chapter=90057&layout=html&Itemid=27/.

Johnson, Samuel (1755) *A Dictionary of the English Language*. Available at: johnsonsdictionaryonline.com/?page_id=7070&i=1/.

Milton, John (1644) *Of Education*. Available at: www.dartmouth.edu/~milton/reading_room/of_education/index.shtml/.

Monahan, Jerome (2004) 'Think Before You Act.' Available at: www.guardian. co.uk/education/2004/may/04/teaching.schools/.

Morgan, Cynthia (2011) 'Deconstructing Christopher Marlowe.' Available at: www.themarlowestudies.org/editorial_cynthia_morgan_9copy.html/.

Murphy Paul, Anne (2012) 'Why Kids Should Learn Cursive (and Math Facts and Word Roots).' Available at: ideas.time.com/(2012/11/08/ why-kids-should-learn-cu-cursive/.

Peirce, Charles Sanders (2007) Works by Charles Sanders Peirce. Available at: www.cspeirce.com/menu/library/bycsp/bycsp.htm/.

Republican Party of Texas (2012) *Report of Platform Committee and Rules Committee.* Available at: www.tfn.org/site/DocServer/20...pdf?docID=3201/.

Robinson, Ken (2006) 'Ken Robinson Says Schools Kill Creativity' [video online]. Available at: www.ted.com/talks/ken_robinson_says_schools_ kill_creativity.html/.

Robinson, Ken (2010) 'Bring on the Learning Revolution!' [video online]. Available at: www.ted.com/talks/sir_ken_robinson_bring_on_the_revolu- tion.html/.

Robinson, Ken (2010) 'Changing Paradigms' [video online]. Available at: www. ted.com/talks/ken_robinson_changing_education_paradigms.html/.

Russell, Bertrand (1951) 'A Liberal Decalogue.' Available at: www.davemckay. co.uk/philosophy/russell/russell.php?name=a.liberal.decalogue/.

Sayers, Dorothy L. (1947) 'The Lost Tools of Learning.' Available at: www.gbt. org/text/sayers.html/.

Soccer History (2010) 'Danny Blanchflower.' Available at: www.soccerhistory. org.uk/DannyBlanchflower.htm/.

Vernon, Mark (2012) 'The Case for Doubt in Politics.' Available at: www.bbc. co.uk/news/uk-politics-17625652/.

Interviews

Aaronovitch, David (2012) Interviewed by the author [audio recording]. London.

Appleyard, Bryan (2012) Interviewed by the author [audio recording]. London.

Baggini, Julian (2012) Interviewed by the author [audio recording]. London.

Benn, Melissa (2012) Interviewed by the author [audio recording]. London.

Bishop, Irene (2012) Interviewed by the author [audio recording]. London.

Blond, Phillip (2011) Interviewed by the author [audio recording]. London.

Botton, Alain de (2011) Interviewed by the author [via email]. London.

Freedman, Sam (2012) Interviewed by the author [audio recording]. London.

Haynes, Natalie (2012) Interviewed by the author [audio recording via Skype]. London.

Jones, Sarah (2012) Interviewed by the author [audio recording]. London.

Katwala, Sunder (2012) Interviewed by the author [audio recording]. London.

Lea, Michael (2012) Interviewed by the author [audio recording]. London.

Mount, Ferdinand (2012) Interviewed by the author [via email]. London.

Pearce, Nick (2012) Interviewed by the author [audio recording]. London.

Seldon, Anthony (2012) Interviewed by the author [audio recording via telephone]. London.

Simons, Jonathan (2012) Interviewed by the author [audio recording]. London.

Taylor, Matthew (2011) Interviewed by the author [audio recording]. London.

Truss, Elizabeth (2012) Interviewed by the author [audio recording]. London.

Willingham, Daniel T. (2012) Interviewed by the author [audio recording via Skype]. London/USA.

Wind-Cowie, Max (2012) Interviewed by the author [audio recording]. London.

Index

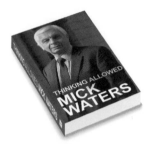

978-1-78135-056-0

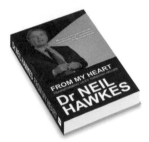

978-1-78135-106-2

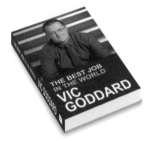

978-1-78135-110-9